The Banker's Daughter

For Viv, always my best critic

The Banker's Daughter

Caroline Thonger

MERTON

First published 2007

Published by
Merton Priory Press Ltd
9 Owen Falls Avenue
Chesterfield S41 0FR

ISBN 1 898937 71 0

ISBN-13 978 1 898937 71 5

Printed by
Dinefwr Press
Rawlings Road, Llandybie
Carmarthenshire SA18 3YD

Contents

Maps and Photographs

Maps

Photographs

Acknowledgements

Photographs 55–9, 61–4 and 66–7 are believed to have been taken by Mr E.V. Breymann of Lima in the 1940s. Photograph 65 is believed to have been taken by Dr O. Welter of Lima in the 1940s. Photographs 68–71 were taken by Eva Vollmann during her stay in Peru in the 1940s. Photographs 55–71 were published in *Along the Roads of Peru* (1945) by Eva writing as Carola Stendell.

Author's Note

History was always my most hated subject at school, and not just because we had to memorise a succession of kings and queens, battles, reforms and endless dates. By the time we had reached that monumental exam question, The Causes of The First World War, the Anglo-centric view of the teachers toward the conflicts of the twentieth century was causing me subconscious discomfort. Even in the 1960s, I was made to feel vaguely guilty towards the German ancestry of my mother.

My sister and I had been brought up not to contradict our elders. Although curious, we never questioned why we should have a grandmother living in Brussels, a grandfather living with another wife in West Germany, and our German-speaking cousins living all over Europe and as far afield as Canada and Brazil. Nor did we understand why our mother should be so reluctant to talk about her past; and most of all why she should seek to suppress any discussion about the Jewish element of our heritage.

It was only after our grandmother and mother died, in 1993 and 2003 respectively, that the extraordinary wealth of personal letters, together with family photographs, documents and possessions came to light. Much had been kept hidden by our mother. It was this discovery, together with my inheritance of my grandmother's journal, which made me decide to research our family history.

The Banker's Daughter is a reverse take on the 'rags to riches' story. It is an account of how a woman, born into a world of privilege and luxury in 1890s Berlin, has her life changed irrevocably by the tumultuous events of the twentieth century. Eva Steinthal was never famous, but she lived through some of the most famous events of recent history. Although based on true facts, a few of the scenes depicted have been fictionalised in order to preserve the flow of the narrative.

I am indebted to the following for their help: Dr Peter Liddle at the Second World War Experience Centre, Leeds; and Donald Crighton, a writer for Lloyds Shipping with whom I corresponded and who directed me to Lloyds Shipping Movements at Informa Press, Paul Street, London; for the wonderfully courteous response via email from the

Maritime Museum in Hamilton, Bermuda; for their hospitable welcome and advice I thank the staff at the Maritime Museums in Southampton and Greenwich, as well as the Guildhall Library at the Barbican in the City of London; and for their endless patience over several visits, the National Archives at Kew, also in London.

In Germany, my gratitude extends to Professors Gisele Erler & Dr Wilfried Henze at the LAB—the Landesarchiv Berlin or Berlin State Archives, for their patient assistance; but most of all my thanks go to Dr Monika Tatzkow, a renowned historical document researcher at Köpenick, Berlin. Through her I was able to access information in the National and Regional Archives in Berlin, Potsdam, Hanover, Düsseldorf and Dresden; as well as searching digitally through the archives of Deutsche Bank and the Dresdner Kunstgallerie (Dresden Gallery of Art).

My thanks go to friends and acquaintances in the writing world (too numerous to mention), and to all other friends who have supported me in this project; to Vinus Schmitt, one of my 'Berlin cousins', whose help was invaluable in deciphering hand-written Sütterlin (German Gothic script) in old family letters; to my sister and her family for their unstinting help; and last but not least to my three children—Tom, Marcus and Sophie—for always believing in me.

Caroline Thonger
Stratford upon Avon
March 2007

Part 1: Prussia

Map 1 Prussia after 1871.

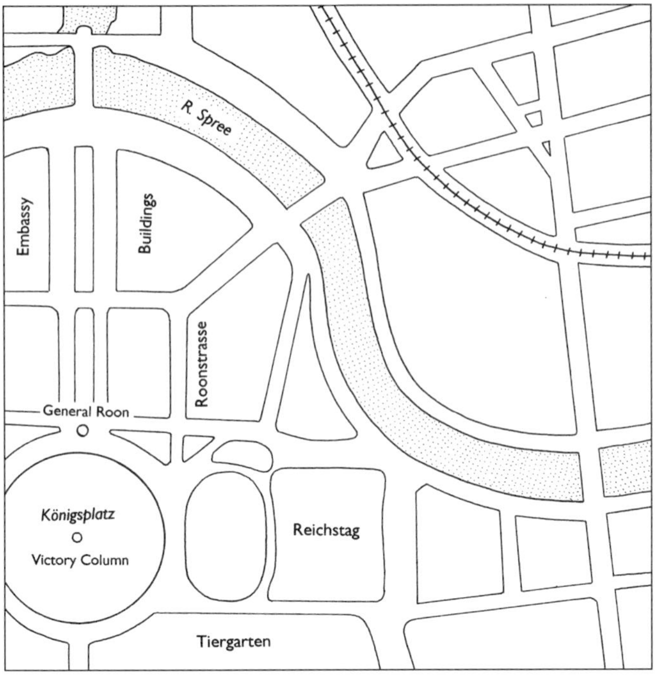

Map 2 Central Berlin *c.*1900, showing Roonstrasse.

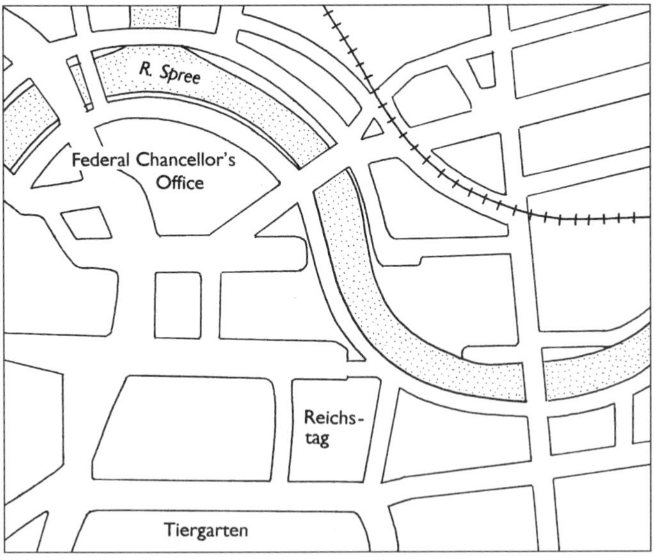

Map 3 Central Berlin today.

1

Born in Berlin

November 1892

'Oh, it's a girl again!' panted the portly midwife. 'But the next one will be a boy, please God.' Beads of perspiration glistened under her thatch of iron-grey hair.

As if to agree with this statement, the last remnants of the feeble winter sun, glistening on the cobbled pavements outside, were extinguished by a sudden black cloud. Pellets of hail rattled against the tall sash windows of the ground floor apartment, and the wind howled.

As the dark-haired, dark-eyed baby was wrapped in clean white sheets and attended to by the waiting doctor, the midwife huffed and fussed around the wide four-poster bed. The damp and exhausted shape, huddled under the soiled and crumpled sheets, could only emit a feeble groan.

Fanny Steinthal was just 26 years old, and this was her third baby in well under two-and-a-half years. By her side, her faithful lady's maid Else mopped her mistress's fevered brow.

'Is the baby—?' whispered Fanny, but her question was interrupted by a raucous scream emitted by an extremely healthy-sounding pair of lungs.

'She's fine, Madame,' Else assured her smiling. 'A beautiful little girl—and won't her sister be pleased?'

'But my hus—Herr Steinthal wants another boy,' moaned Fanny softly, turning her head into the white softness of her lace-fringed pillow.

Else scowled at the red-faced midwife, and wiped a clean cloth over her mistress's face. She had never liked Frau Demel; far too forthright and abrupt for a midwife in her opinion, especially as she always appeared in sombre black dresses more suitable for a funeral. But of course it was not her place to criticise her so-called betters. And anyway, Frau Steinthal had an irrational liking for the woman because her name—the same as the world-renowned Austrian coffee house—reminded her of her native Vienna.

'Oh, come now, Madame,' said Else, whose soothing voice and

capable manner belied her young age, 'the master will be delighted that his wife is safely delivered of a healthy girl, you'll see.'

In the Steinthal household everything was bustle and busy-ness. Next door in the nursery, two-and-a-half-year-old Erich was sitting on a rug, seriously studying the thick card pages of an old-fashioned picture book. His one-year-old sister Daisy was being attended to by their hapless nursemaid Helga. As if already jealous of her new baby sister's birth, she transmitted her own immediate needs by screwing up her face in characteristic temper and bawling loudly. The girl was doing her best to get both children to bed, to guarantee the expected level of peace and quiet for the master's return that evening. The doctor, having ensured the new baby's immediate wellbeing, was glad to escape the noise with a welcome glass of schnapps in the sitting room.

As their exhausted mistress slept in her freshly laundered sheets, the cook-housekeeper was supervising Maria, the maid-of-all-work, in the correct procedure for cleaning soiled sheets in the steaming washtub. Meanwhile, with some foresight, Ernst the coachman-cum-butler crept down the dark and dank cellar steps, to seek out a suitable German *Sekt* with which his master could wet the new baby's head on his return from the bank. In the midst of all this work, whenever they had a chance to chatter, the servants speculated on the name to be given to the new little girl.

The rain was pouring down in sheets when the master of the household, Max Steinthal—whose diminutive figure was protected from the elements by a huge black umbrella and his customary black top hat—finally returned home from his office in Berlin's banking quarter. It was just a month short of his 42nd birthday, and he had already been a director of Deutsche Bank for 19 years. Not only was he the youngest member of the bank to hold that exalted position, but he was also one of the few Jews employed at that level. It had taken him until he was 39 years old before he had taken the momentous, but important decision to find a suitable wife. For a full 16 years his first and only love had been the bank, despite the fact that the young director had often aroused particular attention from mothers whose daughters were of marriageable age.

On the first day of April in 1889, while he was visiting his aunt Amalie Ephraim's house, he was introduced to a young, classically trained pianist from Vienna. It was not so much Fanny's dark-eyed, auburn-haired beauty that aroused his interest, but rather her cold and aloof manner towards him. Quite overcome with unfamiliar feelings, but determined to see this particular young lady again, he finally plucked up courage and managed to engineer a 'chance' meeting with Fräulein

Lindenthal and her mother at a concert at the Singakademie. This time they chatted together, and Max was delighted to be subsequently invited to visit the family's home in the Judengasse during his next stay in Vienna. The ensuing courtship was affectionate, romantic and from Max's inexperienced point of view, probably hopeless. Fanny, however, seemed quite enchanted with the earnest, rather owl-faced gentleman from Berlin, whose excellent wit and good manners more than made up for his short stature and slight build. Less than three weeks later, she finally succumbed to his charms and agreed to become engaged on Good Friday. Max surprised his intended by presenting her with a ring he had purchased at a well-known jeweller's called Friedländer on Berlin's famous Unter den Linden. They married in July 1889 when Fanny was just 23 years old—fully 16 years younger than her new husband.

The wedding took place in the Seitenstettengasse in Vienna's most prominent synagogue, known as the Vienna City Temple. The Chief Rabbi, Dr Adolf Jellinek, one of the most renowned and dazzling preachers of his time, married the couple according to 'civil law and Israelite custom'. As Fanny's mother was already a widow, Max's father Eduard agreed to be their marriage witness.

With determination and considerable self-sacrifice, Fanny decided to forgo her musical career. Instead she would focus on producing a large family and the most supportive of homes, to best help and further her husband's career and his illustrious position at the bank. And so it was that on a dark and rainy day in November, Eva Karola came into the world, the third child of the seven children that Fanny was to bear in just ten years: four boys and three girls.

Even with the birth of their first child Erich, the Steinthal household was already much bigger than any of their neighbours'. Situated in the elegant district of Tiergarten, near both the Reichstag and the Brandenburg Gate, Roonstrasse was an upmarket street of elegant, colonnaded façades in white stucco. Each house number incorporated six individual apartments, the entrance to which was a very solid wooden door topped by a curved fanlight. The ground-floor tenants benefited from the presence of each building's capacious cellars, while those on the second floor had the use of extra attic space. The first and second floors had balconies overlooking the street. Each apartment block was managed by a porter, who would oversee all the comings and goings from his specifically appointed lodge sited at ground level. Every day on his way to the bank, Max would pass by the statue of General Roon, whose heroic exploits in the victorious Franco-Prussian war of 1870 had been celebrated in both a monument in the nearby park and a street named after him.

Most of the residents in the other flats of number 9 were the sole occupants of their apartments. It was a neighbourhood close to both ministerial buildings and ambassadorial residences, reflecting the upper end of Prussian society. Lawyers, bankers, medical doctors, foreign embassy staff, a Captain of Horse in the Prussian Cavalry, an actress and several baronesses were included amongst the residents of Roonstrasse.

Almost as soon as the Steinthals had moved into the spacious apartment on their return from honeymoon in the Engadine in Switzerland, Fanny was pregnant with her first child. She was to spend much of the next four and half years in a state of 'confinement'. Pregnancy at the end of the nineteenth century was very much a condition to be kept hidden from public view, and she would indeed have been mostly 'confined' to the apartment. By the time Eva came into the world, the once roomy ground floor flat was becoming almost overcrowded.

In the Roonstrasse, each apartment consisted of a similar layout: a large and airy sitting room, comfortably furnished and with tall windows looking out onto the street; a dining room long enough to seat six or eight; a master bedroom with an adjacent bathroom; another room which could be used as a study or guest room (but which in the Steinthal household was rapidly converted into a nursery); a kitchen and two small nearby rooms with a washroom for the staff. Fanny soon became very reliant on Else, her loyal *Zofa*—the term for 'lady's maid' but originally meaning the queen's lady-in-waiting. Helga the nursemaid was employed specifically to look after the children. Both girls were in their early twenties and younger than their mistress, but were required to live in, so as to cope with the demands of the young mother and her increasing number of children. The cook-housekeeper and Ernst the coachman-cum-butler walked every day from their own modest homes in order to put in a 16-hour day working in the Steinthal household.

With the careful foresight for which he became renowned at the bank, and while Fanny was pregnant with Eva, Max put in a bid for a sizeable plot of land. A year later, when his second daughter was just five months old and Fanny was pregnant yet again with her fourth child, the first plans were being drawn up for a new house in the Uhlandstrasse. This was a pleasantly leafy avenue in the district of Charlottenburg, soon to become populated by some of the wealthiest professional families in Berlin, many of them Jewish financiers. Max Steinthal's building plans revealed his dream to become not merely just one of, but the most talked-about and indeed famous of Berlin's Charlottenburg families.

On a freezing and snowy day in January, and thirteen months after her birth, Eva's little brother Werner was born. Although Fanny was delighted to have produced a second son, his arrival meant that the nursery was becoming distinctly over-populated. Max had spent long hours in consultation with his chosen architect, the renowned Richard Wolffenstein, whose designs were to include commercial buildings, private villas, a railway station and an academy. Once all the plans had been formally approved by the *Baupolizei* (the Berlin equivalent of city building inspectors), construction on the new villa could begin in earnest. Some time during 1895, three years after its first conception, the Steinthal family moved into their new home at Uhlandstrasse 191. Eva was two-and-a-half, Daisy a year older, while Werner the baby of the family was 17 months and Erich the oldest had just had his fifth birthday.

However elegant the Roonstrasse had been, the villa in Uhlandstrasse was an absolute revelation. Built in a deliberately grandiose and Italianate style, the new house must have seemed enormous to the four young children.

The ground floor alone consisted of at least fifteen rooms, the most stunning of which was the Great Hall. Sumptuously panelled in dark oak and boasting a ceiling as elaborate as a baroque church, its most impressive feature was the large, stained-glass windows at the far end that reached up as far as the second storey. From one side of the Great Hall a sweeping staircase led upstairs to the first floor, entirely surrounded by an ornately carved balcony that looked back down into the Great Hall. Hanging down from the first floor ceiling was an opulent and glittering chandelier. In the centre of one wall was the 'niche'—a semi-circular fireplace completely covered in decorative tiles. The highly polished, dark wooden floor was covered in bright yellow Chinese carpets, which lit up when the sun shone through the stained glass. This whole area was completely out of bounds to the children, who were to spend most of their early days in the large and specially appointed nursery on the first floor, accessible only by the same back stairs as those used by the servants.

The entrance to the whole house included a vestibule, a *garderobe* for coats and a room in which the butler-cum-coachman could keep watch for his master or mistress, or any guest arriving at the new house. The back stairs led off this small room. Apart from the Great Hall, the ground floor consisted of the main living room, a separate boudoir for Fanny, a huge formal dining room leading out onto the terrace, and a breakfast room next to the Winter Garden. This was an indoor conservatory separated by a wall constructed of glass bricks, and heated so that semi-tropical plants could achieve luxuriant growth. Three further rooms at this level also included Max's own study, which he was to furnish in dark woods and plush velvet, the room dominated by his mahogany desk. For Fanny the most important room, apart from her own private salon, was the music room complete with its concert-sized grand piano.

Upstairs, the first floor consisted entirely of sleeping and dressing quarters for the family. Max used one of the smaller bedrooms, which had its own adjacent dressing room. Fanny's bedroom was much larger and had its own en-suite bathroom. There were several children's bedrooms (planned in anticipation of a much larger family), together with their own bathroom. Two small sitting rooms had been included at this level—one for the girls and one for boys. When the family first moved in, it was of course the nursery that was the most important room as far as the children were concerned. This level also contained several guest bedrooms and another bathroom. The girls' sitting room had its own balcony overlooking the garden, and all the windows were quite high.

On the second floor the windows were much smaller, several of them 'mansard' windows (such as would usually be found on steeply-pitched attic roofs). This was the floor entirely taken up by the servants' quarters and consisted of some eight or nine rooms, a small bathroom and corridors leading to the back stairs.

Below stairs, the basement level was another realm entirely. Apart from a huge and capacious kitchen, there were sculleries, larders, wine cellars, washrooms and the female servants' quarters. There was also a room specifically for the boiler and main heating apparatus, and another section for further servants' quarters. The staff would take all their meals below stairs in the kitchen.

The number of staff was the first thing to increase as soon as the family moved into their new home. Fanny was soon to preside over a staff of at least twelve. Her cook-housekeeper was replaced by a Polish cook who had come highly recommended and who was to indulge Fanny's passion for home-made Austrian patisserie. Ernst moved into the household as a live-in coachman, and Else remained as Fanny's personal maid. Helga was replaced by two very capable nursemaids, and as soon as Erich was old enough a governess was employed to begin the process of his home tutoring. Apart from the scullery maid working in the kitchen, at least five maids and under-maids would have been employed (all living in) to keep the enormous villa clean and tidy. Most of their day consisted of polishing woodwork, scrubbing floors or washing laundry, overseen by the formidable housekeeper. Her personality was superseded only by that of the supercilious butler, who was in charge of all the dining and entertaining arrangements in the house.

From the outside, the new villa was very impressive. An ironwork trellis led into the garden, dominated by the large and ornate iron gate leading to the front door. The first-floor balcony overlooked the conservatory, which stood out in a hemispherical shape to one side of the house. The roof was tiled with elegant grey slate, which because of its angle hid the line of the second-floor windows when viewed from the side. From the main entrance the second floor consisted of mansard windows, and the front door, heavily panelled in dark wood itself, was topped by a stone pediment. It was the stained-glass windows, however, that were to become the most talked-about feature of the new villa. Having multi-coloured windows (depicting a very bucolic theme of shepherds and shepherdesses), that rose dramatically from ground level up to the second floor, caused Uhlandstrasse 191 to be given the nickname of *'die Synagogue'*. Whether this was an affectionate or somewhat envious term is hard to determine.

Within six months of settling into the new home, Fanny was pregnant again with her fifth child. As if to celebrate his father's achievement, Eduard was born on Christmas Eve, the day of Max's 46th birthday. After a gap of 17 months, the last two children—Ruth, the third girl and Peter, the fourth boy and youngest child in the household—both arrived within thirteen months of each other and well before the turn of the century. By June 1899 Fanny had produced seven children in fewer than ten years, and was still only 33 years old, whereas her husband was in his 49th year. She had achieved her dearest wish: a 'dynasty'.

Erich was nine years old when his youngest brother was born. Eva was six-and-a-half. For the seven Steinthal children, life in the Uhlandstrasse was indulged and idyllic. The family had become part of Berlin's business elite.

2

The 'Golden Age'

When Max Steinthal was born on Christmas Eve 1850, Germany as a nation did not exist. He was raised in a Jewish community in Berlin, which was the largest city in Prussia. He was the second child of a businessman and wool trader named Eduard Steinthal, who soon before the birth of their first-born son Leopold had brought his young wife Johanna to live at a new address in Neue Friedrichstrasse. He came from a long line of Jewish travelling salesmen—Eduard's great-grandfather was born at the very end of the seventeenth century and had been a bookseller. Eduard Steinthal, however, was the first person in his lineage to move to Berlin, and to establish his family in the capital city of the kingdom of Prussia.

With his older brother and two younger sisters, Max spent his childhood in an exclusively Jewish neighbourhood, where the former ducal palace had been converted into spacious living accommodation. The two houses, which were conjoined by an enormous courtyard in the centre, were inhabited by a wide variety of all classes of tradesmen and craftsmen. These included carpenters and locksmiths, tailors and coopers; while the community itself provided several laundries, a woollen goods factory, a beer garden, a haulage company, a wood store and—most important of all—its own synagogue. Watching the confused but somehow manageable co-existence of all these disparate elements would have given the children an excellent example of the strict work ethic and industrious character so typical of European Jews.

Around the turn of the nineteenth century Napoleon emancipated all Jews in Europe, but by the time of his downfall in 1815 growing nationalism created an atmosphere of resentment and increased repression. There were sporadic outbreaks of violence and riots carried out against certain Jews, which included the destruction of Jewish property. Then during the Europe-wide revolutions of 1848 the pendulum swung back in their favour, bringing a new sense of freedom for all European Jews. It was this momentous year in history that was to herald a period of legal equality for Jews, especially in Germany, where they were to play key roles in the arts and sciences. By the end of the nineteenth century many Jews had become deeply integrated into German society. A select few were to go on to achieve high-ranking political appointments.

A small but significant indication of this period of assimilation, called by some the 'Golden Age' for German Jews, was in the choice of children's names. Whereas Eduard's ancestors had included amongst them the very biblical and Hebrew-sounding names of Eleasar, Jechiel, Lazarus and Zipporah, his four children were given the totally Germanic names of Leopold, Max, Sophie* and Elvira. Max was to continue this tradition in the naming of his own seven children.

By the time Max had completed his education at the local grammar school at the exceptionally young age of sixteen, his predilection for mathematics was clearly manifesting itself. Apart from a certain precocious musicality on the piano and ability for learning long poems off by heart, Max's true potential lay with numbers. He was never happier than when he sat huddled over complex and intractable equations with his private tutor Max Simon, who was to go on to become a professor of mathematics at the University of Strasbourg.

Interestingly, in keeping with the professional, business-based line of his father and grandfather before him, Eduard made no attempt to send either of his sons to university. Two months before his 17th birthday Max was apprenticed to a banking firm called Paderborn's, where after less than 18 months he was asked to make his first important decision: he could either learn more about bookkeeping or else further his knowledge in the Stock Market. His immediate choice of the latter was to have far-reaching consequences on his future career. He had been taken on by the boss of the company because of his excellent references, even though he considered himself to be quite unattractive, a 'young Jewish boy with bad posture and a pair of pince-nez on his nose'. Socially he had always felt himself to be in the shadow of his physically much more attractive older brother Leopold. Max's forte however became arbitrage, and it was soon discovered that he had such a good memory for figures that he was nicknamed 'Rabbi' by the chief dealer.

Max's own talent was not the only reason for what was to be his

* I had no idea when I chose the name Sophie for my only daughter, that I was naming her after a German great-great aunt. And when my sister chose Max as one her twins' names, she insists that she 'just liked the name', rather than choosing to name her child after his great-great-grandfather. Then again, I've only recently discovered that Thomas (the name of my first-born) was the name of an ancestor on my father's side who was a saddler in Bicester in the middle of the eighteenth century and who produced 15 children!

meteoric rise in the banking world. He could not have been born at a more advantageous time in Berlin's history. In the year of his 21st birthday in 1871, after the 'Iron Chancellor' Bismarck's concerted efforts, German unification was completed and Berlin became the capital of the new German nation. Kaiser Wilhelm I was declared Emperor of the new German Empire. This was a time of great opportunity for those involved in the banking business to meet the demands of burgeoning industrialisation, especially in the railways. Before this time banking held its strongest influence in various former German principalities, where because of the Church's ban on usury Jewish bankers had managed finances at court. The best example of this was the Rothschild family, descended from a financial agent for one of the richest of princes, the Elector of Hesse-Kassel. Others such as the Oppenheims in Düsseldorf and the Kaskels in Dresden dominated their respective princely courts. In the *Hansastädte* (free-trade cities) of Bremen and Hamburg, on the other hand, banking was virtually non-existent. Although Jewish bankers had been employed by the Hohenzollerns (the Prussian royal family), their progress had been seriously hampered by the restrictive yoke of Prussian bureaucracy. Berlin's very lack of banking tradition left the way open for the pioneers of modern financial practices in the nineteenth century.*

By the time of unification, Berlin had become not just the administrative capital but also the financial centre of the new Germany. Several very influential Jewish families were instrumental, through their financial acumen and ingenuity, in founding banking institutions that were to sweep away the former private banks, which were completely unable to cope at that time with the exponential demands for capital. One of these new institutions was Deutsche Bank, founded in 1870 as a specialist bank for foreign trade in Berlin by Adelbert Delbruck, a private banker and Ludwig Bamberger, an ambitious politician. Its first branches outside Germany were opened in London, Shanghai and Yokohama. Deutsche Bank acquired the Berliner Bank-Verein and Deutsche Union-Bank in 1876 and became then the largest bank in Germany, surpassing the Disconto-Gesellschaft.

Major projects in its first decades included the Northern Pacific Railroad in the United States and the Baghdad Railway, both in the 1880s. The bank also financed bond offerings for Krupp, the renowned steel manufacturers, and introduced the chemical company Bayer to the Berlin stock market. Just three years after its inception, however, the

* A. Richie, *Faust's Metropolis* (1998), p. 148.

newly unified German economy was to suffer a serious financial setback with the economic crisis of 1873, whose effects were extremely serious and long lasting. Despite this, in that same year Max Steinthal was taken on as a new employee of Deutsche Bank, specifically to deal in foreign trading. With a considerable amount of that delightful Yiddish expression *chutzpah*, when asked if his ambition was to become a clerk in the bank, Max retorted confidently that his sole intention was to become one of its directors. He was just 23 years old. Within a few years he was justifying the other directors' confidence in their new protégé—whose names included Wilhelm Platenius, Georg von Siemens and Hermann Wallich. Before he had reached his 28th birthday, Max Steinthal was invited onto the administrative board of Deutsche Bank.

Around this time Fanny Lindenthal was growing up in Vienna, which was not only the administrative capital of the Austro-Hungarian Empire, but also the cultural and musical heart of Europe. Despite her own somewhat modest upbringing, she would have been surrounded by art, literature and music, sectors of Viennese society in which Jews featured most prominently. It was perhaps fortuitous that at the time she became engaged to Max, Berlin as the capital of the new Germany was also striving to become a prominent centre for European culture. Her appreciation of music and the arts was to have an important influence both on Max and on their growing family.

For the Steinthals as a couple, the most essential factor was assimilation into and full acceptance by Berlin—and therefore German—society.* To this end Max felt it crucial that all his children be baptised into the Protestant faith, which in German is called *'Evangelisch'*. Each child's birth was entered into the appropriate Birth Register, and then usually some four or five months later the child was christened in the local church. Erich's entry in the Register seems very detailed, but it was those very details that were to have such a devastating effect on the family in the next century. In spiky Gothic script the 1890 entry states: 'As proved by his marriage certificate the Director of Deutsche Bank Max Steinthal, living at Roonstrasse 9, of the religion of Moses,** has

* Conversions from Judaism to Christianity in Germany at that time were quite usual, although much frowned upon by the traditionally Orthodox Jewish families (as was marrying 'outside the faith'). Max's belief system was always pragmatic, rather than deeply religious.

** The German term is *'mosaisch'* which means 'of Moses'. It was very important to state the religion of the parents, because all Germans had to register their religious preference (Catholic or Protestant) so that a percentage of their taxes could go to their shown that by his wife Fanni Steinthal née Lindenthal and living with him in his apartment did on 30th June 1890 at 9:15 a.m. bear a male child named Erich Berthold.'

For some reason Eva's christening was delayed until March 1897, when she was four and a half years old. Her godparents were a couple called Mr and Mrs Roland Lücke (whose name sounds Teutonic and not Jewish), and the ceremony took place in the local Louisekirche in Charlottenburg. The most prestigious godparents, however, were present at the youngest child's christening. Peter Steinthal, last of the seven children, was baptised at the age of four months in the presence of none other than Dr Georg von Siemens and his wife Elisa. This must have been a definite indication of how Max Steinthal's family had finally been assimilated into the higher echelons of Berlin society.

Each child was given two Christian names, except for Daisy who had three. Some of the children were known by their second names, while most of them had nicknames. The boys were given the names Erich Berthold, known as Erich; Jacob Werner, always known as Werner and the only child to have an Old Testament first name; Eduard Hans, named after his grandfather and known as Eduard; and Peter Friedrich, usually called Piet. The girls were Margarete Daisy Lea, always called Daisy; Eva Karola, nicknamed Pevchen; and Bertha Ruth, named after her maternal grandmother Bertha Lindenthal but always known as Rütchen or 'Little Ruth'.

Max and Fanny Steinthal's seven children, born in the decade spanning the 1890s, made their appearance into the world at the height of the expansion of Imperial Berlin. Imbued as he was with the Jewish work ethic, Max strove principally in his 'first love', Deutsche Bank, to advance the progress of Germany into the new century, and at home to provide for his large family of wife and seven children. German society at the end of the nineteenth century contrasted completely with the example of an English family at that time, where a public school education (certainly for the boys), followed by an appointment to high political office and possibly a peerage, could have propelled an erstwhile industrial family into the upper reaches of the establishment. This would have been impossible in Berlin where political, military and social life was completely controlled by a mere one per cent of the population: the 7,000 Junkers in the capital city and its surrounding areas. A distinct line

preferred church. Jews did not have to pay 'Church Tax' but their religion would have been officially registered.

had been drawn between these aristocrats and everyone else in Berlin, and crossing that line was nigh on impossible.

The propertied middle classes were becoming rich beyond their wildest dreams in Berlin's burgeoning industrialisation. Those belonging to the old *Bildungsbürgertum* (the usually liberal educated middle class) had become marginalised. While they continued to live in Tiergarten—that quiet and elegant part of the city where Max and Fanny Steinthal had started out in married life—reading journals and attending lectures at the university, they could not compete against the onslaught of Berlin's brassy new culture. It was a classic example of 'old' versus 'new' money—with new money winning. Names such as Siemens (Max Steinthal's fellow director at Deutsche Bank) were becoming synonymous with the new affluence, and in many ways it was these up and coming millionaire families that were creating the new wealth of Berlin.

Rather than founding their own independent culture, this newly rich middle class attempted to copy the upper echelons from whose membership they were excluded, vying with another for imperial recognition. Some even attempted to get their sons into the officer corps and marry off their daughters to the younger sons of minor aristocrats. At the height of the Empire the quest for orders, medals and distinctions reached an absolutely ridiculous level amongst the bourgeoisie. Although again exempt from noble orders (such as 'the Red Eagle of the Crown' and the 'Black Eagle'), businessmen and professionals would fight over the lesser orders which could be handed out at the Kaiser's annual *Ordenfest.* Berliners further became obsessed with the idea of rank, and it was fashionable for not only the man, but also his wife, to be recognised by his title: women would insist on being addressed as *'Frau Doktor'* or *'Frau Professor'* in acknowledgement of the rank or position achieved by their respective husbands.

Ironically, Max had already received two awards for services to foreign powers before his first child had been born. His first, a Spanish Order, was awarded 'in recognition by the Spanish government for services rendered in financial matters'. The second award, received just a month after his marriage to Fanny, was awarded by the Sultan of Turkey for his 'services to the Anatolian Railway'. This was a section of the great Berlin-to-Baghdad Railway, part of Kaiser Wilhelm II's great push for expansion towards the east.* These were the first in a long line of awards that Max was to receive in his lengthy career with the Bank.

As the new and brash bourgeoisie, of which the Steinthals were very

* Wilhelm II became Kaiser in 1888.

much a part, expanded in wealth, so their living quarters likewise had to expand to accommodate their new lifestyle. Huge new apartment houses and pseudo-palaces were erected in the Steinthals' neighbourhood of Charlottenburg, some of them very impressive on the outside but frequently consisting simply of cheap brick smothered in stucco and plaster. This was certainly not the case with the Steinthal home at Uhlandstrasse 191, designed and built as it was by one of the best contemporary architects, but some elements of the villa-style house did certainly conform to the bourgeois fashion of the time. The hall was enormous, lined with dark panelling and approached on the inside by an impressive sweeping staircase. The tall stained-glass windows were exactly in keeping with the latest fashions demanded by this newly enriched class of Berlin society. And Max's new-found interest in collecting modern art, together with his maintaining a keen interest in a whole variety of charitable works (for the Jewish section of the population), accorded exactly with the pursuits of his fellow professionals in this new middle class.

Previously unexposed to western fashion trends, Berliners were now keen to make up for lost time and everyone wanted to keep up with the latest demands of fashion. For the men, this meant copying the 'emperor's sideboards' so favoured by Franz Joseph of Austria and Kaiser Wilhelm of Germany. Beards, which had previously been avoided because of their liberal connotations, were now the height of fashion. It would have been difficult to find any man without some sort of facial hair; and this also applied to Max. For the wives and daughters, meanwhile, the most important thing was to be well dressed for the dinners and balls they frequented, and for promenades along Unter den Linden. Paris styles were not merely copied but seriously embellished, so that the Berlin manufacturers could outshine Paris. The demure Empire-line dresses and ringlets of the Biedermeier epoch were a thing of the past. Rather than women being made to look more like mother than mistress, now opulence was everything.

While the Steinthal family were not exactly slaves to the new fashion trends, they certainly wished to maintain a very serious hold on their social status in society. Max made sure that family portraits were taken at frequent intervals. There were photographs taken of Max at various stages in his life: clean-shaven as a young man, but by the time he was photographed on the occasion of the Bank's ten-year anniversary, he was already sporting a moustache and beard. This had grown considerably by his 39th year, on the day of his wedding. From his very early youth, the photographs of Max portray a man who always wore a stiff, starched white collar, a bow tie, full waistcoat and usually a tailcoat and formal trousers.

Despite the relatively high standing of the Steinthal family and their staff of at least twelve, thrift would have been one of the virtues that Fanny brought with her from Vienna. Daisy's dresses would have been passed down to her sister Eva, and then to Ruth. All through their childhood, Eva retained her jealousy of her older sister Daisy, whom she considered to be unfairly beautiful and to have the best legs of the three of them. What Rütchen inherited from her mother was her hair, and her dark tresses were to turn deep auburn. Her younger sister's 'crowning glory' provided yet another source of envy for Eva.

3

Prussian High Life

By the time Fanny had recovered from the birth of her seventh child, she was already firmly established as mistress of the huge house on the Uhlandstrasse. As Max spent long hours away from home because of his work, it was left entirely to his wife to run the household. And this Fanny did with a rod of iron and not some little temper. Although always known somewhat affectionately as *Mutting* to her seven children (the equivalent of 'Mumsie' in English), she would have been a severe and autocratic presence during their childhood. Eva shared her bedroom with her older sister Daisy, and together with the rest of the children they would have spent their early formative years in their sizeable nursery on the first floor, possibly feeling much closer to their nurse-maids than to their parents. Even in the far less spacious surroundings of the apartment in the Roonstrasse, Fanny would never have changed a nappy or even bottle-fed the babies herself. By the time Eva was five years old, Erich had been privately tutored for two years and Daisy had been learning her first lessons with a governess. When the children were a little older, they would group together in a part of the ground floor and recite the poems of Schiller and Goethe off by heart. The three girls would receive all their education at home, with private governesses, whereas it would have been expected for the boys to attend one of the local *Gymnasien*, or grammar schools.

Max and Fanny adored each other and were never to have a cross word in all the years of their long marriage. She always called him '*Schatzi*', which means 'Little Treasure'. Even so, their bedroom arrangements upstairs were completely separate. Max had a small bedroom with his own dressing room—which he found perfectly adequate. Every day his personal valet would lay out his master's formal wear for the day. Fanny, meanwhile, had an entire 'suite' to herself, consisting of a very pretty bedroom, her own bathroom and a sitting room. Her bedroom always smelled of violets.

The Polish cook became renowned, not only amongst the Steinthals' close family but also in their wider circle of friends and acquaintances. She made the most wonderful meals, from complicated dinner parties for

36 down to *Wuerstchen mit Kartoffel* (sausage and mash) for the children. Entertaining became a very important part of life with the Steinthals, but an element from which the children were completely excluded. However, the business of eating could take part in various sections of the house and on different levels. The children would eat in the nursery on the first floor, together with their nursemaids and governesses. Perhaps when they were older they were allowed to join their parents in the *Gartensaal*, the everyday breakfast room that adjoined the conservatory and from which it was separated by its spectacular glass wall. Fanny loved crocheting and could make entire Biedermeier crocheted covers and tablecloths. The decor of the *Gartensaal* was also in Biedermeier style, and this was a very pleasant room, especially when the sun shone.

Every day Seelbinder the gardener would choose flowers, from his treasured collection of semi-tropical plants, for the mistress of the house to arrange opulently in large vases in the 'niche' in the centre of one side of the Great Hall. She also had smaller vases dotted about her favourite salon, in which she entertained ladies to tea and for which her Polish cook made a show of baking her speciality of Viennese patisserie. For evening dinner parties of course the formal dining room was used, where the long mahogany table could seat 36 under a sparkling chandelier, and extravagant five- or six-course meals would be served with an excellent selection German wines from the well-stocked cellar, together with the obligatory champagne.

The staff took all their meals below stairs, seated in their respective uniforms at a long wooden table and fed once again by the capable Polish cook. Sometimes as a special treat, when she was baking cakes the children would be allowed to stick their fingers into the mixing bowls. While the children enjoyed a relaxed relationship with their nursemaids and also most likely with the lower-ranking members of staff, Fanny became a very autocratic mistress. Her loyal lady's maid Else was soon nicknamed *'die Maus'* ('little mouse'). Fanny treated her very roughly and rudely, especially as she would tend to drop food down her front every mealtime, which Else then had to spend hours washing off her dresses. Although frequently caught at the sharp end of Fanny's bad temper and querulous moods, Else remained ever loyal to her mistress. She was also a very skilled with her hands, and would spend her spare time knitting or sewing some complicated piece of embroidery for Fanny.

Most sumptuous of all were the musical evenings and grand balls given by the Steinthals. The daughter of the composer Franz Liszt lived in the neighbourhood, and apart from offering piano lessons to the family she would help Fanny plan specifically themed programmes for the concerts that were held in the Great Hall. The children were strictly excluded from attending these elegant events, and could only listen from the upstairs balcony. The most magnificent evenings of all were the dances and balls, in which up to 120 figures could swirl and twirl in the Great Hall to the strains of a live orchestra.

For the children, possibly the best time of year was Christmas. In a life regulated by nursemaids, governesses and tutors; of learning by rote and Sunday school for confirmation; where learning good manners and formal deportment became a matter of course; and who saw very little of their parents except on Sundays and on holiday, Christmas must have been a magical time. An enormous fir tree would be erected in the Great Hall and beautifully decorated all over in red and silver baubles, complete with dozens of red candles. If the parents had both been brought up in the Jewish tradition, there was certainly no evidence of this by the time the family moved to the house in the Uhlandstrasse. The staff, who would have been given perhaps half a day off a month, were each given a present that accorded with their rank in the household. For the girls this was a bolt of cloth with which they could make their own dresses. The higher their position in the household, the larger the amount of cloth—all of which had been carefully measured out beforehand by Fanny.

Christmas was celebrated in true German fashion with an enormous carp as the main dish, and with traditional German *Pfefferkuchen* (gingerbread biscuits) cut into stars and gingerbread men and moons and circles. Eva and her sisters would wear their prettiest dresses, and the boys would be put either into their sailor suits or the more formal adult suits with stiff collars. Fanny would be dressed in a vision of white flounces with her hair dressed up into a chic chignon, while Max would wear the same dress suit he always wore to the bank.

The first decade of the new century was to bring momentous changes to the Steinthal household. When Eva was in her tenth year and her youngest brother Peter was just three, Erich the oldest was sent away to the Bismarck-Gymnasium. He was to show a keen interest in literature from an early age, but to his father's great chagrin not even an inkling of mathematical brilliance or indeed the slightest leaning towards the world of business. Earlier that year of 1902 and at the age of 51, Max had been awarded the title of *'Kommerzienrat'*—a business honour for which he had to pay 300 marks, securing his own place in the world of finance. Fanny could now assure her own position in Prussian society by being addressed as *'Frau Kommerzienrat'*.

Three years later, after a spell in the Clara Emilia Sanatorium (probably for a 'rest cure' because of overwork), another award from Italy and the momentous opening of the new and exciting Berlin Underground system, Max decided to leave the administrative board and join the supervisory board of Deutsche Bank. That way, he told his family, he could 'sit at table at home at least once a week'.

There is one family portrait taken in the music room in the spring of 1906—the only one to include all seven children. Fanny is seated at the grand piano, while Ruth the second youngest child is standing on her mother's left, playing the violin. She is about seven years old. To her left sits her older sister Eva, aged about 13 with her youngest brother Peter sitting on her lap, at around six years old. Standing next to him with his hand on the piano is Eduard, aged around ten. To Fanny's right, ranged along the side of the piano, are first Werner aged 12, his big sister Daisy aged just 14 and finally Erich the oldest aged 15. All three girls are wearing calf-length white dresses with frilly bows at the waist, and the older girls have decorous high collars. The ages of the boys can be distinguished fairly accurately by the clothes they are wearing.

In another, earlier photo of Eva with her sister Ruth, together with their two brothers Peter and Eduard, the youngest Peter is in a sailor outfit that looks like a dress, because he was only about a year old. Once the boys had reached their third birthday they would be dressed in proper sailor suits, with shorts and a wide-collared top. In the 1906 photo Peter is wearing a typical sailor suit in marine blue, with white stripes on the wide collar. His two older brothers Werner and Eduard are wearing suits that look more like school uniform, with small white collars. They both have severe side partings and their hair has been combed rigorously over their heads. As the oldest, Erich is wearing clothes that are a junior variation of those worn by his father: a smart jacket and high wing-collar that looks at once very grown-up and uncomfortable. The three girls have their dark long hair tied back in ponytails on top of their heads, with white ribbons. Every child is wearing small-buttoned boots.

The children all look very serious, but Erich looks sad, Daisy looks knowing and Eva somehow looks worried. Fanny looks particularly pleased with herself, as if she were showing off her best achievement of producing seven children—even if they had breached the usually child-free sanctum of her music room. Yet how could any of them predict the course of events that would soon affect the family so catastrophically?

Just a couple of months after the photograph was taken, Eva fell very seriously ill with meningitis. For days, while Daisy was put into one of the guest bedrooms, Eva burned with high fever. Two nurses were on permanent duty over the sick child, and the rest of the household had to creep about so as not to disturb her. This was an extremely dangerous illness whose outcome could have been fatal, and it was a very anxious time for the whole family. The worst consequences could have been permanent brain damage. Miraculously, the reverse seemed to be the case and Eva found the strength to pull through. Daisy, who was always jealous when attention was not focused on her, was later to make some very spiteful remarks about her younger sister. As far as she was concerned, before the illness Eva had been a particularly slow learner who had problems in keeping up with her reading and writing. Once she was fully recovered from the disease, however, she seemed to sparkle with a new wit and intelligence.

That summer, in order to celebrate Eva's recovery, Max took his whole family away on holiday in the Tatra Mountains.* A few months later, in the spring of 1907, Daisy was invited to tea at the home of very wealthy Jewish friends, whose house was 'like a castle'. She had grown into a very beautiful young woman, whose haughty looks belied her 15 years. There she caught the eye of a very handsome young man some five years her senior. Her return home that same day sent shockwaves through the Steinthal household, as she announced in a determined voice that she had fallen in love and was going to marry Lutz Reichenheim, and nobody could stop her. Eva and Ruth pretended to be scandalised at this news, but Eva was secretly in awe of her sister's boldness.

As if to divert attention from his wayward elder daughter's behaviour, and ever keen on investing in the modern age, Max purchased two new automobiles for the family. Ernst the coachman, who up until then had been in charge of taking members of the family around Berlin in a pony and trap, was sent away to driving school. Max had always used the horse-drawn trolleybus to get to work. The new machines were of course the invention of Mr Benz, who was to christen the latest version of his new-fangled machine after his daughter Mercedes. The huge models, with coach lamps on the front, running boards and plush leather seats, were a wonder of brass and wood and steel.

On a beautiful spring day an expedition was organised to take the entire family on an outing through the woods. Erich, Daisy and Eva were in the front car, driven by Ernst, while the younger children were in the second car driven by Ernst's underling, an under-coachman. Inordinately

* Today the Tatra Mountains are in Poland, south of Krakow and near the Slovakian border. At that time they were on the fringes of Eastern Prussia and so still part of the German Empire.

proud that they were one of the first families in Berlin to own motorcars, the party set off in high spirits. Some time later on that day, disaster struck. Ernst lost control—possibly attempting to avoid a rider whose uncontrollable horse had taken fright at the shiny and utterly alien machine. The children and staff in the second car could only watch in horror as the front car crashed, and tipped over into a ditch. Daisy escaped, shaken but unhurt. Eva was concussed and confused, but it was Erich who was the most severely damaged. Completely unconscious, he lay in the damp grass with a cracked skull and blood gushing out of a hole in his temple.

While one of the governesses comforted the terrified children, and the under-coachman ran for help, Fanny took control of the situation. She told Daisy to put her finger in the hole in Erich's head, to stop the bleeding. It probably saved his life. Erich was to spend months in hospital recovering from an operation that inserted a silver plate in his head. Eva was left with a facial tic, but Erich was to remain physically and mentally affected for the rest of his life. The fact that this was one of the first automobile accidents in Germany did little to alleviate the trauma on the family.

In August of that year, a couple of months after her oldest son's 17th birthday, Fanny took Erich away from home for a 'cure' holiday. Max joined the remaining six children and their usual large posse of staff for a holiday in Grevesmühlen, a town right up in the north of Germany near the Baltic coast in the state of Mecklenburg. At the start of the new school year, it became obvious that Erich would be unable to continue his studies at the Bismarck Grammar School. In his 18th year he became the first Steinthal child to leave home. He went to live in Weimar, where a private tutor was engaged so that he could complete his studies for his *Abitur* at his own (considerably hampered) pace. For the girls, life continued at home much as usual, but the younger boys must have felt the absence of their older brother. Werner was also at grammar school—having overcome a bout of polo that was to leave him with problems in his legs for the rest of his life. Eduard, the most naughty but least able of the four boys, would be sent away to school the following year.

This alarming accident did nothing to deter Fanny from having a go at driving herself. On another occasion she went on an unaccompanied drive along the Koenigsberger Allee—the 1,000-kilometre-long highway that led eastwards out of Berlin all the way to Koenigsberg in what was then Eastern Prussia, and which is today the port of Kaliningrad in Russia. Despite severe protestations from her chauffeur, she insisted on attempting to drive the large and unwieldy motorcar herself. Needless to say her recklessness caused another near-fatal accident. Unable to maintain control, Fanny caused the car almost to capsize into a ditch on the side of the road, which would have consisted of many potholes and would have had various sections that were completely unmetalled. Fanny survived the mishap entirely unscathed. Without compunction, she swore the hapless chauffeur to secrecy about the whole incident, by making sure that he would confess that he had been the one driving Madame in the car.

A further prerequisite for the new-fangled driving experience was membership of the Kaiser's Automobile Club. Access to membership was severely restricted—usually to members of the Junker class. It is debatable whether Max, who despite his aspirations still belonged to the professional classes and certainly not the topmost echelons of Berlin society, would have been granted membership.

While the boys were growing up to experience the beginnings of independence by being sent away to school (although still being educated in a very disciplined atmosphere), the girls would have been chaperoned wherever they went. Whether being tutored at home, going for walks and promenades, being entertained to tea at other rich families' houses—they were never on their own, nor were they allowed to mix with 'rough' company. The servants were considered a different category of person, each having their allotted place in life. Fanny had her own dressmaker but there might have been the occasional outing for the girls to visit one of the highlights of Berlin society: the department store.

At the end of the nineteenth century the new department stores were to become the symbol of not only local, but also even national pride. Since unification Berliners had become keenly aware of their status compared to other major capitals of Europe. Having defeated Austria and France in war, they were now determined to outdo their European rivals of Vienna and Paris in terms of pomp and luxury. Synonymous with the new urban Berlin were the names of Tietz, KaDeWe and Wertheim's, which were to provide their eager customers with an amazing supply of new and wonderful goods from all around the world. At breakfast, Max would often read Fanny paragraphs from his daily paper, pleasing her most when he told her of the latest store to be opened in their city.

Hermann Tietz was a typical example of the new, energetic, optimistic and daring Berliner, much approved of by the Steinthals. He delighted in introducing new goods into the city. His attitude was reflected in the development of parallel advances, such as the construction of a new over- and underground system, much of which was funded by Deutsche Bank and which was a project very dear to Max Steinthal's heart. Tietz's emporium was soon joined by the *Kaufhaus des Westens*, subsequently only known by its acronym of KaDeWe. The building was unusually refined and restrained in design. Its innovation lay in that it offered not only the sale of an extensive choice of goods, but also combined this with a whole range of services that previously could only have been found in separate stores and outlets. These included not only a café and a beauty salon, but also a central ticket office for all travel and entertainment.

Both these stores, however, were ignored by Fanny, because she wanted to take the girls to the most sumptuous new department store of all: Wertheim's. Max had told her all about the new store, built on the site of the demolished Sarotti shop in the prestigious area of Leipziger Strasse, and costing an almost unimaginable twelve million marks. On the day of their visit, the three girls stared in wonder at its grand entrance hall, resplendent with extravagant chandeliers hanging from the ceilings, and at the staircases sweeping past walls adorned with mosaics and mirrors. Ruth could not believe that foaming fountains and real live palm trees could exist inside a store, while an uncountable number of lights illuminated the wide staircases. To give the building an airy feel, solid walls had been replaced by glass—like a greatly magnified version of the Steinthals' own *Gartensaal* at home. The tiles were in a soft rose-pink, and had apparently been supplied by a factory owned by the Kaiser.

For the girls, as for the thousands of Berliners flocking to the new store, Wertheim's was an absolutely magical place. Berliners of all classes simply loved this new 'shop', which was quickly dubbed 'the greatest department store in the world'. People would throng through the doors of Wertheim's to make ostentatious purchases from the huge array of goods on display; but more often than not they would simply come to watch their fellow shoppers and to be seen.[*]

Such a visit would have been a rare event for the Steinthal girls. In their teenage years, however, their somewhat narrow knowledge of the world was expanded with the appointment of an English governess called Miss Florie, together with two girls from the *Suisse Romande* region of Switzerland. Thus they were taught English and French at home, which all the Steinthal children were able to speak quite competently. Another activity considered suitable for a young lady was horse riding. A photo of the two older girls, taken in front of the villa, shows them mounted on beautiful horses: Daisy aged about 19 on a magnificent chestnut, looking very haughty and knowing, Eva on a dapple-grey, looking calm

[*] Richie, *Faust's Metropolis*, p. 211.

and confident. Their governess as chaperone is seated on a pretty roan, and looks unsure of herself. All three young women are wearing full-length skirts with long hunting jackets, with straw boaters on their heads and long whips in their hands, seated elegantly side-saddle. The horses are all fitted with curbed bits to hold their heads up, and they have obviously been groomed to a lustrous shine.

At the beginning of 1911 Max and Fanny decided to expand their two elder daughters' education by travelling even further afield, and an exotic, six-week holiday was planned. Leaving their brothers and sister at home in Berlin, Daisy and Eva were to be taken by steamship on the trip of a lifetime to uncover the mysteries of Egypt.

4

Bridal Trips and Betrothals

A few days into the New Year, the steamship *Prince Henry* set off from the Bay of Naples on its cruise eastwards across the Mediterranean towards Egypt. Apart from the usual complement of passengers, whose trunks were loaded strictly by number into the capacious hold below decks, its main cargo consisted of sacks of flour. Fanny and Eva, the Steinthals' enthusiastic chroniclers of their adventures to the family back home in Berlin, watched in fascination as giant cranes lifted 20 sacks at a time off the quayside, to fill the yawning belly of the ship.

The family had travelled by train in first-class comfort as far as Naples. Here they were taken on a drive towards the lava-strewn but fertile slopes of Mount Vesuvius, which Fanny later described as 'most interesting and unusual with its stink of sulphur'. Further cultural activities included a visit to the *Museo Nazionale*—marvelling at the collection of bronzes—followed by a trip to the Aquarium. On one evening they all attended a magnificent performance of *Tosca*.

Once the ship was out on the open sea, the family were invited to lunch at the captain's table. It was here that *Herr und Frau Kommerzienrat* Steinthal, of Deutsche Bank, together with their two daughters, could be formally introduced to the German vice-consul at Cairo, whom Fanny found 'charming and easy-going'. She was obviously keeping a sharp eye out for suitable introductions for Eva—indeed in the new century many families of similar standing to the Steinthals would undertake such 'exotic' journeys, for the specific purpose of finding suitable husbands for their daughters. Such 'arranged' marriages were considered not only acceptable but socially advantageous.

As Daisy and Eva had begged to share their mother's cabin, the three of them soon found their living space to be somewhat cramped, even though the thoughtful captain had offered them a second stateroom on the deck below. Max, meanwhile (as perhaps befitted his status and age), was given a beautifully large cabin in which he could indulge in his favourite pastime on holiday: three-hour, after-lunch naps. The calm routine of life on board ship, which included watching the flickering glow of Stromboli, a volcano in the sea, and the most beautiful sunset—'a palette of the deepest violet to the palest orange' as Fanny later described it—was soon to be interrupted by extremely inclement weather. Fanny proved to be the best sailor and was entirely unaffected by the heavy rolling of the ship, but the other three were all seasick. Worst off was Rosa, Fanny's personal maid, who had probably never ventured that far from home before and was simply unable to cope with such unfamiliar and adverse conditions. On the morning they were due to disembark in Egypt, Fanny herself had to take control of all the packing. Eva wrote to her grandmother Bertha, who had been left in charge of the remaining four children in Berlin, 'Saturday was much windier and on Sunday the weather turned into an out and out cataclysm. But Mama behaved like a true hero.'

Egypt proved to be even more fascinating, charming and alien than any of them could have imagined. In several letters back home, both Fanny and Eva described their progress from the port of Alexandria to Cairo, where they stayed in the Savoy Hotel and were taken on a tour of the old city, including beautiful mosques, and then on a drive out into the desert to visit the Pyramids. Eva was captivated and astounded by the ancient construction of Cheops and its two lesser pyramids (where massive stones were simply laid on top of each other without any mortar in between), and even found the gigantic forms of the sphinxes, mutilated as they were almost a hundred years previously by Napoleon's soldiers, something to marvel at. While Daisy was probably spending most of her time pining for her Lutz back home, Eva hinted in her letters that she was beginning to find men attractive. She told her grandmother, 'You can see many beautiful people here—but I'm referring only to the men of course, because the women are always veiled.'

From Cairo the family took a train to Assiut (known as Asyut in ancient times), from where they were to board the Nile steamer that would take them southwards upriver to Luxor and then to Aswan. Before embarking on this stage of the journey, they had taken part in an Arab wedding and had also watched a chaotic but exciting desert race, whose participants rode a bewilderingly motley collection of camels, donkeys, oxen and motorcars. The Nile cruise was to last around three weeks, and the leisurely pace of the trip was made even more pleasant by the fact that there were only 24 passengers on board, instead of the usual 70. Fanny was as excited by the discovery of acquaintances (probably from Berlin) on board ship, as she was at the passing scenery. She wrote, 'The Nile is big and wide, yellow and green, while its banks are flat and barren. From time to time you can see a village or the Nile mud crowned with a few date palms, while dozens of sailing boats glide past us and a delightful whiff of oil wafts over the ship.'

In Luxor Max was to receive news of a great crisis back home in Berlin. The continuing construction of the Berlin Underground system, much of which had been financed and backed by Deutsche Bank and which of all projects at that time was the one dearest to his heart, had run into apparently intractable problems. Determined to be of some help, even at this great distance, Max sent a telegram from Luxor to Deutsche Bank in Berlin, offering a typically practical solution. The yellowing document has been kept in the bank's archives to this day.

On the way back across the Mediterranean, from where they enjoyed a marvellous view of the French Riviera, Fanny wrote to her mother, 'The children really are amassing fabulous memories of this trip which they can treasure for ever, a fact which brings me daily pleasure. Who knows what life will bring them later? At least we'll have been able to fashion this part for them.' Her words were to be very prophetic.

The journey home included a visit to Pompeii and then another first-class train journey across Italy. On one particular day Fanny was standing in the corridor of the sleeping car as they pulled to a stop in Trieste (where the statue of Dante stands proudly in the town square). 'Suddenly a tall chap stumbled inside and embraced me round the neck,' wrote Fanny in her next letter home. She was delighted to find it was none other than Lutz (Daisy must have been even more pleased)—he had apparently been on some sort of cure, possibly after an illness, because Fanny described him as having put on eight kilos since she had last seen him.

After meeting up with Viennese friends in Merano and visiting a local castle by pony and trap, Fanny wrote her last letter home, saying that unfortunately Max would have to break off his holiday in order to come home early to attend to urgent business. The letter included a severe warning to the household to have everything spick and span for the master's arrival back in Berlin. She also chided Erich for not wanting to join the two girls in Merano. 'You would like it very much,' she wrote, 'and since there's a theatre and good concerts here, you couldn't possibly be bored.'

It had been a wonderful trip, which kindled in Eva a lifelong fascination with archaeology, and a passion for culture and artefacts from the ancient world.

In the summer of 1912 the entire Steinthal family undertook their annual holiday to the Engadine in Switzerland. Once again, in accordance with Max's support of modern forms of transport, he would have insisted that the whole family travel from Berlin by train. The chauffeur would have driven them in their latest Mercedes Benz to the station. An entire first-class carriage would be reserved for the Steinthals, because again each child would have had their own governess or maid, with all the clothes and necessities being packed into a stack of large trunks. The overnight journey took them from Berlin to Zurich, changing next morning to continue to Chur, and then along the spectacular mountain railway to St Moritz. They stayed in the village of Sils Maria, high up in the mountains and bordering a series of three lakes each surrounded by lush evergreen forests. The scenery was simply stunning, the elegant town of St Moritz itself being dominated by the towering, 11,000-ft peaks of the Corvatsch.

It is quite possible that Lutz, who was by now very much a favourite of Fanny's, accompanied the family on this holiday as well, because it so happened during the summer of 1912 that Daisy became the first of the seven Steinthal children to be betrothed. She was 20 years old, a dark-haired beauty, while her fiancé was 25 and by all standards a very handsome young man.

Although there were no cable cars at that time, Swiss ingenuity had already come up with the idea of the funicular railway, where the up-train was pulled up an extremely steep gradient by the counterbalance of the down-train. The best method, however, of getting high up into the mountains was by pony and trap. The siblings delighted in riding uphill in their hired wooden cart pulled by a feisty and fat little Haflinger pony, cheerfully urged on by a nut-brown local lad. High above the grandeur of the hotel glittered the everlasting snows of the glacier, tantalisingly out of reach.

It was a delightful place, and while the hotel itself offered every luxury, the finest wines and the best haute cuisine, the most health-giving element was the pure mountain air that infused the whole area. For city-dwellers such as the Steinthals this was truly a 'breath of fresh air'. By this time Max was in his 62nd year and his beard had already turned white, giving him a rather benevolent and patrician air. For Eva these holidays were the best time, because it gave her beloved but very busy father time to join in the family activities. Fanny in her mid-forties was an attractive and dynamic woman.

On one particular day well into the holidays it was decided that the whole family would undertake a walk in the mountains. Fanny and the girls would have been dressed in long skirts and long jackets made of felt or heavy tweed, while the boys wore britches and Loden jackets. They all wore stout walking shoes and would have been accompanied by at least four or five staff from their household. The whole party therefore consisted of some fifteen people. Ahead of them walked their Swiss mountain guide. As they came along a ridge bordered with steep crags, they met a party coming along the other way. In front was a youngish looking man of excellent physique, wearing green climbing britches, woolly socks, stout walking boots, a green felt jacket and a peaked cap set at a jaunty angle from which a feather was sticking out. He smiled broadly at the large number of adults and young people coming towards him, and doffed his cap in greeting.

'Fine morning,' he shouted warmly, giving a little bow. 'Vollmann at your service! And whom do I have the honour of addressing?'

As Fanny was by far the most adept at coping with new social encounters, she took command of the situation.

'This is my husband, the esteemed banker Max Steinthal,' she said, indicating Max with a wave of her hand. 'And these are my seven children.' The boys all bowed slightly, as they had been taught to do by their tutors. The girls stood where they were, believing that a rocky path in the mountains of Switzerland did not merit a curtsey from any of them.

Further pleasantries were exchanged, and once Max understood that the newcomer Richard Vollmann was also spending his summer holidays in the mountains round Sils Maria, he issued an invitation for the young man to join them one evening for drinks in their hotel.

'Well, what d'you think of that?' whispered Ruth to her older sister. 'You're the one he was looking at.' Feeling herself momentarily lost for words, Eva did not reply for a few moments.

'Why Pevchen!' exclaimed Ruth, staring intently at her sister. 'You're blushing!'

'Hush!' hissed Eva, pulling her sister to one side. 'I'm doing no such thing.'

'But what d'you think of him?' persisted Ruth, whispering even more quietly so as to remain out of hearing range of either of their parents.

'Well,' said Eva, recovering her composure slightly. 'His hair was so blond, wasn't it? Almost as white as snow.'

Several days later Richard Vollmann presented himself for drinks at the Steinthals' hotel. It was a pleasant enough evening. The day before the family were due to return to Berlin, Max Steinthal decided it would be a good idea to invite the earnest young man to dinner with the whole family. Richard Vollmann turned out to be an entertaining speaker, and kept the younger members of the family regaled with an apparently unending flow of stories about his latest exploits climbing in the mountains. Several times during the seven-course meal Eva found herself blushing for no reason that she could think of.

Friedrich Eduard Richard Vollmann was born on 3rd September 1883 in

Sebnitz in Saxony. At the time this was a small manufacturing town on the banks of the River Elbe, in the east of the state of Saxony. Today it lies very close to the border with the Czech Republic. Situated some 60 kilometres east of Dresden, Sebnitz had a solid and hard-working population whose lives revolved around a strict Protestant work ethic. Most of the citizens were Lutheran by faith, in keeping with many cities and towns in the north of Germany.

Friedrich, who was always known as Richard, was the elder son of Richard Vollmann, a factory owner. Together with his younger brother Walter the two boys were intellectually fed on a diet of sound business principles, as their father was the owner of a factory called Mey & Co., which made artificial silk flowers. Rather than send his boys away to university, Richard Vollmann senior decided that their education would be best served by inviting them on a round-the-world trip when they had reached their 18th birthday. This was not an opportunity, however, that their father thought to present to the youngest member of the family, a girl christened Helene but always known as Lene. She would have been brought up on a rigid diet of *'Kinder Kirche Küche'* (children, church and cooking) and told that her main aim in life was to find a suitable husband and produce children.

So it was that at the turn of the century young Richard went on the trip of a lifetime, most of it by train and packet steamer, to all the four corners of the world. He saw Australia and New Zealand, learned about manufacturing in Japan and Hong Kong, visited his father's business subsidiary in New York, was entertained in various parts of South America, and spent some time at several factories in Manchester in order to absorb English business practices. He visited remote family in Brazil and Peru, where certain of his mother's relatives had emigrated to run plantations. At one stage he took his bicycle and walked with it on his shoulders all the way to the top of Snowdon in Wales. An inveterate explorer and fitness enthusiast, Richard had been manifesting physical prowess, especially in rock and mountain climbing, from a very young age. And to round off his education, it was in Brazil and Peru that the more worldly of his cousins introduced him to the tantalising milieu of the red-light district, and where he developed a liking for the more exotic kind of prostitutes.

When Richard got home to Sebnitz after his summer trip in the Swiss mountains, he told his mother and father all about the dark-haired beauty he had met, together with her family from Berlin. His father at once pricked up his ears at hearing the name of Max Steinthal coupled with that of Deutsche Bank, while his mother began immediate matchmaking.

The Saxon firm of Mey & Co. had been a client of Deutsche Bank's for years.

'After all, son,' said Frau Vollmann persuasively, 'you're nearly 29 years old, the son of a well-established factory owner and by now certainly in need of a wife. She sounds like the perfect match for you.'

'And it's always a good idea for a young man to seek out the daughter of a wealthy professional,' added his father, with a twinkle in his eye. 'What could be better than for the son of a proud manufacturing family to match up with the daughter of a prosperous banking family, eh? As you know, it is the custom for the bride's father to provide his new son-in-law with a good start in married life.'

Richard looked sideways at his father, the thickness of his round glasses magnifying his myopic blue eyes. With a grin, he nodded his white-blond head. 'So you think this would be a good match, father?' he asked.

'Well, you need to think of providing a son who can follow in your footsteps,' replied his father.

Back in Berlin, all thoughts of the Vollmanns vanished from Max's mind as Lutz Reichenheim approached his father-in-law to be, and formally asked for his daughter Daisy's hand in marriage. All Daisy could think about was how handsome her fiancé looked in his uniform: the striped trousers, tightly-fitting smart jacket with gold buttons, and shining highly polished boots with spurs. But Frau Reichenheim meanwhile had invited Daisy to tea on several occasions, in order to plead with her not to marry her son, whom she described as 'a feckless wastrel'. Daisy with her feisty and determined spirit would have none of it, and refused to let go of her dream to be married to Lutz, despite some of the adults' protestations. She probably had a good ally in her own mother, who was very taken with the handsome young man.

By this time Max's net worth had increased exponentially to 12.4 million marks, putting the family well into the millionaire bracket. Some three years previously, to Fanny's great delight, her husband had been awarded the title of *'Geheim Kommerzienrat'*. It translates literally as 'Privy Counsellor', but was a business rather than a political honour. With considerable pomp, this honour was conferred upon Max Steinthal by the minister for trade and industry in the name of the Emperor. From now onwards Max would be addressed as *'Herr Geheimrat'*.

For some years now Max had been investing in works of art, and had been employing as his trusted adviser a certain Wilhelm de Bode, the director of the Berlin Art Gallery and one of the most respected art connoisseurs of the time. Having originally purchased what could almost be described as a 'job lot' of paintings from the Sussex estate of a deceased Rothschild living in England, Max had by now acquired a sizeable collection of modern art, much of which hung up the stairs and in his study in the family villa. Fanny, meanwhile, had become an avid collector of miniatures. Yet when de Bode approached Max after the announcement of Daisy's engagement, requesting permission to travel to Italy to acquire further paintings, Max refused to give him his blessing. Despite the family's very considerable fortune, Max complained that the arrangements for his oldest daughter's forthcoming wedding 'had completely pumped him dry'. Thrift was still the watchword of the day.

It was the first wedding in the Steinthal household, taking place just before Daisy's 21st birthday, and so of course Eva and Ruth were bridesmaids for their sister. Eva was 20 and Ruth a very young 14. The marriage took place in the fashionable Marienkirche in Charlottenburg, for which momentous occasion Max would have given his oldest daughter a sizeable dowry, together with a generous monthly allowance. Although Eva was secretly extremely jealous of her older sister, her wedding marked the end of the hitherto frequent exchange of confidences between the two girls. For Eva the main benefit of the whole affair was that she now had a bedroom all to herself.

Unbeknown to anyone, Daisy's honeymoon signalled the rocky path along which her marriage was to travel. Already an inveterate gambler, Lutz spent his honeymoon night risking ever-higher stakes at the gaming tables, finally hocking his new wife's jewellery to back his mountainous debts. Despite this abhorrent behaviour, within two months Daisy was pregnant with her first child, and the birth of the Steinthals' first grandchild was predicted for September 1913.

That summer the Steinthal and Vollmann families were to get together. Daisy, in her state of confinement and six months pregnant, stayed at home in Berlin. She and her husband Lutz had generously been given their own apartment on the first floor in the house in the Uhlandstrasse.

Travelling once again to the village of Sils Maria in Switzerland, the Steinthals were to meet the Vollmanns for the first time. Max Steinthal had several earnest discussions with Richard Vollmann senior, while Fanny entertained Frau Vollmann to coffee with whipped cream in the elegant lounge of their luxurious hotel. Meanwhile Richard was allowed to take Eva out for walks, during which he delighted in showing off his physical fitness by giving her little demonstrations of rock-climbing.

A few evenings later, when everyone in both families had got suitably dressed up, the engagement between Eva Steinthal, daughter of the Berlin banker, and Richard Vollmann, son of the Saxon manufacturer, was announced. It was July, but in keeping with the traditions of the time (as had happened with Daisy's engagement and subsequent marriage), the wedding was immediately set for the following November—a mere four months later. During all this time Richard had been charm itself towards his dark-haired, petite and somewhat shy intended. They made a striking couple, despite their nine-year difference in age.

If Richard Vollmann senior had any reservations about his son marrying into a Jewish family (although aware that all the children had been baptised into the Lutheran faith), then he kept them to himself. The prospect of having wealthy in-laws from Berlin, as well as a guaranteed dowry and good financial support for his son's future, was a compelling attraction. As far as their respective backgrounds were concerned, while the Steinthals came from a fairly modest line of travelling salesmen, the Vollmanns had been descended from a much more highly respected trade. From the mid sixteenth century Vollmans had worked as highly skilled craftsmen, forging armour and weapons for various Saxon nobles and proud to pass on the title of *Waffenschmied*, or armourer, from father to son.

That autumn, a momentous event precipitated the forthcoming wedding plans for Max's second daughter. It was September and Daisy was into her ninth month of pregnancy, but for some reason the whole family was out of the house. In the end Daisy's waters broke much too soon, and she found herself alone with only Lutz to help. Before he could even send for the doctor, his wife was well advanced into labour. There was no alternative but for him to roll up his sleeves and assist his wife with the birth of their first child. Monica came into the world on 18 September, a red-haired, healthy girl whose lively temper made an immediate impression on her father. Completely humbled by this experience, he was to remain in awe of his first-born daughter.

Not long after the precipitous arrival of the Steinthals' first grandchild into the family, it was the beginning of October and time for Max to spend the only day in the year when he immersed himself completely in the religion of his forefathers: Yom Kippur or the Day of Atonement. On this, the most important religious festival in the Jewish calendar, he would don the full Orthodox clothing—long dark coat, black hat, prayer shawl—and walk to the great Synagogue on Fasanenstrasse. There he would present the Rabbi with a very generous cheque. Fanny would never take part in this particular custom and, even though she supported her husband's patronage of Jewish arts, culture and education in Berlin, she never made reference to her Jewish past.

A month before his second daughter's wedding, Max rang for his personal valet and asked him to show Fräulein Eva into his study. Whereas this very masculine preserve could in no way reflect Max's mild-mannered and loving nature, Fanny's feminine and soft-featured salon was in sharp contrast to her own forceful and dominant personality. With some trepidation Eva opened the heavy oak door into the unfamiliar surroundings of her father's study.

He was sitting behind his enormous, leather-covered, mahogany desk, surrounded by dark panelling, sombre-coloured velvet curtains and shelves lined with gold-embossed books. Eva saw that her father's hair was turning an even more distinguished shade of silvery-grey.

'Well, Evi,' he beamed at her, 'do you remember our trip to Egypt?'

'How can I ever forget, Papali?' breathed Eva. 'All that wonderful art and culture, museums, people, the Pyramids and the Sphinx and — '

With a smile, Max raised a hand to cut off his younger daughter's flow of enthusiasm. 'I'm glad our voyage left such an impression on you,' he said. 'But before I give my blessing for my second daughter to belong to another man, I would just like your honest opinion of my favourite piece of art.' And he pointed to the large oil painting hanging on the wall behind him, a treasure that she had never been allowed to see before.

Eva walked round her father's desk, completely absorbed in the task. The painting was one that Max had acquired some six years previously, only a year after the artist had completed it. Tipping her head back for a better view, Eva studied the composition.

'Well, Papali,' she said frankly, 'I love the colours and I can almost feel the power of the wind and the waves. I think it tells a story of fishing on the high seas—the three sailing boats belong to the fishermen, while their wives are poor but hard-working women who are carrying baskets to collect shellfish on the beach, and one woman has to bring her baby and she has no money to buy shoes.'

Max nodded his approval. 'You have a good eye for art, Evi,' he told her. 'Can you promise me that you'll make sure to visit many museums and art galleries in your new life? There's always benefit in appreciating beautiful art.'

'Should I know this artist, Papa?' asked Eva.

'Indeed, I believe one day he will become very well known. He's a Spanish painter from Valencia called Sorolla y Bastida, and this painting is called *Las Tres Velas* which means The Three Sails.'

As Eva turned to leave her father's study, he leaned forward in his plush leather armchair. 'And remember this, Evi,' he said. 'It is always well to remember those less fortunate than ourselves.'

'Yes, Papa,' said Eva seriously.

Two days before her 21st birthday, Eva was married to Richard.

5

The End of Innocence

It was a splendid affair, although the celebrations taxed even Fanny's renowned powers of organisation and social management to the full. First of all there was the engagement photo to be taken. Eva was clothed in a beautiful dress of soft white voile, embroidered with little flowers, with three-quarter length sleeves and a high-waisted broad ribbon, tied at the back. It had a simple little collar. She wore her hair in an elegant French bun, pinned at the back of her head. In the photo the only piece of jewellery she is wearing is a plain platinum bangle on her right wrist, and she is even hiding her left hand with its diamond-encrusted engagement ring. Richard, meanwhile, is looking very serious in his pinstriped trousers, fully buttoned-up waistcoat, stiff white collar, silk tie and well-cut tailcoat. His blond hair gleams in the light of the photographer's studio, and his round glasses give his face a rather bookish air. Eva's small oval face has no need of the embellishment of make-up, and her somewhat sultry dark eyes look directly at the camera under finely arched and dark eyebrows. They are indeed a very handsome couple. In a second picture taken at the time, Eva was photographed on her own, wearing a breathtaking white and high-waisted lace and muslin dress with matching handbag, and with a charming, wide-brimmed black hat that emphasised the delicate features of her face.

The wedding ceremony itself took place at the Louisekirche in the fashionable district of Charlottenburg. This time Eva's dress was completely full-length and made of satin and silk. She wore white satin slippers and white gloves. Richard was in full top hat and tails, with a white bow tie. After the service the whole family returned to the villa in Uhlandstrasse but, unlike the custom in England, the wedding breakfast took place the next evening. Seated in Fanny's magnificent dining room, with all her best Bohemian crystal and Meissen chinaware, the family partook of an eight-course meal, accompanied by a ten-piece orchestra playing a selection of suitably romantic wedding music. This included *Norwegian Wedding March* by Grieg, tunes from Puccini's *Madame Butterfly*, extracts from Wagner's *Meistersinger*, waltzes from *Rosenkavalier* by Strauss, fantasies from Puccini's *La Bohème* and finally themes from Wagner's *Lohengrin*.

The meal itself was sumptuous and accompanied by a selection of very fine wines. It was all very much to Richard's taste, being an inveterate gourmand and enthusiastic participant in *Esskultur* (the culture of fine dining). He might even have considered the number of courses to be quite moderate. During a visit to Lima in 1906 he had been invited to a stiffly formal dinner given in honour of one of his Gaffron cousins. On that occasion there had been no fewer than fifteen courses.

In the Steinthals' magnificent, festively decorated dining room there was caviar to start, followed by beef broth. The next course was shoulder of young wild boar with vegetables. The wine was a 20-year-old Haut Brion Bressac. This was followed by crayfish with a 1900 German wine by the splendid name of Eitelsbacher Karthäuser Hofberger. The next course was a dish of quail, served together with Vino Santo, followed by *poularde* (fatted chicken) with goose liver, with which an 1881 Corton was drunk. After a suitable interval the next course was pears in double cream to the accompaniment of a 1904 Erbacher Herrnberg Schloss Reinhartshausen Cabinet. To finish up there was fresh pineapple, after which a toast was drunk to the happy couple with Pommery & Greno champagne. For those who still had a few spaces left, there was cheese, fruit and 'pudding' as a final afterthought.

One example of the wedding 'menu' which contains on one side this splendid feast, in the middle the architect's drawing of Uhlandstrasse 191, and on the other side the programme of wedding music, also has a photo on the front of Eva and Richard, surrounded by somewhat sentimental flowers. 'Herr Richard Vollmann', inscribed underneath in gold ink in a beautifully cursive script, refers to Richard's father. It was his personal invitation to the wedding.

During their honeymoon in Austria Richard's true character began to make itself manifest. After a visit to Biarritz on the French Atlantic coast, Richard had insisted on a sporting holiday, and took his young bride skiing at a high resort in the Dolomites. It must be remembered that in 1913, skiing was an exclusive and relatively unknown sport that was particularly physically taxing. There were no cable cars, no lifts up the slopes, and the skis themselves were up to two metres long, very heavy and made entirely of wood. Eva fell over constantly, which caused Richard huge amusement. He would frequently leave her lying helplessly in the snow, mocking her until she could get herself up again.

Within a month of their wedding, Eva was pregnant. It was to be an extremely difficult pregnancy, during which she felt very unwell most of the time. Again as was the custom, the young couple were living in Sebnitz with the Vollmanns, Eva's parents-in-law, at the time. Richard would be away frequently all day, either at his father's factory or out of town on business, and sometimes he would stay away overnight. This suited Eva, who was ignorant of where her husband stayed when he chose to spend the night away. Although she would never have dared to confess as much to her mother, and even less to her mother-in-law, all Eva's romantic notions of her wedding night had been cruelly broken by Richard's rough handling of his new bride, whom he found to be rather timid and lacking in passion. This was due in no small measure to her ignorance in matters of physical relations, despite having four brothers. She was so innocent that when her mother had asked her to come back to Berlin for a short while to assist her at a home for 'unfortunate girls', she was quite happy to help with the babies, but had no idea where they had come from. In her mind, girls who were not married had no way of creating babies. (This was one of Fanny's charitable interests, and she took her daughter there with the intention of getting her mind off the unpleasant effects of her pregnancy.)

It is very possible that Richard actually raped his wife, more especially if he had come into the honeymoon bedroom somewhat the worse for wear from copious amounts of alcohol. However, their physical relations would have stopped altogether just a few weeks into her pregnancy, because Eva would have been quite unable to tolerate his being near her. Richard was perfectly happy to go off with his brother in search of physical relief amongst the red-light district of Dresden—an occupation about which Eva was blissfully unaware.

By the early summer of 1914 a heat wave had taken hold of most of Germany. It was to last many weeks and made life for Eva almost unbearable. Yet despite his wife being by now into her seventh month of pregnancy, Richard insisted that she accompany him on a trip to Hochbusch, a picturesque but very hilly section of the area bordering the River Elbe know as 'Saxon Switzerland', where he indulged in many long walks. She found the heat stifling and her husband's attitude incomprehensible and unsympathetic. But he was her husband and she felt she had to do as he insisted.

Eva probably found little sympathy from either her mother or elder sister. For Fanny, despite the restrictions of confinement during each pregnancy, childbirth had been a relatively uncomplicated affair. Daisy by now was pregnant with her second child, which was due two months after Eva's first baby. She had little time for her younger sister, having marital problems of her own. Having been so determined to marry Lutz, Daisy now felt she had to lie in the bed that she had made, without ever giving the slightest hint of a problem to any other member of her close family. And despite everything, the truth was that Eva adored Richard, and was to put him on a pedestal for the rest of their marriage.

At the end of September, when the long heat wave had finally broken, Eva went into labour. Alarmed by her younger daughter's physical symptoms, Fanny had insisted she return to Berlin. So Eva was back in her own bedroom in her parents' house, and the labour was to be protracted and beset with dangerous complications. The family doctor, urgently called out together with the midwife, became extremely concerned for Eva's wellbeing. The baby seemed to be too large for her narrow pelvis, and thus to be having considerable problems in getting out of its mother. Finally, late into the afternoon of 29 September a healthy baby girl was born, whose appearance into this world very nearly caused the departure of her mother into the next one. It had been an extremely difficult birth, just ten months after the wedding, and once Eva had slightly recovered the doctor thought it his duty to tell his patient that it would be too dangerous for her health for her ever to contemplate having any more children. This pronouncement was almost the last straw for the exhausted Eva, who simply lay limp and huddled on the bed and wept bitter tears into the pillow. Not only had she failed in her mission to create a large family like her mother, but more importantly she had failed to produce a son and heir to follow in his father's footsteps.

The baby was christened Ruth Ursula, but in keeping with the family tradition she was always known as Ursula. She was the second grand-child to be born in the house in Uhlandstrasse. Her arrival, however, was greatly overshadowed by the onrush of world events. War had been declared at the beginning of August, and the younger boys in the Steinthal household were almost dizzy with patriotic fervour, as Werner immediately got ready to join the army. For the oldest Steinthal boy, however, fighting was out of the question, and Erich at 24 was to spend the war years in Frankfurt am Main, at which time he indulged his passion for books and started his first bibliophile's collection. Werner was 20 and Eduard was 17. Lutz (whom Fanny always regarded as one of the family) was some 11 years older at 28—all three young men were of an age to become soldiers. Peter was still at school and only 15 at the time, but nevertheless raring to follow in his older brothers' footsteps and probably in awe of his brother-in-law. He did feel rather grown-up even so, in that the birth of the two baby girls within a year of each other had made him an uncle twice over.

Eva was to find herself in an almost impossible position. While her father's very martial political attitude reflected the national enthusiasm in favour of war that was sweeping across Germany, as did that of her three brothers and brother-in-law, her own husband showed no such passion at all. In fact, he deliberately refused to fight.

6

Letters to the Front

Eva was seven months pregnant when war was declared following the assassination of Archduke Ferdinand. The Great War would have been hard enough for Eva to bear, if her husband had chosen to go away to battle and join his fellow Germans in the great tide of patriotism that swept across the country. But he would have nothing to do with a war against France, Russia and subsequently England that was to be fought, on the Western front, in the muddy fields of Flanders. Eva found herself married to a man who was immediately dubbed 'anti-patriotic', which made her own position with regards to her family almost unbearable. Max Steinthal believed with all his heart in the necessity of war—not least because of the considerable wealth it would bring to those industrialists with the foresight to supply and finance the Kaiser's great military endeavour.

Berliners, who only months ago had been showing doubt in their Kaiser, now rallied behind him in the thrill of the prospect of war. It brought all Berliners together under one banner for the first time in history, ironing out the once-strict demarcation lines that had separated ordinary people from the middle classes, and the bourgeoisie from the Junker class. Each group desired something different from the forthcoming conflict. The Junkers and military, mindful of the decisive German defeat of France during the Franco-Prussian War, could only visualise a similarly certain victory and the prestige it would bring, together with an increased chance to maintain their grip on power. The government saw war as a chance to divert public focus away from domestic difficulties to the excitement of imperial foreign policy. The mighty industrialists of Berlin, backed by financiers such as Max Steinthal, saw a golden opportunity to provide weapons, rolling stock, electrical goods, chemicals and textiles, thereby increasing their markets abroad. The youth of Berlin, as typified by the Steinthal boys, saw an opportunity to relieve the boredom of their comfortable yet stifling middle class world. Even the socialists and workers saw in the war a chance to finish off despotic Russia and the mighty British Empire.

Max Steinthal, who by the outset of war had been working for

Deutsche Bank for over 40 years and was in his 64th year, was a fervent nationalist who believed in the strength of Germany as a nation. He saw it as his bounden duty to support all the efforts of the Kaiser, and considered that victory was an inevitable outcome.

Richard Vollmann's views on the impending situation could not have been more diametrically opposed to those of his father-in-law and brothers-in-law, the latter of whom—even Lutz—he viewed with cynical detachment as eager young puppies, just spoiling for a fight without really understanding the consequences. The business education he had received on his world tour had embedded in Richard a deep belief in free trade and the business principles practised by the United States of America. He saw no reason to follow nationalist ideals, but rather considered that the only way forward for the enrichment of Germany and other nations was internationalism. Narrow and inward-looking interests would only harm the country in the long run. It was a view that was extremely unpopular and against all current thinking. Nationalist fervour was sweeping like fire all over Germany, and in Berlin young men were scrambling over each other in their eagerness to join up in the army.

Just three weeks into the war, eight-months pregnant Eva wrote the first of a whole series of war-letters to her brother Werner from the house of her parents-in-law in Sebnitz. He had already been sent away for training with the *Autocorps* (mechanised motor unit), after joining up as soon as war had been announced. Eva seemed to be experiencing an unfamiliar mixture of intense pride and patriotism, combined with possible fear for her unborn baby. In order to relieve the unpleasant symptoms of her advanced pregnancy, she would take herself for slow and gentle walks up the local hill known as the Knöchel. She wrote to her brother:

> Here we're really not affected yet by events in the outside world. It's so peaceful on Sunday while the bells carry on ringing just as they've always done, and summer resides in the streets. Sometimes I go for a walk in the evening up to the Knöchel, to watch the sunset and listen to the sounds of dusk. I could almost weep at the irony of Nature's simple-minded and obdurate lack of reason, she who smiles down so benignly while allowing millions to kill themselves.

Despite her husband's anti-war stance, Eva threw herself into the war effort with passion and enthusiasm. Perhaps mindful of her father's words to her before her wedding, and so that she could make her own contribution to the community, she attempted to do as much as possible for the local townspeople. Eva considered her own efforts were only 'a tiny splash on a hot stone' (a drop in the ocean), but nonetheless she felt compelled to do her bit. In keeping with towns all over Germany, Sebnitz began providing free daily food for all the families whose fathers were away fighting, consisting of a hot midday meal. Eva herself campaigned very hard for the working classes in the town that had become her home. She realised that in this industrial town, known to all as 'the city of artificial flowers', these workers amounted to several thousands. She even took to feeding a few women and children 'at home' in the house of Richard's parents. A women's committee was set up to give the local women work, such as sewing shirts and handkerchiefs as well as socks and pullovers, all intended for the soldiers who were away fighting. Having never been schooled in any sort of handicraft, Eva was sad to discover that she was not particularly competent at needlework. Moreover, in her advanced state of pregnancy she was unable to bear more than a short period at a time at the sewing sessions, before becoming too tired to continue.

Eva was obviously very close to her brother, and she wrote in her next letter how much she missed being able to talk to him. This was written from Berlin when baby Ursula was just a month old, and was an attempt to explain the very new and unfamiliar feelings she was experiencing as a first-time mother. Werner was to be his second niece's godfather, and by this time he had already been sent to France.

> I believe that such a welter of feelings, as are felt with the birth of the first child, can never be experienced by a man and only once in her life by a woman. Everything that's sacred and good in mankind is evoked by the arrival of a child into the world; it's as if there were a halo round its little head, because it's still so completely innocent and so touchingly pure. And it's a remarkable thing, how a woman loves her first child so much that everything she does is only on demand for her child and not for herself. Only by attending to the happiness and wellbeing of her child can she ensure her own happiness. My little one is sleeping next to me in her basket; she moves her little fists and breathes so deeply and evenly. When I look at my child I can't imagine that such joy can exist anywhere else, because the whole world is in such pandemonium. And yet this blessed feeling is at the same time such a burden to bear because of this terrible war, with all its misery and suffering. I simply can't get rid of the constant sensation of a kind of heaviness—dreaming at night and waiting for news by day. You can imagine how delighted we are here with the tiniest message

> bearing good news, but up until now we've been receiving so terribly little by way of information … a bit from the Western front but not really very much more.

In the same letter she expressed sympathy for her older sister Daisy, who by then was eight months pregnant with her second child and whose husband Lutz was also away fighting. Even though she was still very weak and frail after such a difficult birth, Eva and Richard intended to move from Berlin back to his parents' house in Sebnitz. His father's factory was working again, making Eva 'enormously happy' for the workforce, which included cottage workers on piecework in their homes. Richard—who was always known as Dick—had been spending his time travelling backwards and forwards between Berlin and Sebnitz. Apart from helping to manage the factory, Dick was now working at the Central Office for [Inland] Provisions in Berlin, all of which was keeping him very busy. While Peter was away at school, Eva's younger sister Rütchen, who of course still lived at home as she was only 16, did her own bit by helping out twice a week at a local welfare office.

Despite Richard's strong stance against taking active part in war, the concept of 'conscientious objectors' did not exist and he still had to carry his militia document with him at all times. From the age of 21, all young men in Germany were eligible for service in the *Landsturm*, a kind of alternative but obligatory military service that could be called up in times of war. Richard probably felt that his work at the factory, which afforded so many jobs to the people of Sebnitz, would exempt him from any possibility of military duty. His younger brother Walter had perhaps been a little more perspicacious in that regard. As soon as war was declared, he applied to be the driver for a general in Berlin who was guaranteed to remain in the capital behind a desk, rather than on any sort of active duty.

By December, just a year after Eva's honeymoon and when her only daughter was less than three months old, Werner was captured on the Western front and taken to a French prisoner-of-war camp. In order for any post to reach the German prisoners, all letters had to be written in French. Eva wrote an impassioned and bitter letter to her beloved brother, despising 'this hateful language'.

'It seems grotesque,' she wrote in French, 'that I have to write to you in the language of those with whom we find ourselves at war, in the language of the race that will hate us to the very end of its days, and which will not forget its hatred of us for as long as it draws breath.' And then in a particularly xenophobic outburst, she blamed the French and English politicians for causing the war, apparently ignorant and in complete denial of the Kaiser's aggressive stance:

> I know very well that it's not the French people themselves to whom we owe this insane war, but those [men] Poincaré, Izvolski and Grey,* as much as the newspapers. And again, it's the pride of those men leading that nation which is forcing us to spill the blood of the flower of our youth, and to whom we are to be thankful for an ailing and anaemic generation coming out of those ditches, those trenches from which half of our strong and good young men will emerge with perpetual ill-health. At the moment I haven't a shred of sympathy or pity for the French nation. May it die the death! It's not we who demanded its blood! But I do have pity for the men, for the poor soldiers who have to die because of the faults of their leaders.

By the spring of 1915 Eva was again experiencing mixed emotions of pride and loss, as Eduard was given his marching orders. At only 18, he was the youngest member of his unit, and even though he was being sent to the Russian front just as his brother-in-law Lutz had been already, he could not have been a more ardent volunteer. Together with both parents and her younger sister Ruth, Eva had been driven to Mainz to wave goodbye to him 'without any tears or sentimentality'. The sight of Eduard, known affectionately as *'Dickerlein'* or 'Fatty', in uniform made Eva exclaim in her letter to Werner, 'Thank God we've still got boys like this in Germany!'

Yet while her second brother marched off to war, Eva was undergoing a personal battle of her own. Six months after the birth of her child she was still feeling wretchedly unwell, and unable to undertake any sort of physical exertion. But worse than that was the fact that just 16 months into her marriage, her relationship with Richard seemed to be practically non-existent, and he appeared to display no sympathy whatsoever for his wife's continued ill health.

> And I've been running around from pillar to post [she complained to her brother] and there isn't a single doctor who can find out what the matter with me is. I've had endless examinations and they all say: take it easy, take it easy and then they find nothing wrong, or else they just say that things will gradually get better of

* Raymond Poincaré was then president of France, Alexander Izvolsky the Russian ambassador to France, and Sir Edward Grey the British Foreign Secretary.

> their own accord. I doubt that very much, but even so I'm not allowed to bring any of this to Dick's attention. Look, what sort of marriage is it where the man refuses to take part in *anything* to do with his wife? I could howl like a baby. It's not so much that I'm suffering with all this, but mainly (1) the fact that I feel I'm no sort of companion for Dick; (2) that any sort of work has come to a standstill and (3) there can be no guarantee that my situation will ever get better.

Despite all this, Eva did appreciate the luxury of having a husband at home with her—feeling keenly for her sister whose second child had been born in the previous November, just two months after Ursula. The boy was called Hans Gebhardt, but his birth had been completely missed by his father Lutz. It was to have a severe effect on their future relationship. Lutz always treated his only son brutally, frequently beating him with his whip. Eva was later to call him a 'sadist'.

She wrote, 'If I didn't have the compensation of having my child, I would plunge into depression. In every other respect I can state without reservation that I have a good life. The fact that Dick is here and will stay here is denied thousands of others, and I can at least take some comfort because at the moment I'm not hanging my head in absolute misery.'

By July 1915 Werner had been transferred from the French POW camp at Landrécies, near Cambrai in northern France, to a military hospital in Nauheim, near Nuremberg in southern Germany. Unbeknown to the family he had been shot in the head, and was to lose an eye. Whatever the circumstances, Eva was pleased to have her brother back on German soil and even expressed the hope of being driven to the military hospital to see him. Fanny had taken Ruth to Oberdorf in Bavaria, perhaps for a short holiday, and in order to encourage his recovery Eva told Werner that they might be able to visit him there as well. She knew that the hospital at Nauheim was now a convalescent home for many wounded and recovering officers. By this time letters were infrequent and unreliable, and it often took many months for news from the Western and Eastern fronts to filter through to those waiting back home.

In her next letter, written a couple of weeks later, Eva was pleased to tell her brother that—possibly because he had been wounded—Richard was being very 'touching' with her and that he'd set aside ten days so that he could drive Eva to visit her brother in hospital. It was obviously expected that he would have to stay there for some time.

And then in another burst of patriotism, she told Werner how excited she had been at the latest news: Hindenburg had captured 29,000 Russians. 'May this be the way forward to even greater things,' she wrote. 'And if it turns out to be true that this brings peace, how can anybody measure the bliss we'll feel when our boys and all our loyal men come home?' For her, men like Hindenburg were heroes, whose very name gave one faith in the future.

Meanwhile Lutz had managed to send back news from somewhere on the Russian front, but there had been no word from Eduard for months. On the second anniversary of their engagement, Richard suddenly presented his wife with a real dog, a Russian greyhound of rare size and beauty. Eva was overwhelmed at the generous gesture, and despite everything she had told her brother about her marital situation in previous letters, she felt that she did not deserve to be 'so spoiled'. There is a charming photo of Richard and Eva sitting in the breakfast room in the Vollmann house in Sebnitz, with the greyhound standing obediently by his new mistress.

Ten days before Christmas Eva's dark moods were back again, and even though she had been to see her brother in September she could not find the strength of character to evoke the true spirit of Christmas. 'I did go to the market myself with Dick,' she wrote to her brother, 'to buy a very sweet little tree for Urslein and us, but all the trees in all of Berlin can't make up the spirit of Christmas!' She enclosed a small cigarette case with her letter as a present to her brother.

In the same parcel Eva also enclosed a book—containing the famous short story by Leo Tolstoy called *The Kreutzer Sonata*.* She considered it a very thought-provoking read, which seemed an appropriate present as she and her brother had often indulged in deep and spirited philosophical discussions. She did admit to him, though, that it simply threw into the dust a lot of what she held sacred, and in some parts its frank language was 'plain disgusting'. Her letter continued by discussing the

* In 1802 Beethoven published his Violin Sonata No 9 in A major. It was very briefly known as the Bridgetower Sonata, named after the half-Polish, half-West Indian violinist George Bridgetower (1779–1860) who performed with Beethoven at the premiere. However, after the performance, while the two were drinking, Bridgetower insulted the morals of a woman who turned out to be an acquaintance of Beethoven's. Enraged, Beethoven changed the name of the piece to the Kreutzer Sonata, dedicating the piece to Rudolphe Kreutzer, considered the finest violinist of the day. Ironically, Kreutzer never performed it, and believed it to be unplayable.

In 1889 Leo Tolstoy published a short story entitled *The Kreutzer Sonata*, using the Beethoven piece as an example of how people can be led astray by their unruly passions.

The latter story in turn gave rise to Czech composer Leos Janacek's first string quartet, of the same name.

points raised by Tolstoy in his short story, some of which she agreed with and some of which went against everything she believed in. 'It negates *everything* of significance,' she wrote, 'as bestial and beneath our dignity.' She did however agree with Tolstoy's opinions on the status of women. 'It is the worst mistake in the life of a woman,' she wrote, 'for her to think that she can live only for love and on love alone. It's even more difficult for a married woman to find an ally, so that she won't simply sink into the morass of love and children. Sometimes I think I've only just reached this stage of development in my own life.'

Further on in the letter she went on to express sympathy for the plight of prostitutes—which indicated that by this time she must have become more of a woman of the world, even though still completely ignorant of her husband's proclivity in that direction. Perhaps she could only talk about such things with her brother. 'It's utterly disgraceful,' she wrote frankly, 'that thousands and thousands [of women] should die a horrible death just because others consider it necessary for their health.' She was perhaps making a veiled reference to the dangers for prostitutes of contracting diseases acquired by frequent sexual activity.

Both Beethoven and Tolstoy had obviously affected Eva deeply, as she went on to explain, 'In one respect I found it very interesting to read what he had to say about the Kreutzer Sonata, because the day before I'd been to a concert and heard Veczey playing a Beethoven concerto. Remarkably I had exactly the same impressions as he describes: a daemonic kind of power was lurking in the music, and all the time that Veczey was playing what was going through my head is something that thank God I'm unable to describe to you. The spell was broken as soon as the music stopped.'

In all other respects, Eva's life was carrying on as normally as was possible in the circumstances. She had resumed her singing lessons with a lady called Fräulein Ohlhoff, and even though her mother had told her that she had lost some sensitivity in her voice, Eva had found pleasure in being accompanied on the piano. (For all three of the Steinthal girls music had been an important part of their upbringing: Daisy played the piano like her mother, Ruth was quite an accomplished violinist and Eva had a very pleasant soprano voice.)

Christmas was a busy time in the industrial town of Sebnitz, and Eva as the wife and daughter-in-law of the principal employers in the town became very involved in the life of the factory. She had personally packed fifty parcels for 'our workers' on her own initiative. She also allowed a note of pride about her 14-month-old daughter to creep into the letter. 'Ursel is even more marvellous,' she wrote. 'She's already crawling as fast as the wind through every room, and she loves her father best of all. If I let her crawl wherever she wants to, she always goes to his dressing room and she's already able to call out "Papa"! She really can understand quite a bit. Soon it will be time for her training so that she learns how to behave, and is decent and clean.' It would be the nursemaid and subsequent governess, however, who would undertake and be solely responsible for the successful completion of that primordially important stage in a child's development known to the English as 'potty training'.

Two days later 16-year-old Peter wrote his own Christmas letter to his soldier brother. Still at school he had left home to live in lodgings, and was able to boast about his latest exam results. 'In my new school my achievements have been pretty good (even in Maths). I'm 11th out of 22 students and hope that by putting in a bit of effort and especially by moderating my behaviour I'll be able to achieve my ambition of getting into the Upper School.' Peter was to be the brightest of all the four Steinthal boys, and at that time most likely to follow in his father's footsteps. He also told his brother about what life was like in Berlin in the middle of war. 'We're slowly beginning to feel something of the war,' he wrote, 'especially as far as butter is concerned, as well as other things, which is in scant supply. But that's so trivial compared to what you're going through.' He finished the letter with a touchingly emotional farewell that said, 'I wish you a very happy Christmas from the bottom of my heart, as well as good luck for the New Year, and if it should be our destiny, to be able to see each other again for ever. In friendship, your brother Peter.'

In the New Year Eva had a photo taken of Ursula and put onto a postcard for her godfather Werner. The child, aged 15 months, is sitting up in large Silver Cross style pram, wearing a white jacket and with her unruly dark curls held in place by a charming white bonnet. Her nursemaid is standing behind the pram: an attractive, dark-eyed young girl (probably French) whose buttoned-up coat shows the stiff white collar of her uniform, and whose hair is tied back with a large ribbon. She is staring confidently at the camera.

By the spring of 1916 Eva seemed to be dividing her time between her parents-in-law in Sebnitz and her family in Berlin, and in an uncharacteristically enthusiastic letter described how much a three-week holiday to Oberdorf in Bavaria had done her good. Even though Richard was able to join his wife for only four days out of the twenty-one, and although much of her stay there was interrupted by visits from relatives, Eva considered that this was the best rest she had enjoyed in a long time. 'It was almost as if we'd rediscovered, after such a long time, that which we had no time for in our everyday life,' she wrote. She went on, 'I've come back from Oberdorf with so many good intentions, especially not to let myself be so affected by my frequent and silly moods, which have lately made my life so unpleasant with Dick.'

Yet even though Eva had been having such problems in her relationship with her husband, when she felt better about herself she was almost ashamed to admit her feelings of happiness to her brother, in the midst of the turmoil of war. 'Most of all, my dear Schnodel,' she wrote (this was her pet name for her brother), 'can I tell you this in the midst of such unhappy times? I am now happier than I've ever been. Is it callous of me to tell you that? It would seem so ungrateful if I didn't acknowledge this fact. I often feel that Dick and I have been taking considerable pains to stay on the straight and narrow, and then there's the child! I'm so happy when I have her next to me, when she's asleep or playing or recognises me so sweetly and is so content in herself. You know, sometimes I think I should feel ashamed to have such a rich life, when at this very moment others see their life as so pitiably bitter.'

There was another thing that caused even more joy in Eva, and that was the greatly improved relationship between Richard and his father-in-law Max Steinthal. Perhaps both men had come to realise that in such straitened circumstances, it was more important to have a person of similar intellectual standing with whom to discuss matters and exchange views, rather than to keep rigidly to one's own deeply entrenched beliefs. 'For Papa it is a relief to have a knowledgeable man in the family,' wrote Eva, 'and especially to be able to talk to somebody who understands his own business, and for Dick it's a good thing for hundreds of reasons.'

While Eva had been away in Bavaria, Fanny had been working 'like a whirlwind' in the local rest home for soldiers in Berlin. By this time she was a fully qualified nurse, and had thrown herself into her work. More than anyone in the family, she had felt the keen pain of the absence of her two sons and favourite son-in-law, and this was a way of taking her mind off her very real feelings of loneliness. It was hard but satisfying work, and on one occasion when Eva visited her mother briefly after her holiday, she was able to describe her as 'much fresher, calmer, and more sociable'. Being so deeply involved in nursing work meant that Fanny was no longer so enmeshed in the everyday running of the household in the Uhlandstrasse, which had caused her frequently to work herself up into an extreme state of stress and nerves. This must have been a great relief to all the household staff. What is not mentioned in any of the letters is what happened to the English governesses, including Miss Florie, at the beginning of the war. They must have been sent home as soon as war was declared.

Much impressed by her mother's example, but still very unsure of her own abilities, Eva continued her letter by asking for her brother's honest opinion about his sister's capacity for work. She had just had her 23rd birthday, but still considered herself to be very young and inexperienced. One possibility was assisting her mother in the rest home for soldiers, where competent staff were always urgently needed. She had been offered another opening at the military hospital. This was to act in the role of what today would be called a counsellor, but at that time was a kind of liaison for the families of married soldiers who had been seriously wounded on the battlefields, and whose injuries were permanent. This included soldiers whose limbs had been amputated, those who had lost their hearing in the thick of gunfire, and those who had suffered the loss of an eye (as Werner had).

The applicants had to be 'married and serious-minded women', and their role was 'to encourage [the patients] from their particular hospital back onto the path to life, earning and work. And to reawaken their joy for work, and if possible return them to employment'. The most important function would be 'to communicate with their families, especially where a poor wife considered that her crippled husband would be nothing more than a burden to her and an unemployed mouth to feed.' This further involved making it clear to her that the loss of a leg, an eye, an arm and so on did not have to be such a terrible impediment that it would cause her nothing but immediate suffering. Eva went on, 'We would be expected to build up the contact between the married couple, in which the wife is taught how to be prepared for the degree of mobility of her husband, or possibly to show the youngest war brides that they have to fulfil their duty by their husband and not that they should drag him unwillingly through life just as an unpleasant duty.'

This was work that Eva felt would be a very difficult task, 'and it's doubtful whether they'll take me on,' she admitted, 'because I'm still too young.' She was determined to go ahead with her application, nevertheless. 'I'm going to try and see if I'm good enough to achieve this,' she told her brother, 'because it's something I'd really like to do. Most of all I feel I'm lacking in life experience, in contrast to Mama for example, which is a distinct disadvantage. In a few days' time I'm going to go the appropriate office to discuss whether they'll consider taking me on.'

Meanwhile she had received word from two of the boys: Eduard wrote a 'blissfully happy letter' telling his sister that he was right in the thick of things. Instead of this news making her anxious, Eva told Werner, 'It's such a joy that the boy is taking part with all his heart. Let him just come back home to us well and healthy!' At the same time Lutz was fighting hard on the Eastern front near the Russian border in Galicia.

She finished the letter on rather a soulful note that pleaded, 'Don't pretend like most people do, who say they're happy and don't need anybody else. One would like to partake in another person's happiness as well and most of the time one is as lonely being happy as being unhappy.'

In October of that year Lutz was able to come home on leave and meet his son for the first time. Daisy was soon pregnant with her third child: Monika was three and her baby brother just under two years old. But coupled with this happy announcement was the news that Max's younger sister Elvira had died in somewhat equivocal circumstances. Always known as 'Lieschen', she had been born with 'something wrong' that was never talked about in the family, but which meant that she could never live on her own and would always have to be looked after. She had lived with both parents until their respective deaths. Eduard, Max's father, died in 1896 (not long after his son's move to the villa in the Uhlandstrasse). His mother Johanna died in 1910, and from that time he was to keep a portrait of her above his bed. He then took the necessary steps to ensure that his younger sister was safely installed in a flat opposite the family villa, and a permanent nurse was engaged to look after the problematic young woman. Whether she died of neglect or carelessness is unknown, but there were rumours that the nurse had left her charge alone in the bathroom, and that Lieschen had slipped down into the bath and drowned.

7

War and after

While 1917 was to bring great changes to the outcome of the fighting on two fronts, with the Russian Revolution and America's eventual entry into the war, back home in Germany circumstances were becoming ever more difficult. Goods were in short supply, and life was getting far harder for the citizens who had so fervently supported the Kaiser. Eva's next letter was written to her brother from Schloss Caputh, where she had been forced to move with her young baby and frequently absent husband. The *Gartenhaus*, or gardener's house—part of a small estate of the country house belonging to a local Junker that Max used to rent occasionally in summer—stood by a lake that froze over to a depth of several inches in the harsh and unmerciful cold of the Prussian winter.

By this time Eva was finding it much harder to express herself, and she found writing to her brother very awkward. 'Ever since you went away again,' she wrote, 'I've been going over in my mind why we weren't able to speak to each other this time as freely as we usually do. I finally came to the conclusion that I'm probably just as much to blame as you are. Now that our reason for being consists entirely of the struggle for existence, that's to say one's head is full of everyday bits and pieces and trivial but essential things, then of course it's much harder to get back to the sort of writing we used to manage to do every day.' Although she had been able to take a maid with her, it had become impossible to find a children's nurse, and Eva now found life a constant effort.

Meanwhile Daisy's third child was born in Berlin in July, a girl who was called Gisèle but who would always be known as 'Baby' and treated very much as such in the Reichenheim family. Once again Lutz was away fighting and had missed his second daughter's appearance into the world. While Monica was to remain her parents' favourite child, both Hans—as the only boy—and Gisèle as the youngest child were to have a persistently troubled relationship with their father.*

Caputh was to become renowned throughout the world as the town where Albert Einstein would spend most of the year in his favourite summer house between 1929 and 1932. He was later to write 'sailing ships, far-reaching views, solitary walks in autumn, relative silence .... [This place] is paradise'.

This contrasted greatly with Eva's opinion of the place, to which she was forced to move with her two-year-old daughter Ursula. The population of the town was approximately 3,000 and the local people lived mainly off fruit growing, fishing and trade from visitors. This supposed jewel of the region lying south-west of Potsdam, sandwiched as it was between two very scenic lakes, had little effect on Eva, whose overriding thoughts were focused on how best to survive the difficult living conditions. She had by this time volunteered to help out at a local military hospital. Despite having no training, she proved to be a capable and unflappable nursing assistant. One doctor told her that she had all the makings of a good nurse, because she had an absolutely steady hand. This might have temporarily boosted her morale, but did little to alleviate the almost unbearable conditions she now found herself living under.

Perhaps existing in what was little more than a farmhouse would not have caused so many problems to a family of lower social standing. But Eva had come from an upper middle class family in Berlin, where her every need was catered for by a maid or some other servant. She had never been taught to cook, and would have been clueless about how to wash and mend clothes. Like her mother before her, she certainly would have had absolutely no idea how to change, never mind wash, a baby's nappy.

While Ursula grew into a sturdy toddler, food was becoming much less plentiful in Germany. There was an ever-present and insistent clamour for increasing amounts of supplies to furnish the war effort. For the population left at home conditions were becoming even more difficult. Eva had to learn how to plant her own vegetables, with young Ursula helping to pick beans at the age of three or four. In the cruel

* In much later life Gisèle was to remark that she wished her mother had fallen for some handsome Egyptian princeling during their famous trip to Egypt, instead of marrying a man who, despite his undoubted bravery in the war, was to spend the rest of his married life living off his wife.

winter months, Eva had to break up coal with her bare hands. Meanwhile Richard would be out all day working in Berlin or Sebnitz, leaving the women to fend for themselves. Marital relations were strained to the utmost, which Richard was able to relieve with his local drinking buddies with whom he would pay frequent visits to the local hostelry for evenings of heavy drinking and carousing. One of these was a gentleman by the name of Stauss, who was an employee of Deutsche Bank.

Throughout the course of the 'war to end all wars', the hopes of Berliners were kept alive by constant and ever more shrill propaganda, which was spread throughout the city. When the Bolshevik Revolution broke out in February of 1917, there was a widespread belief maintained in Berlin that a separate peace with Russia would bring about an end to the war, and guaranteed victory in Germany. It was not to be. The expected military benefits arising from the long drawn-out negotiations for the Treaty of Brest-Litovsk never came. The troops had to remain on the Eastern front to maintain order, and grain from Ukraine took far longer to materialise than had been hoped. In the end it was the American entry into the war in 1917, rather than the Russian collapse, which was to end the war, making it inevitable that Germany would be defeated.

For Fanny and especially Max, as for millions of fellow Germans, this prospect was simply unimaginable. She continued her valiant exertions to support the German war effort, writing frequent letters and sending generous food parcels to the Western front. A letter from the central depot for voluntary contributions was received in gratitude for Fanny's contribution sent to Werner's Regiment at the 12th Battery Field Artillery, where he held the position of sergeant of the reserve.

> The depot has received by freight … at the forwarding office at the instigation of *Frau Geheimrat* [Madame Privy Counsellor] Steinthal the voluntary contribution from her hands to the 12th Battery, Field Artillery, Regiment 12 as follows:
>
>> one crate containing Christmas goods for 50 men and in addition 30 Viking books; one crate containing 300 officers' cigars, a thousand cigarettes, 25 packets biscuits, 25 packets tea, 25 packets sweets, 25 packets smoking tobacco, 6 wallets, 6 notebooks for 1918, 20 pocket-knives, 10 pairs of braces, 24 pieces soap, 10 pounds sugar; one crate containing 12 boxes of asparagus; one crate containing 24 packets (dried) fruit, 6 shag pipes; one crate containing games; one crate containing 12 bottles of wine.

It was a magnificent gift, which must have brought cheer to the beleaguered soldiers, who by now had endured almost three years in the trenches.

Ever eager to join his brothers, Peter presented himself to his local recruiting centre on the day of his 18th birthday in June 1917, and would be wounded in action less than a year later. As soon as he was taken to be treated in a military hospital, Fanny was to fight like a tiger for the right to take him home and care for him in Berlin. By February 1918 Werner, aged 24, held the position of 'Deputy Master of the Watch'. Eva sent him a postcard of the garden house in Schloss Caputh. 'As I might not always be able to get a letter to you in the near future, at least I can send you a good luck wish to tell you I'm thinking of you and to thank you for your letter. The weather here's getting better every day, and there are thick clumps of snowdrops blooming everywhere. Where are you hiding? Are you also in Normandy?'

Despite her optimistic tone, the course of the war was doomed to disaster. Defeat, however, was impossible for nationalistic Berliners to envisage, especially Max and Fanny Steinthal. Addressing the American Senate in 1917, it was Hiram Johnson who quoting Aeschylus had uttered the words: 'The first casualty when war comes is the truth'. Since 1916 the German High Command had taken complete control of all affairs, both military and civilian, which included information and propaganda. The government decided from the outset not to inform the population about the reversals of German fortune on the Western front. They felt it was essential to 'deny defeat' and that they should 'nurse the patriotic feelings of the German people'. They were so successful in the dissemination of this propaganda that most Berliners believed the German army was encountering only success in its mission to dominate Europe, and that a glorious victory was imminent. On 21st March 1918 Paul von Hindenburg—whose exploits in Russia had so impressed Eva—and Erich von Ludendorff announced the great German offensive on the Western front, which caused the Berlin newspapers to publish headlines that screamed 'Now We Have Them!' They could not have been more wrong. Despite the 6,000 heavy guns and three-quarters of a million men set against the Allies, they were repulsed. The next attempt in July at the Marne also resulted in defeat. Germany was to suffer 800,000 casualties in those campaigns alone, which were such an enormous failure that Hindenburg forbade anyone to mention the true situation unless they had something positive to say. Morale at the front began to crumble, and was close to total collapse by the autumn of 1918. In the face of imminent defeat, Ludendorff still had the audacity to report to Berlin that 'complete victory was within his grasp'. Unaware of how much they had been lied to, most Berliners entered the last month of the war still fervently hopeful of victory. This could not have been further from the truth.

The war brutalised and impoverished Berlin, and the unimaginable ghost of the loss of the war was to haunt its citizens for years to come. The shocking news of the defeat on the Western front hit the unsuspecting city like a thunderbolt. The two Steinthal boys and their brother-in-law Lutz must have finally come home from war in a state of utter and abject demoralisation. Even though Fanny welcomed them with open arms, aware as she was of the huge sacrifice made by the youth of Germany who were slaughtered in the trenches (as were the flower of British and French youth and their allies), the ensuing years would have been extremely hard for them to bear.

In Caputh Eva was fighting her own private battle. While grateful that she still had a husband, unlike the thousands of young widows left to fend for themselves in the aftermath of war, the whole situation had done nothing to bring the couple any closer together. Quite the opposite was true. Throughout the long four years of war, Richard had remained aloof of his wife and insisted that they sleep in separate bedrooms. Eva found this particularly hard to bear, for in her mind she came to believe that sharing physical relations was a sign that your husband loved you. If he no longer wished to sleep with her, then there must surely be something wrong with him. More than anything she wished to disprove the doctor's gloomy prognostications about her inability to have a second child. All her romantic dreams of a happy marriage and dozens of children were crumbling to dust.

It was a terrible time for Germany. By 1918 the city of Berlin had lost all its pre-war affluence. Food rations were cut yet again, there was hardly any coal and the demoralised population soon became prey to the deadly influenza epidemic sweeping across Europe, that was to claim three hundred people—mostly young men and women—a day.

Unbeknown to the authorities at the time, it was the American entry into the war that was to provide a double-edged sword: both a blessing and a curse. Without the American contribution, the Kaiser's army would never have been defeated. But at the same time it was the young men crowded into troop ships and transported across the Atlantic that were bringing with them a deadly virus: an unstoppable and untreatable strain of influenza. The outbreak had started in the early autumn of 1918 in the United States, and soon spread countrywide because of the extensive mobilisation of troops to furnish the war effort. After some time various measures were put in place by the beleaguered authorities, but to no avail. Every citizen was urged to wear a mask, but as one commentator was later to note rather laconically, 'it was like attempting to stop dust with chicken wire'. While as many doctors and nurses as possible had been sent across the Atlantic in the Liberty ships, to assist in the field hospitals treating the atrocious casualties of the trenches, the medical staff left behind in the USA had to cope with an impossible number of dead and dying.

By October the influenza had spread all over the world, because of the mass movement of troops through the war. In South Africa and Australia, approaching ships were kept away from land and attempts were made to put them into quarantine—but to no avail. This was an airborne virus and all measures to contain it were futile. A concerted effort was made by the remaining doctors and scientists throughout the United States to create a vaccine, but unbeknown to them the science of the day simply was simply not sufficiently advanced. What they thought was a bacterium (visible through their microscopes) would in fact take several more decades to discover with the advent of the electron microscope. And even more alarming was the fact that unlike other strains of influenza, this one was not attacking the elderly, the infirm and the very young. It was the flower of youth, those aged between 21 and 29, who were being cut down in their prime.

In the end, at the time of the Armistice on 11th November 1918, some 15 million soldiers had been killed in the World War. About double that number, some 30 million people, were killed by the pandemic. It had infected the entire population of the world, around a billion people, and was as merciless in its effect as the Black Death. In the end, as quickly as it had started, the death rate started to go down. The flu had run out of humans to infect, and had burned itself out. The whole episode was so frightening to most American citizens that they simply wanted to forget about those terrifying few months. The influenza, popularly dubbed 'the Spanish flu', became known as America's 'forgotten pandemic'.

In Europe in the aftermath of war, the outbreak of influenza was just one more thing to beset the populations whose young men had been massacred so horribly in the trenches.

In Germany the government was in chaos, as Bolshevism spread through the rank and file of the army and navy. This heralded the era of Liebknecht and Rosa Luxemburg, the leaders of what became known as the Spartakist movement, and brought about waves of Communism and near anarchy throughout Germany. The Spartacus Uprising was nipped in the bud in the most violent way possible: in January 1919 both Liebknecht and Rosa Luxemburg were murdered. Luxemburg's body was left to rot in the Landwehr canal, while Liebknecht was shot in the back in the Tiergarten, possibly not far from the Steinthals' first apartment.

To compound all these economic, political and health problems, the final straw came when Germany was hit by the infamous period of inflation. In part this had been due to failed imperial fiscal policy. The war had been financed by loans and bonds, rather than by the government raising taxes, which was a direct cause of the devaluation of the mark. The leaders had taken a big risk, convinced that the money would be amply repaid by the defeated Allies. While the government's gamble had failed, it was the Paris Conference in January 1921 held to fix the level of reparations exacted by the Allies that finally triggered hyperinflation. The amount originally set in Paris was eventually reduced a few months later in London—but it was still astronomic. Germany was expected to pay 132 billion gold marks, an amount that was impossible to comprehend. It caused the Berlin press to protest angrily that their children would languish for years in 'debt slavery'. Much to Richard Vollmann's disgust, inflation was then further fuelled by finance minister Wirth's ill-fated 'Policy of Fulfilment' in 1921, which allowed the value of the currency to founder in the vain hope that the Allies would take pity on the despairing nation.

When France marched into the Ruhr in 1923, with the obvious intent of splitting the Rhineland and the Ruhr from the rest of Germany, it caused the final push into rampant and runaway hyperinflation. Berlin was to become the suicide capital of Europe. Reports abounded of desperate people withdrawing their entire savings—filling wheelbarrows with piles of worthless notes—before jumping out of windows to commit suicide.

8

The Villa on the Elbe

The post-war years were to bring a mixture of tragedy and new hope to both the Steinthal and Vollmann families. What was certain, however, was that unlike many of their unfortunate compatriots, the combined wealth of both families had managed to cushion them from the worst effects of the dire post-war economic situation.

In Berlin, although he had first been recommended for it, Max Steinthal ensured that his wife Fanny was the one to receive the Service Medal for her assistance with the war effort. Not many months after this, Max's feeling of pride in his wife's achievements was to be overwhelmed by sadness at the news of his older brother Leopold's death in Rotterdam. This occurred quite suddenly while he had gone to Holland to fetch a 'poor relation' who had managed to escape with her young children from South Africa. Perhaps the last dregs of the Spanish flu caught him unawares. Whatever the reason, Leopold had only just reached his 70th year. His daughter Agathe was one of Eva's favourite cousins.*

As if to counterbalance this tragedy, the Vollmanns were invited to the wedding of one of Richard's cousins. Held in Sebnitz, it was a much less grand affair than Richard and Eva's matrimonial ceremony in Berlin, but nevertheless it must have offered a much-needed reason to celebrate after all the years of wartime shortages. A fairly generous nine-course menu, featuring typical Saxon dishes, was offered to the accompaniment of a selection of music very similar to that played at the wedding breakfast in the Uhlandstrasse.

Richard and Eva had been living with his parents in their capacious

* Agathe had married a man called Paul Schippert, whose father had been a famous general in the war. His sister, meanwhile, had married a farmer who had taken his new wife to start a different life in South Africa. The couple had three children, but as soon as war was declared all German nationals were interned by the government, as South Africa was then a dominion in the British Empire. Tragically the husband died in prison. In 1919 she was allowed to return to Holland as a widow with her children, and Leopold arranged to meet her in Rotterdam, where he suddenly became ill and died.

house in Sebnitz, where several photos were taken of young Ursula. Not long after their attendance at his cousin's wedding, Richard took Eva away on a three-week trip to Lugano on the Italian Lakes, perhaps in order to chase away all the stresses and strains of the previous four years. Five-year-old Ursula would have been left in the care of her Vollmann grandmother. Eva was later to write how 'blissfully happy' she had been on this particular holiday.

Max Steinthal and Richard Vollmann had one trait in common: they both demonstrated acute business acumen in their different spheres—Max in the world of high finance and Richard in the world of manufacturing. This ability in both men assured the wellbeing of their respective families, and meant that despite all Germany's post-war problems they would be able to weather the economic storm and maintain a prosperous lifestyle.

On the occasion of his 70th birthday in 1920, Fanny Steinthal presented her husband with a small book she had written to celebrate his life, as a souvenir and for the edification of his seven children and four grandchildren. It represented Max Steinthal as a man of innate genius and of great determination, who was instrumental in the flowering of Germany's economy from the turn of the new century, and whose devotion to Deutsche Bank had greatly increased that important institution's fortunes.

In 1921 Richard was approaching his 40th birthday and decided that it was time his family set up their own home. After a considerable amount of searching, he found a villa on the Pillnitzer Landstrasse near the village of Wachwitz, just outside Dresden. Although the house was located some 60 kilometres away from Sebnitz and the factory where he worked as director every day, he considered the position of the house near Saxony's state capital to be of extreme importance. He assured Eva, who was still only 29, that she would love Dresden, and that Wachwitz would be an excellent place in which to bring up their young daughter Ursula.

Wachwitzhöhe, as its name suggests, stood on a steep hillside high above the river Elbe and had originally been built as a tavern in 1880. Its Italianate tower had once served as a dramatic viewing platform for the guests. To one side, an almost vertical flight of steps led to a small grotto in the hillside. The house was surrounded by a wood of oak and horse chestnut trees, and included various small cottages for staff. The picturesque nature of the landscape around the house had acted like a magnet, as much to artists as to summer guests.

Ursula was just six years old when her parents moved with her into their new home. It was to take a lot of getting used to—not for Richard, who spent most of his days away at the factory in Sebnitz, but certainly for Eva, who found herself suddenly confronted with having to cope with a staff of some ten or so local people. Most fearsome of all was the cook, a large lady of formidable temper who took an instant dislike to her new mistress. The rumour soon spread amongst the staff that behind her back, the commander of the kitchen referred to the wife of the new owner as 'that stuck-up Berlin bitch'. It took Eva a significant time to gain her staff's respect and to assume her position as mistress of the household.

Saxons have always been fiercely proud of their history and independence, and while Richard Vollmann was of course considered local and 'one of us', Eva coming from the nation's capital was treated for some considerable time as an outsider. It was not even so much that she came from Berlin, the most important city of Germany, but that she had been born and raised in Prussia. She might even have encountered initial difficulties with understanding the harshly gutteral Saxon accent.

Ursula, however, was oblivious to all these problems. Her nursery was established up on the second floor, near the tower that overlooked the garden and the steep hillside that led down to the broad meanders of the river Elbe. A governess was appointed to instruct the young girl, and a pattern was soon established that echoed Eva's own upbringing. Even though she was an only child, Ursula would have spent most of her time in the nursery, and would certainly not have joined her parents for their evening meal until she was much older. It meant that the relationship between mother and daughter was not always the easiest, and there was to come a time when young Ursula would be strongly influenced by one of her governesses against her own mother.

Richard was away for long hours working at the factory, whose management he had completely taken over by now (Richard Vollmann senior had fully retired by this time and left the running of the production of artificial silk flowers to his two sons). Every lunchtime he would join his brother at his parents' house, to be fed on his mother's substantial Saxon cuisine. This included heavy stew-like dishes of pork with dumplings, accompanied by vegetables and potatoes frequently smothered in thick, floury sauces. On his return home to Wachwitz he would also consume the evening meal organised by Eva and prepared by their own Saxon cook. His once-slim physique was succumbing to good living, and he was to assume a rather portly figure for the rest of his life.

Eva meanwhile set to with a will and put all her effort and energy into furnishing her new home. Much of the furniture and decoration were to come from abroad, the result of frequent trips to Switzerland and England. The display of tasteful and unusual artefacts, collected on later business trips undertaken by Richard to places such as Japan and Central Africa, added an exotic and well-travelled feel to the house.

Downstairs the villa consisted of an assembly of fairly large rooms. The main sitting room was arranged in a big square, from which French windows led onto the terrace. This was a much-favoured spot on which to have tea and coffee served in the summer months. The double-line of linden trees below it formed a roof with their leaves. The oak sideboard was English, and filled with the modern Dresden chinaware that had been presented to the Vollmanns on their wedding day from Eva's Steinthal parents. It was part of a whole series of furniture purchased abroad. Eva was to accompany her husband on several of his business trips, and whenever he travelled to London she would go with him. During the time he spent in business meetings, she would run around 'like a cat', as she later described it, visiting quaint little antique shops and buying up all sorts of furniture for their home.

As befitted a principal sitting room, a large gilt mirror hung on one wall, completely filling in the space over the corner fireplace. A collection of chairs was clustered round a delicate coffee table, standing on a beautiful Aubusson carpet. Richard's desk was finely carved and had 'lion' feet. The walls were lined with leather-bound, gold-tooled books and there were elegant silver candlesticks on the mantelpiece. One wall consisted entirely of a large Gobelin tapestry, which matched the colours of the different carpets that covered the highly polished parquet floor. The whole room was dubbed *'der Gartensaal'* (the Garden Room just like the Uhlandstrasse) because it led out through the French windows onto the terrace and so into the garden.

Next to this large room was the music room. Ursula was never destined to follow in her mother's or grandmother's footsteps, in that she was born with no apparent musical ability whatsoever. That did not deter Eva from furnishing this room with all the accoutrements for music-making. It also contained what she was later to call a 'funny' style of furniture—chairs with very short legs. These were Eva's first purchase in terms of furnishings, but something that she came to regard as an ill-considered and impulsive choice later on in life. There was a roll-top desk that was only there for decoration, because it was much too small to write on. The room included another writing desk that became her 'real' desk, which she was eventually to decorate with a collection of small bronze horses by Gaul.

The dining room contained a large, oval, highly polished mahogany table, big enough to hold 24 places (somewhat smaller than that of Fanny in their home in Berlin, which had seated 36, but nevertheless quite sizeable by Dresden standards). Some of the chairs were antiques—purportedly Chippendale or Sheraton purchased in London. Eva would probably have found a maximum of six such chairs in the antique shops of London, and the rest would have been carefully constructed copies, made by local craftsmen. Over the table hung a large chandelier and, in keeping with Richard's business lifestyle, the couple would hold frequent dinner parties for up to 22 guests. Business acquaintances of Richard's would have mingled with specially invited members of Dresden's high society.

In pride of place in one corner of the dining room stood a *Kachelofen*, a wonderful example of tiled oven that Eva had purchased during a trip to Switzerland. It was heated with coal and cleverly designed to stay warm all night. The dining room was therefore the warmest room in the house. The oven had been disassembled in Switzerland, transported in pieces back to Wachwitz, and then reconstructed brick by brick and tile by tile by a local mason. The fireplace was designed in the classic style, and also included hand-painted tiles typical of this region of Saxony.

Richard was an inveterate collector, and would frequently bring back samples of local arts and crafts from his trips abroad. He had already amassed a large collection of items from Peru, which he had purchased even at the young age of 18 during his round-the-world trip. Another journey to Africa resulted in a wonderful collection of Benin bronzes, spears and assegais. During several trips to Japan taken at different times, Richard brought back various fine examples of Netsuke. The couple began collecting paintings from the first year that they lived in the villa, but the progress of Eva's appreciation of fine art, initiated by her father's example, was to arise through quite another relationship. Her encounter with Professor Emil Waldmann, director of the museum of art in Bremen known as the *Kunsthalle*, was to have far-reaching and extremely serious consequences for the whole family.

During this time, and by now in his seventies, Max bought a summer house called *Gut Neumuehle* on a lake nicknamed *'Maxsee'* in his honour, which all members of his family could use for holidays. This was in the district known as Mark Brandenburg some 100 kilometres north of Berlin in the direction of the Baltic Sea. In winter the lake would completely freeze over, making it possible for members of the family to skate from the house to the local village shops a few kilometres away.

Once the Vollmanns had firmly established themselves in the villa on the Elbe, they had very little to do with their Berlin relatives. At about the time that they moved into the new house Richard's sister Lene married Dr Schweizer, whose family had an estate in Silesia.* A year later her only son Ulrich was born, Ursula's first cousin on the Vollmann side of the family and always known as Ulli. Not long afterwards, tragedy hit the young family. Finding himself enmeshed in gambling debts, Lene's husband felt compelled to uphold the family honour and took the only way out for a former Prussian officer and member of the Junker class: he shot himself in the head. Having to look after her son prevented the young widow from losing the will to live, but she never fully recovered from the tragedy.

About a year after these sad events, there was an exchange of letters between Eva and her younger brother Werner, who in breathless fashion had announced his imminent engagement to a charming girl called Helene Barth. Eva wrote back immediately, offering sisterly advice and her own strong opinion about the suitability of this particular girl as a companion for Werner in his chosen career. Eva was sure that her brother would soon be following in their father's footsteps by forging his own career in Deutsche Bank, and hinted that Helene might be somewhat too childish and naive of character to be a suitable banker's wife. Werner probably smiled at his sister's frankness, but he certainly did not heed her advice because later on that year the young couple were married in Berlin. Werner was the first of the Steinthal boys to be married. He was 29 years old.

An old photograph album contains pictures of Eva during her honeymoon and a few months later when she was three months pregnant, which belie any difficulties she might have been encountering as a newly married woman. In December 1913 the young couple were in Biarritz and Eva is shown leaning over a balustrade and gazing back at the camera from the sea. She is wearing a warm woolly hat pulled down over her ears, and a long, thick woollen cardigan. Some three months later Richard was taking her on frequent visits to what is known as the *Sächsische Schweiz* (Saxon Switzerland), the area of outstanding natural beauty of steep rocks and cliff-faces along the banks of the river Elbe to the east of Dresden. The cliffs rise to almost 700 feet above the level of the river, and the air there is supposed to be absolutely clear and intoxicating in its freshness. Eva is sitting on a rock looking out over the river—she obviously had no fear of heights. Beside her are a small black-and-white terrier and a beautiful looking Irish Setter. Her hair is

* This was formerly in Eastern Prussia and today forms part of Poland.

tied back in its usual bun and she is looking completely relaxed. Perhaps she was taken there as a cure for her undoubted morning sickness and general feeling of being unwell during her pregnancy. In the next photo the setter is standing on a rock next to its mistress, who is sitting and cuddling the dog with great affection.

A year later in Easter 1915 (when young Ursula would have been just six months old) Eva is photographed by the Ilse Falls in a thick pine and fir forest, part of the Harz Mountains. Perhaps it was still possible at that stage in the war for the Vollmanns to take brief holidays in the local mountains. It is obvious that the baby would have been left with her nurse and not taken away at that stage in her life. Another photo shows Eva standing in the snow, dressed in a thick tweed suit of long skirt and jacket with large buttons, wide pockets and velvet collar, with a kind of 'flower pot' hat on her head, outside an Alpine style of building. This was taken in Brocken, another scenic spot in the Harz Mountains and today part of the Harz national park. Later on that day (for she is wearing the same tweed suit), she is pictured at a local restaurant called the Red Trout looking over a lake with charming little low-roofed houses nearby, at a place called Ilseburg.

The theme of her parents taking their holidays apart from their daughter was to be reiterated all through Ursula's young childhood. At eight-and-a-half she is photographed with her mother in the garden at Wachwitz. But while Eva is looking at the camera—or rather, squinting, because the sun is probably very bright—Ursula is determinedly looking away from the photographer (probably her father). Both mother and daughter are sitting on rustic benches at a wooden table, and by their side sits an Alsatian dog, his ears pricked to attention. The grass is long and meadow-like, and bordered by a thick hedge of tall trees. Ursula has very long plaits, a pretty white blouse with short sleeves and a gingham skirt. Her mother is dressed with a similar white summer blouse and is wearing a patterned summer skirt.

The next photograph is very dramatic, showing Richard halfway up a vertiginous cliff-face in the mountains of Arolla, in the Valais canton of Switzerland, and is dated summer 1923. On this particular occasion he took his wife with him to share in his passion for mountain climbing. The rock-face is called *'Petit Dent de Veisini'*. Arolla at that time was famous for its 'cure' hotels, its principal one being the eponymous Kurhotel in the centre of the village.

Eva seemed keen to partake in her husband's activities, and with her slim figure dressed in stout britches, heavy woollen socks, sturdy mountain boots and a hat, with a rope round her waist, she is shown halfway up a rock-face with her hands and feet correctly positioned in the surrounding crevices to balance her weight for the climb. The next photo shows that Richard and Eva took a mountain guide with them on their various climbs into the mountains, and that they would have spent nights in the various mountain huts. Eva has an extremely suntanned face, so their holiday must have lasted for several weeks. The hut is a simple wooden construction, but as sturdy as all Swiss huts are to withstand the rigours of their harsh winters. Around Eva and her guide is a vertical cliff-face of jagged-looking rocks. This particular hut called *Cabane Berthol* features in the next photo, which includes Eva in thick jumper and britches and her guide who is wearing sunglasses on his forehead. Between the two of them stands an absolute giant of a man with his arms stretched out. He must have been over two metres tall. A vista of snow-bedecked mountains extends behind the group.

Mountains and heights seemed to hold absolutely no fear for Eva, which was probably an excellent thing considering her husband's passion for climbing. In the next photograph Eva is standing between two men (one of them is probably the guide and the other one might be Richard). They are in the middle of a high mountain glacier, each of them carrying stout walking sticks but nevertheless looking relaxed amid the rugged scenery. The edge of the glacier is melting into a mountain stream, but their guide must have been very sure of where to walk to avoid crevasses.

In the next photo Eva is sitting on a pile of rocks, probably a cairn at the summit of one of the peaks. Their guide is semi-lying near her, and his ice pick has been planted with the pick-side upwards into a pile of rocks. The Alpine meadow is dotted with little flowers, and behind them soars the snowy peaks of a mountain range. This was most likely their picnic stop.

Richard had been used to travelling all over the world from the relatively young age of 18. Eva on the other hand, while used to train travel and coming from a family who had possessed one of the first family cars in Germany, had little experience of other forms of travel—apart from proving herself a bad sailor during the voyage to Egypt. The final photo of this series taken in 1923 shows her standing by a Junkers plane on very rough terrain, which is labelled 'Zurich 1923'. The plane is a tail-dragger and its fuselage seems to be constructed out of corrugated aluminium.* It must have been possible at that time to fly

* This was possibly a Junkers F13, originally built by the Hugo Junkers corporation as the first aircraft in the world to take passengers. This flight took place three years before the inception of Lufthansa.

from Zurich to Berlin, a trip that would have entailed an overnight journey by train. Eva is dressed once again in her long tweed suit, with her hat pulled firmly down over her eyes but nevertheless smiling at the camera. She seems quite unfazed by this adventurous form of travel.

On the surface, this seemed to be an extremely physical and enjoyable holiday for both Richard and Eva. But she was to write much later in a letter that 23rd April was the last time in which he came close to her 'in that way'. To all intents and purposes she would endure seven years of celibacy, and Richard's refusal to have any sort of physical relations with his wife was to cause untold misery to both of them. The subsequent 'treatment' that Richard underwent to remedy his 'condition' would have been impossible to envisage in any country other than Germany. Yet Berlin was at the forefront of the treatment of psychiatric conditions (following the principles of Vienna's renowned Dr Sigmund Freud). Not only was it possible to find practitioners of psychoanalysis at least 50 years before this method became popular in England, but Berlin was to have the first institute of sexology in the world.

Max at 23

Max at 50

Fanny in her 20s

Fanny aged around 40

Roonstrasse (no. 9 at top end)

Uhlandstrasse 191

Great Hall showing stained-glass window

Great Hall showing 'baroque' ceiling

Fanny in her music room with her 7 children

A 1912 Mercedes

Mey & Co.,
Sebnitz, Saxony

Eva and Daisy with their governess (L) out riding

Eva on her engagement

Eva and Richard's engagement

Eva and Richard's wedding, November 1913

Eva on honeymoon in Biarritz

Eva & setter on the cliffs above the Elbe

Eva with baby Ursula (1914)

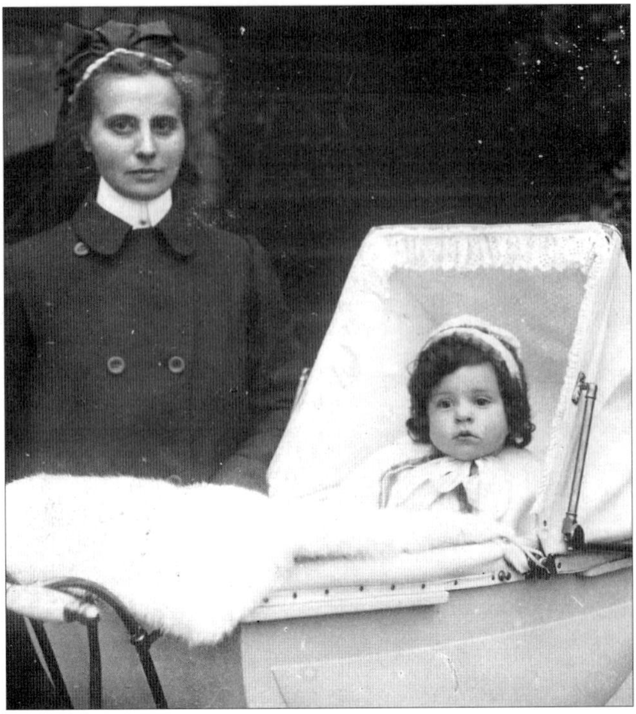

Ursula with her French nursemaid (1915)

Eva & Richard with the Russian greyhound (1915)

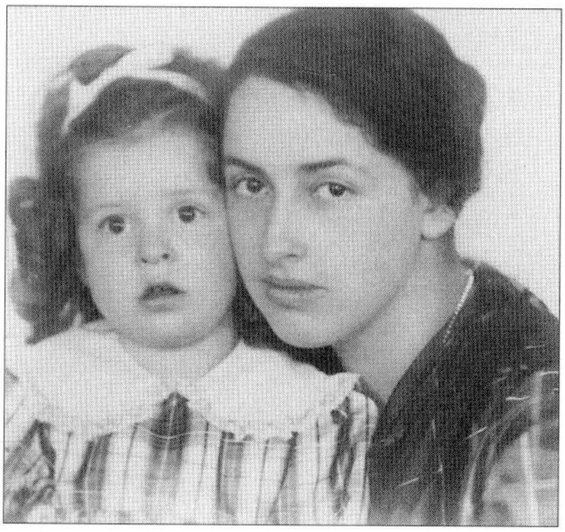

Eva and Ursula (1916)

Eva and Ursula in Caputh (around 1917)

Eva in 1918

Ursula with her grandfather Max 1919

Eva & Richard 1922

The Vollmann villa at Wachwitz

9

Of Art and Psychiatry

Magnus Hirschfeld was a German Jewish doctor whose studies in human sexuality were to make him a pioneer in a taboo subject, far ahead of his time. He was a homosexual and transvestite himself, coining the term 'transvestism'. His Scientific Humanitarian Committee, founded in 1897, advocated the emancipation of all homosexuals. Hirschfeld campaigned tirelessly against Paragraph 175, which was implemented in 1871 after the founding of the German Empire. This reversed the previously liberal French laws adopted by some of the German kingdoms, and made carnal intimacy between men illegal throughout the Empire.

In 1919, under the relatively more liberal atmosphere of the newly founded Weimar Republic, Hirschfeld opened his *Institut für Sexualwissenschaft* (Institute for Sexual Research) in Berlin. The institute housed an immense library and collection of books on sex, and provided educational services and medical consultations. Though much of Hirschfeld's work rested largely on scientific investigation and political argument, the apparent success of the committee at mobilising what they regarded as large sectors of German and European society on behalf of homosexual emancipation was due entirely to Hirschfeld's own personality. He was a dynamic speaker and toured all over Europe, attracting sizeable crowds. He adamantly believed that sexual honesty was a prerequisite for healthy living, and as a pioneer he often found himself not only as an educator, but also as a father confessor. His controversial reputation meant that he was frequently sought-after as a party guest, whilst simultaneously being one of the most reviled public figures in Germany.

Dr Bernhard Schapiro was a Jew born in Latvia, where he had first attended Rabbinical School, following which he then completed his studies in medicine in Zurich. He came to Berlin in 1922 and joined Magnus Hirschfeld at his institute. His speciality was the diagnosis and treatment of impotence, for which he developed several pharmaceutical products.

It is not surprising that Richard Vollmann was later to refer to the institute in Berlin as 'infamous'. He was very much a man's man and would have been extremely unlikely to hold even slightly liberal views about homosexuals. However, it was Dr Schapiro who was the expert in the matter of impotence, and it was for this condition that Richard was reluctantly to submit himself in early 1925. Eva must have been absolutely desperate to have another child, a loss for which she compensated by always having dogs in the house. She was to possess a series of purebred red Irish Setters that she adored with a passion, despite her inability to train them properly. For years the family was to endure a series of irate protestations from their farming neighbours. At least once a week the back door would be thumped by an angry fist, and there would stand a local farmer with a face like thunder demanding immediate compensation, because one of Eva's dogs had got into his hen-house and had killed his chickens.

Somehow it was decided that Eva's enforced celibacy must be due to some mental problem in Richard, one that was preventing him from indulging in any sort of physical relations with his wife. He was persuaded to attend Dr Schapiro at the 'infamous' Institute for Sexology in Berlin, while Eva was away in Switzerland with Ursula. The institute employed Freud's method of psychoanalysis, a process that Richard was to find exceptionally painful. He stayed in the Hotel Eden during his treatment, and was to maintain later that he had suffered a lot with 'this damned psychoanalysis', describing his treatment as 'awful'.

Success in Richard's treatment was ultimately impossible—not because of any refusal on his part to cooperate. The main reason at that time for the incipient failure of the marriage was Eva's relationship with another man, a man who was to become a dominant part of her life for years to come. Despite all her subsequent protestations of innocence, Eva was to indulge in an impassioned love affair with a man 12 years her senior, married with two sons. The relationship was to create untold problems in her marriage, and was even to cause Ursula to be sent away to school because of the poisoned atmosphere at home. While Eva thought that by having a physical relationship with another man she would somehow be able to cement her own marriage, Richard wanted nothing further to do with a faithless wife and found the whole situation unbearable. Eva, who considered she was being so discreet and that her husband was quite unaware of her 'dalliance', could not conceive why her husband would not understand and agree with her need for contact of a physical nature. At the same time, it did not occur to him for a moment that his wife imagined she could hide the whole affair from him.

Richard's business took him away on ever more frequent trips abroad. He was looking to expand the markets for the factory in Sebnitz and increase the sales of artificial silk flowers. In later years he would be away from home for up to eight months of the year. When he was home, Richard and Eva would give frequent dinner parties for up to 22 guests, as well as musical evenings and society gatherings.

'People were very glad to be invited to our house, you know,' she was to say later in her life. While Ursula would be looked after and tutored at home by her governess, Eva would spend mornings or afternoons in Dresden, exploring the quaint little streets and visiting the art galleries and museums. On the surface it was an indulged life, the life of lady of leisure whose main occupations were to keep on top of a staff of ten running a large household, and deciding what flowers to have in the hall that day or what that night's menu was to be. However in her heart Eva was nursing a deep hurt, a painful longing that created a hole in the very centre of her being and left her feeling abandoned and starved of affection. She loved her daughter but was unable get very close to her, and adored her dogs. But something was missing from her life, and the longer her husband refused to touch her physically the worse became this yearning.

Matters came to a head when Eva met Professor Emil Waldmann. She had first been introduced to the rather ascetic looking lecturer in fine art in 1921, when Ursula was still only about seven years old. It is quite likely that this would have been in Dresden, when the professor was possibly conducting research in various art galleries for his series of books on renowned Old Masters. He ran a succession of well-attended lectures on different aspects of fine art, and over the next few years Eva was to become his 'best student' and his 'most attentive audience'. He was invited to the house in Wachwitz on several occasions, ostensibly to advise the Vollmanns on the purchase of works of art. He even accompanied the couple on a culture trip to Italy, although he had a wife of his own called Minerva and two sons. She must have been as used to her husband's absences from home as Eva was.

Emil Waldmann was without doubt a good-looking man. He was tall and elegantly dressed, and his patrician face contained deep-set and sensitive eyes of a deep blue colour. His fair hair was later to turn white. His fingers were long and tapered, and his whole demeanour exuded a sparkling intelligence and keen sense of humour. From his point of view, Eva when he first met her in 1921 was still only 29 years old and an extremely attractive young woman. Despite her own lack of confidence in herself, she would have been a petite and alluring vision of dark-eyed and dark-haired beauty amongst the brunettes and blondes of the professor's otherwise Saxon audience. The attraction between the two of them was instant and electric, and the very danger of commencing any sort of relationship would have added to the excitement felt between the two of them.

Eva was later to assert that all she did was conduct many years of correspondence with the professor, but that was not the way Richard saw it. At the height of the troublesome episode of hyperinflation in Germany, he discovered a letter written by Eva to her cousin-by-marriage Eduard Gaffron, with whom she had become very good friends by letter. She wrote boldly to her cousin that she had no intention of going through life as a 'small and unknown woman', and that she had finally found the man who could bring about the opportunity for her to achieve such a bold ambition. This caused Richard to prick up his ears with regard to his wife, and when the very man in question turned up at their home, it made Richard determined to present a different face to his wife. In a future letter he gave vent to the bitterness of his feelings. 'One hour after she was due to arrive home,' he would later write, 'I phoned her from Berlin to welcome her and that's when I heard that she wasn't in Wachwitz, but that she'd gone directly from Switzerland to Berlin. Since she wasn't in the Uhlandstrasse and she had contacted neither the family there nor me, it was obvious that she'd gone to her lover. So an extremely amusing French farce took place, in which wife and lover engage in loving dalliances, while the stupid cuckold and wretched simpleton makes desperate efforts through the psychoanalysis of Dr Freud to get physically closer to his wife.'

Eva in her turn was to refute utterly any claims by her husband that she had been having an affair. These protestations, however, seem rather hollow, as during 1926 there was a passionate exchange of letters between Eva and Emil Waldmann. From the tone of the letters, it would appear that Waldmann was able to offer the romance and affection that she so desperately craved, even though their respective positions were hopeless and they were both married to other people. In the winter months the professor would undertake Hellenic cruises in the Mediterranean, on which he would give lectures to the passengers about ancient Greek culture. He seemed to have no qualms about sitting on deck next to some German government official, while writing passionate letters to his mistress. His wife Minerva's cousin was the German consul, and the clientele on these cruises included people from Dresden who were well acquainted with the Vollmanns. Waldmann seemed to enjoy indulging in florid descriptions, but the last paragraph of one particular such letter is the most telling, because his words indicate a deeply physical relationship with Eva.

Darling, darling, how beautiful it is, and how much more beautiful it would be if only you could be with me, my beloved creation. The landscape in Corfu is amongst the loveliest I know. We went on a long drive by car over the back of the mountains to the west coast of the island, with the husband of my wife's best friend driving. We passed bays carved deeply into the rock, islands and peninsulas, foothills and steep coast with pines and cypresses, fig trees, silver-grey olive trees, aloes, giant cacti, distant purple mountain ranges, cliffs and rocks in the sea. And then the sea itself—how absolutely divine it is, especially at sunset. It's deep blue and purple near the coast, turning to turquoise and the richest emerald green further out. Then when the sun streams over the whole thing like a dazzling opal and the sky is the clearest blue with air as pure as silver—it's just heavenly. I went for a short walk on my own, just thinking of you. There was nobody else around, not a house nor even a monastery—it was delightful beyond words.

You know how much I love you. Will we ever be able to enjoy this together? But that's just the reason why you're always uppermost in my thoughts. This island has the richest variety of vegetation in all of Greece (which is otherwise somewhat barren), so we drove for ages through lemon groves, and then through ancient olive groves, and then past orange trees whose branches were weighed down with just-ripe oranges; through vineyards and eucalyptus woods, where everything was in flower and the scents in the air were indescribably strong and sweet. I'm fine myself and I'm really enjoying this way of life.

So, now I've got to work on my lecture; it's hard when the audience have such a patchy knowledge of culture and I've got engage their interest so that hopefully people don't go away either bored or disappointed.

My beloved, beautiful creature, in my mind I'm kissing your enchantingly beautiful eyes that I love almost more than any other part of you, and your gorgeous mouth. My great big hands are stroking your beautifully soft skin—when I'm feeling good in myself I love you more than practically anything else, if that's even possible.

Eva for her part showed herself to be equally passionate. She carried out work for Waldmann as a kind of personal assistant, translating certain texts from French and Italian. It gave them the opportunity to meet for legitimate reasons. In one letter—the only one in existence from Eva to Waldmann—she wrote by hand in French first of all and finally in German, as if the language of romance were the only method by which she could express her passion. It is inconceivable that she would have thought of her husband in the same terms, or that he would have offered her any terms of such endearment or demonstrations of pure tenderness.

> My darling love, if I'm writing to you today by hand and not with the typewriter, it's so that I can be closer to you. You see: today is one of those 'tomorrows'—yesterday you told me, 'the spoken word melts away, but the written word stays for ever'. Well what I want to tell you needs to survive permanently—even if these lines don't reach you for a long time. And what I want to say to you is very short and very simple, and it's that I'm happy—so blissfully happy from the depth of my heart. You told me I'm looking younger, and I really believe it to be true, because nobody can understand those things they haven't yet experienced nor what it means to live without love. I'm asking you to believe this 'great thought' without fear or doubt: I love you. I want to share all my ideas with you, even if I'm so far away from you; every book I read, every picture I look at, even every dress I put on, I do with my eyes on you, I could even say just for you. I've finally found a resting place for my heart, which after all these years of neglect is such indescribable joy—I thank you for it. May God protect us and give us a few more years of this happiness. I've got so much more that I want to say to you, but with my soul in such turmoil it's hard to capture this in words. But I wanted you to know that when I'm close to you and when I give myself to you, it's not just with my body, it's with my whole self and with every fibre of my being. Because I love you and you are the world to me. Thank you for the happiness you give me.

Perhaps the most telling indication of the state of this relationship was one letter sent by Waldman to Eva consisting of nothing but a poem, called 'To Werther'. For anyone imbued in Germany's cultural heritage, this literary allusion contained a very clear message. In 1774 Johann von Goethe had published *The Sorrows of Young Werther*, a loosely autobiographical novella of unrequited love for another man's wife. In the story, the young hero Werther commits suicide. The publication of the book engendered the first example of copycat suicides in Europe. Apparently some two thousand people killed themselves after reading Goethe's heart-rending but romantic story.

Throughout all this emotional turmoil, Eva found she was confiding in her sister-in-law Lene (Richard's sister), rather than her own mother in Berlin or her older sister. Daisy was experiencing problems in her own marriage, with an increasingly brutal and uncaring husband, while Fanny would probably have been somewhat unsympathetic to Eva's situation. She would most likely have told her daughter in no uncertain terms that it was a wife's duty to keep her husband happy.

10

A Saxon Childhood

As she was an only child, parts of Ursula's childhood were rather solitary and devoid of the company of other children. The manifestation of the second child that her mother so desperately craved turned out to be nothing more than a pipedream. Ursula was consequently brought up in a large villa, where her father was frequently absent and her mother engaged in social functions or in running the household. She did not go to school until she was 12 or 13, and so had few friends amongst the local neighbouring houses.

Ursula's favourite companions were her three Berlin cousins, who used to come and visit from time to time. Monica, the oldest of Daisy's three children, was a domineering, bossy and confident child who always took the lead in any games they were playing. Hans Gebhardt, later to be known as John and almost the same age as Ursula, proved to be a good playmate and later introduced her to the game of 'doctors and nurses' (the only way Ursula was going to get any sort of inkling about the physical differences between girls and boys). Gisèle was three years younger than Ursula, and four years younger than her older sister. She was always referred to as 'Baby' and treated accordingly by everyone else.

One of Ursula's happiest memories of childhood games occurred one September just before her birthday. It was of sitting on the wall that snaked along the steep hillside below the family villa, parallel to the road leading to the village of Wachwitz. Armed with baskets of fallen apples and with bare legs dangling in the warm autumn sunshine, John taught his cousin Ursula how to pelt passing cars with rotten fruit. Needless to say, had such naughtiness and unseemly tomboy behaviour been discovered by their respective governesses, then the children would have been severely reprimanded. John, however, was sly enough to work out a foolproof escape route. As soon as there was the slightest whisper of the imminent arrival of any grown-ups, John would whisk Ursula away from danger by pulling her by the hand, breathless with excitement, up the moss-covered steps leading steeply upwards towards the grotto.

Meanwhile there were three more grandchildren born to Max and

Fanny Steinthal. Werner's marriage to Helene was to remain childless, but Eva's younger brother Eduard married a girl called Gabriele Gebhardt. They produced two sons christened Michael and Frank, the first born when Ursula was 10 and the second when she was 12. Their mother was an attractive but shallow woman, whom Eduard was always to put on a pedestal but who also adored having bevies of male admirers at her feet. At the same time Eva's younger sister Ruth married a sculptor called Julius Nimptsch (shortened to 'Uli'), and they produced just one son named Peter in 1926. This was after Ruth had first suffered a miscarriage. She was to mourn the loss of her baby daughter for the rest of her life.

By this time Max was in his mid seventies and he and Fanny would spend most of their summers at their holiday residence, *Gut Neumühle*, surrounded by an area of thick forests and smooth lakes. The grandchildren would also be invited there, and one photo shows Ursula in a one-piece bathing suit, aged around nine, stepping gingerly into the Maxsee in which her cousin John stands waist-deep, while a stern-looking manservant is watching over both the children. Even when he was on holiday and relaxing, Max would not relinquish his old-fashioned style of dress. Another photo shows their fifth grandson Michael, at the age of about six months, sitting on a rug with his white-haired grandmother Fanny looking on proudly. Max is kneeling upright, wearing a top hat, white shirt and tie, and a long jacket.

Ursula, being an only child, developed some very strong likes and dislikes from quite an early age. An insistence on being fed an assortment of milk puddings as a child created a loathing in her for the rest of her life for anything to do with milk. And she never really got on with her Berlin grandmother. During one rare visit to the Uhlandstrasse, Fanny decided to take her granddaughter out to a particularly fine patisserie as a special treat. In the café, crowded with its upmarket clientele, Ursula was forced to watch what to her was a shamelessly unapologetic display of distinctly Austrian manners. When she wanted to catch the waiter's attention, her grandmother pinged loudly and impatiently against her wine glass with her cake-smothered fork, while uttering in a stridently high-pitched voice, *'Herr Ober! Herr Ober!'* ('Waiter, I say waiter!'). Ursula was utterly mortified and wanted the earth to swallow her up. She had been brought up on strict Saxon principles advocating discreet and modest behaviour in restaurants, and this display of Viennese habits was just too much. It made her take against her own grandmother and was something she could never forgive her for.

As for the Vollmann grandparents, they seem to have been held in somewhat greater affection by their granddaughter. Richard's father was a tiny, gnome-like figure of a man whose white beard exuded a benevolent air. His head was completely bald, and like his counterpart in Berlin he always wore a smartly formal suit with a white shirt and tie, even after he had completely retired from the factory in Sebnitz. A photo taken probably on the occasion of his 75th birthday shows him sitting at a table, with Ursula aged 10 sitting next to him. She is frowning deeply and has her finger in her mouth, her long plaits swinging down her white blouse.

Although Eva and Richard did take Ursula on occasional visits to Berlin, and probably on much more frequent visits to her grandparents in Sebnitz, it happened on many more occasions that their home itself in Wachwitz would be used for Vollmann family gatherings. In the early 1920s Richard's younger brother Walter had married into a titled family, the von Hammersteins. His wife Jutta was stunningly beautiful and the marriage would later give rise to a family joke: while Richard had married into the world of high finance, Walter had married into true nobility. Just as his own mother had before him, within two years Walter's wife had presented him with two sons called Dieter and Christian, and then four years later a girl who was christened Gisela but always known as Gila. All three children were ash-blond. Ursula was 14 when her newest cousin Gila was born.

Shortly after her youngest cousin's birth, a great Vollmann family celebration was held at the house in Wachwitz. The photo shows Ursula all dressed up, standing at the bottom of the flight of steps leading down from the terrace outside the *Gartensaal*. Her Vollmann grandparents are standing behind her, grandfather in tailcoat and grandmother in elegant long dress. Several members of Mey & Co., as well as various cousins, stand assembled behind the anniversary couple. Hidden amongst them, as if denying her very presence, is Eva. Once again Ursula is frowning into the camera, as if disliking the whole idea of parties and celebrations. On the right, Walter stands tall and proud (he was always to retain his slim figure), while his wife looks particularly chic with a luxuriant white fur draped over her shoulders.

Despite Ursula's apparent dislike for her Berlin grandmother, she was to retain some very strong impressions of the grand house in the Uhlandstrasse. She had vivid recollections of occasional Christmases spent there, with the whole family gathered in the Great Hall, in which rose the traditionally enormous Christmas tree decorated in red and silver baubles. Ursula was always impressed at how her grandmother could run what to her seemed a huge house, together with its large staff, with competence and precision. For Daisy's children however, always known to Ursula as 'the Berlin cousins', the villa in the Uhlandstrasse was treated like a second home. Fanny would still arrange musical evenings, from which grandchildren would be excluded as their parents had been before them. The story went that on one particularly prestigious occasion, Daisy and Lutz had been invited to listen to the chamber concert that played in the great hall of Villa Steinthal. Their three children were listening from the floor above, trying to catch a glimpse through the balustrade of the ladies and gentlemen in all their finery. As Monica was craning her neck to get a better view, her head got completely stuck in the banisters. Despite her obvious distress at this calamitous occurrence, their governess was so much in awe of Fanny's temper that she dared not move until the end of the concert to raise the alarm. The whole affair created a great rumpus because the fire brigade had to be called—and it was only years later that Monica was to discover how her uncle Eduard (always the naughtiest of the Steinthal children) had caused exactly the same thing to happen during a concert many years previously.

Rather than being a forbidding figure, Max was an adoring grandfather who loved playing with his grandchildren on Sundays. In later life Gisèle was to acquire a picture of an elderly Flemish burgher in velvet and fur robes, with a beautifully painted head, much in the style of the school of Rembrandt. To her this was the exact image of her grandfather, with his white beard and his head tilted in one of his hands, a gesture which could be regarded as very Jewish. In contract to Fanny with her irascible temper, Max was very mild-mannered and loveable. He would play games with his children and grandchildren, such as 'The Wolf and the Seven Little Goats', his own version of hide-and-seek.

Ursula also retained vivid memories of Christmas dinner in the formal dining room, where the enormous oval table would be groaning with food for the Christmas Eve meal taken in the evening, in accordance with German custom. The main dish served was frequently a great big carp from one of the local lakes, a fish that Ursula regarded with particular disgust because however it was dressed it always tasted of mud. But that was not the only off-putting thing about formal dining with her Berlin grandparents. Over the table on the opposite wall hung a large and imposing oil painting entitled 'Still Life With Melon'. It was not the melon that was the object of Ursula's fascination, but rather the dead hare hanging upside down and the dead birds strewn over the table in the picture. At that young age it did not impress her in the least that this was an old master by the sixteenth-century Dutch artist Snijders, who would have painted that particular still life at around the time William Shakespeare was born. All she could think about was that those dead animals were somehow staring at her, while she was trying to be on her best behaviour and appearing to be enjoying her Christmas meal with her grandparents.

Another clear memory was of her grandmother Fanny sitting in her own sitting room, where the walls were covered in the little miniatures that Fanny collected with such passion. By her side, or sometimes on her lap, was her little French bulldog called Bibo, who was inordinately spoiled and who would snuffle asthmatically at all newcomers.

Ursula also had other Berlin cousins: Eva's cousin Agathe's three daughters. The family of Max's older brother Leopold, however, were always treated somewhat as 'poor relations', and very rarely invited to the villa in the Uhlandstrasse. For Ursula's cousin Bärbel, aged about eight, being presented to her great-uncle Max was a scary and uncomfortable experience, completely unlike that of Gisèle. Her abiding impression was of a dark and gloomy office with a fearsomely hook-nosed, white-bearded and rather formidable looking old man sitting behind a huge mahogany desk.

When Ursula was around 12 or 13 years old it was decided that she should attend the local grammar school for girls, so that she could learn to socialise with girls of her own age. There was one other companion, however, who used to come and visit during the school holidays. Ursula was encouraged to have an English penfriend in order to improve her knowledge of that language. She became best friends with Joyce, a girl from a middle-class background whose family lived in the lush, rolling downs of Sussex. Joyce visited Ursula and her family on quite a few occasions, and it was mainly from this girl that she obtained her knowledge of English. In her early teenage years, Ursula was sent over to England to spend some of the summer holidays with Joyce and her family.

The climate around Dresden was one of extremes: in winter the snow piled up outside their house and the ground would be frozen for weeks; in summer it was frequently hot enough for the local schools to grant the children *Hitze Frei*—time off because it was simply too hot for lessons. Ursula was taught to ski at a very early age, engendering in the young girl a love of winter sports that was to remain with her well into her later years. A photo taken in the early 1920s shows her aged about nine, wearing thick tights, a woolly skirt and woolly jumper, her long hair braided into plaits, practising her turns on a pair of wooden skis. Her teacher was a much older man. All around them are tall fir trees, their branches completely laden with thick snow.

Towards the end of the 1920s, just after Ursula's fourteenth birthday, it was determined in the Vollmann household—most probably on Richard's insistence—that she needed a new governess. Eva may well have objected at the time, but with the marital difficulties experienced by the couple her husband perhaps felt that she was in no position to countermand his wishes. He felt that Ursula needed to be protected from the frequently stressful atmosphere in the house in Wachwitz, and that her studies would be all the more advanced with individual teaching from an experienced person.

Eva was encountering her own difficulties in the household at the time. The cook still regarded her mistress with scant respect, and felt that as she did not know the first thing about cooking she had no place in criticising her efforts. This woman ruled the kitchen with a rod of iron, and was the scourge of the other servants, all of whom had to be fed by this terrifying personage. At some point there were even rumours that the cook was jealous of one of the housemaids, whom she regarded as her own personal property. Eva would not have had the faintest clue about the concept of lesbianism, choosing to believe (rather like Queen Victoria) that such a thing could not possibly exist.

None of this had any direct bearing on Ursula's upbringing, and Eva would certainly have gone to tremendous lengths to ensure there was no evidence of disharmony amongst the staff, in particular whenever they organised one of their famous dinner parties. Yet all Eva's efforts at smoothing things over were to come crashing round her ears. Naively assuming that Ursula was far too young to be aware of any disagreements between her parents, Eva was shattered on arriving home late one afternoon by the calamitous news waiting to greet her. Ursula was missing.

The house was in uproar. While the chauffeur had fetched the master home early from the factory, a frantic search of the house and gardens by their mortified staff had revealed nothing. With his master almost too apoplectic with rage to speak, and his mistress dissolving into helpless tears, it was left to the trustworthy chauffeur to take the family car and search the roads leading to the village of Wachwitz and beyond. Much to his relief, some time later he spied the young girl, wrapped in her long school coat and standing on the bridge that led out of the village and spanned the wide river Elbe. To his consternation, however, she appeared to be in close conversation with a man who looked at least twice her age.

Ever mindful of Herr Vollmann's volatile temper, the chauffeur got out of the elegant Rover and called urgently to Ursula, 'Fräulein, Fräulein, you must come with me at once.' Bundling the young girl into the car's plush leather seats, he drove off with some trepidation back to the Vollmann villa. Ursula was sent straight to bed, but not before the whole sorry story had come out.

Although usually chaperoned every time she went out, it had been during the famous *Elbehang*, a local fair that took place every June, that Ursula had somehow managed to meet a man who was twice her age—30 at least—with whom she later arranged a daring and secret assignation in the local village. A few weeks later, just after her fifteenth birthday, she managed to give her governess the slip. With some skill and out of sight of any of the staff, she succeeded in crawling out of one of the upstairs windows, and then climbed down to ground level, using as a makeshift ladder the hefty creeper that wound its way up the balcony to the second floor. With her heart pounding, the young girl ran down the road, all the way to the village, to meet her 'young' man on the bridge known as the *Blaue Wunder*.

For hours after her return and in the relative safety of her bedroom on the second floor, Ursula's ears rang with the sound of raised voices and the banging of doors downstairs. Richard accused Eva of neglecting her daughter's needs for her own selfish pleasures. It was only his trusty chauffeur's timely intervention that had prevented anything worse happening to *his* young daughter. This near-disastrous adventure, however, had given Richard the perfect ammunition to improve the situation, without the need to have his wife's approval.

As far as Richard was concerned, the fault for this whole sorry affair lay entirely on Eva's shoulders. Despite his long hours at the factory, he was kept well informed of Eva's lengthy afternoon sessions spent in Dresden, leaving her daughter on her own for long periods of time. Even worse, according to him and as he was later to confide in his mother-in-law, Ursula had already been made aware of her mother's love affair even before this near-disastrous event. Her current governess was sacked on the spot.

Thus it was that Fräulein Franke, the new governess, made her first appearance at the house at Wachwitzhöhe. This enterprising young woman of very determined political views was soon able to befriend the young girl, and to instil in her new 'ward' some radical ideas of her own. A woman with an unusually sharp nose for any sort of scandal, Fräulein Franke* soon sniffed out the situation with Eva and her frequent visits to Dresden. Within a few months, from Eva's point of

* Eva's dislike of this young woman was very apparent in later letters. While she frequently called her lady's maid, later to become the family's housekeeper, by her first name (Helene), this governess was only ever referred to as 'Franke' or sometimes just 'F'.

view, the new governess had poisoned her daughter's mind against her own mother. But despite Eva's frequent protestations to Richard about the unsuitability of the woman, he was adamant that she was very good for Ursula's wellbeing and insisted that she stay in the household. His bitterness towards his wife had not abated.

Before the distressing events of Ursula's disappearance, however, a much happier event was to take place. During the summer of 1930 her grandfather Max Steinthal celebrated his 80th birthday with a party, to which a considerable number of members of Deutsche Bank were invited. Although his birthday was on Christmas Eve, the party took place at the end of the previous June, perhaps so that this momentous occasion would be blessed by good weather. By this time, Max had been honoured by the Overhead Train Company, as well as receiving many other awards. He had been a director of the bank for 57 years, the last six of which were spent in the prestigious role of chairman. As such, just the previous year he had presided over the largest merger in German history: with the Disconto-Gesellschaft. Meanwhile, in honour of his years of service as their chairman, the directors of Mannesmann had commissioned a portrait of Max by a contemporary and very well known artist, which had remained hanging in the boardroom from around 1910.

At the same time Richard was also having his status in local society considerably elevated. In 1926 he was granted the title of 'Consul for Belgium in Dresden', and received a beautifully inscribed scroll that had been personally signed by Alfred I, King of the Belgians. This meant that whereas his father-in-law was always addressed as *'Herr Geheimrat'*, Richard would henceforth be known as *'Herr Konsul'*. Later Richard was to commission a portrait of himself in his new role by a rather well known contemporary artist called Slevogt, who belonged to the German Expressionist movement and managed to capture Richard's likeness in a particularly effective way. One person missing from the birthday celebrations was Herman Wallich, one of the original directors of Deutsche Bank. He had died two years before Max's 80th birthday, and at his extremely well attended memorial service Max was asked to give the oration.

A group photo was taken, with Max and Fanny seated in the middle. By this time Max's beard was completely white, giving him a very benevolent air. Fanny was 64 and still a very elegantly dressed woman. Seated around them were the female employees of the bank, and behind them stood a whole group of men, all in stiff white collars and formal suits. Included amongst these were Lutz Reichenheim, Daisy's husband, and Eva's two younger brothers Werner and Peter, both of whom worked for their father in the bank. Also included in the group, standing right at the back, was Richard Vollmann. Ursula and her Berlin cousins would certainly have attended this milestone occasion, but probably in the Uhlandstrasse. Because this photo was taken at the premises of Deutsche Bank, no children were included.

The local Berlin newspapers were full of articles extolling the virtues of the banker Max Steinthal. The evening paper wrote how Max had given 57 years of unbroken service to the bank, interrupted only by short periods of holiday in order to recuperate. Included amongst all the paeans of praise were good wishes sent from none other than *Reichspräsident* Hindenburg.

11

All Change

Back home in Wachwitz, the atmosphere at home was becoming unbearably tense, with frequent episodes of explosions of temper and slamming of doors. Fräulein Franke used the situation with skill and clever manipulation in order to get close to her employer, the Belgian consul for Dresden. A year later Ursula had taken her *Reifeprüfung* (matriculation) at school, coming top of the class, much to the jealousy of the other girls. It was now 1931 and already the ogre of anti-Semitism was raising its ugly head. After the exams, a group of girls, most of them the daughters of impoverished local aristocracy, gathered round Ursula and asked her what sort of family her mother had come from. This was a perfectly normal notion in Saxon society, as the mother's family was the most important element in the marriage from the point of view of status and 'old' money. A good example of this was in Richard's brother Walter's marriage: his wife belonged to the von Hammerstein clan, who by their very appellation could be regarded as minor aristocracy and therefore as bringing an added dimension of 'good breeding' into the Vollmann family.

'Was für eine Geborene war deine Mutter?' they asked her curiously. This usually translates as, 'What was your mother's maiden name?' but the implied meaning is, 'What sort of family was your mother born into?' Ursula told the girls quite innocently that her mother had been born a Steinthal. 'Oh, but that means you're Jewish!' they exclaimed, and ran away laughing. Somewhat puzzled, Ursula came home and confronted her mother by repeating the words that the girls had all taunted her with. 'What do they mean, we come from a Jewish family?' demanded Ursula, glaring at her mother. Religion, for Ursula, had always consisted of weekly attendance at their local Lutheran church, sitting on uncomfortably hard pews in stark and unadorned surroundings, listening to hour-long sermons of the 'fire and brimstone' variety. For the whole of her life, there had never been any mention of Jewishness or talk of the concept of Judaism in Ursula's close family.

After an embarrassed pause, Eva looked at her daughter and sighed. 'There is an element of truth in what those girls are saying,' she finally admitted. Ursula, baptised and confirmed in the strict Lutheran faith, could not have been more shocked. In complete confusion, she ran upstairs to her bedroom, where she was found some time later by her governess. This episode caused an even greater rift between mother and daughter.

When Richard came home that night to an even stranger feeling in the house than usual, he decided enough was enough and that his daughter had to be removed from the poisonous atmosphere. Fräulein Franke, with her usual efficiency, had made sure that her employer was fully apprised of his daughter's experience at school. It was the summer of 1931, and this latest episode had provided him with just the excuse he needed. Without blinking an eye, Richard announced to a flabbergasted Eva that he was going to take Ursula away to the South of France, with her governess. The explanation given to 16-year-old Ursula was that she would go on suffering taunts about her Jewish antecedents if she stayed in Germany.

Before she left with her governess, another Vollmann event was held at Ursula's home. Once again all the members of the family attended: Ursula's grandmother and aunts, including her uncle Walther and aunt Jutta. Posing for the usual family photograph, at the top of the steps stood her youngest cousin Gila, aged about three and dressed angelically in a white dress with a white crown round her blond ringlets. Ursula was wearing a very pretty summer frock, while ranged towards the bottom of the steps were her three male cousins, Ulli, Dieter and Christian, all wearing identical sailor tops with shorts that showed their skinny legs and bare knees.

Eva must have taken little comfort from such a happy family occasion, because she was to be left on her own and deprived of her daughter's company for over six months. Richard, in his usually dominant way, persuaded her forcefully that it was in Ursula's best interest to attend school in Cannes in the South of France, in the company of her governess Fräulein Franke. For Eva, separation from her daughter could not have been more devastating, but at the time this was not a feeling that was reciprocated. Ursula, then only 16, probably considered it quite a daring adventure to be leaving home at that age with her governess.

As he would write years later in letters to Fanny his mother-in-law, Richard knew of every detail of his wife's love for Waldmann. Every morning Eva was driven into the city, to go on shopping trips and to collect her mail from the post office; in the afternoon she would write to Waldmann or would do translations for him. There was no stopping her ill-fated passion for this man, according to Richard. Just a few hours after he had left home on business for Paris or London, Eva would also go haring off from there to meet her lover. It was clear that this could not remain hidden from their staff: every one of them knew precisely about her relationship with this man, even the 'people upstairs' in Sebnitz (the employees of the factory of Mey & Co.). As far as Richard was concerned and to his great regret, Ursula had been 'made aware down to the last detail about the *grande passion* of her mother'. That was the reason for her distant behaviour in regard to Eva and her very close attachment to Fräulein Franke, because according to her father Ursel felt lonely while Eva was occupied in the afternoon with her lover. Too young to appreciate her mother's behaviour and without any explanation to the contrary, Ursel had concluded that it must be expected for her to get herself a boyfriend.

After a particularly explosive argument with his wife, Richard had flung accusations at Eva about her relationship with her lover. Completely shocked at her husband's awareness of her affair, Eva had forthwith arranged to be driven to a hotel in Dresden in order to collect her thoughts, from where she wrote him a letter.

'The simple thought that you could ever find out about this has made me utterly ill,' she wrote, 'and I don't think I've ever wished for anything more fervently than that I should spare you all this. But since you know all about it, we have to come to terms with the fait accompli.' She continued, 'I feel completely sure that I'm now in a position to break off my relationship—but what will you do with an embittered wife, who might become so hysterical that she would only cause problems in your life? And so I turn my thoughts to Ursel, now that such lack of ambiguity exists between us, and I wonder whether the atmosphere will be better and easier for her than it has been up to now?'

Richard's reaction was unequivocal. 'What on earth was Pev thinking?' he later thundered in correspondence with his mother-in-law Fanny. 'Should I share my marriage bed with Waldmann? It was absolutely clear that she wasn't going to give him up.' Quite contrary to Eva's beliefs, the atmosphere was now unnaturally and artificially held together in Wachwitz, because on every trip to her lover Eva had to seek out the greatest variety of excuses and apologies, especially to the staff. Richard suspected that his wife had an accomplice amongst the staff—most likely her trusted lady's maid Helene—who must have arranged how incoming telephone calls from Berlin would be directed. Eva would also have been able to call back using telegrams, just in case Richard came home earlier than expected from his trips to London or Paris.

Ursula was blissfully ignorant of this stress and strife between her parents, and apart from occasional visits home for Christmas and summer holidays together, Ursula was to spend the rest of the 1930s away from her home in Wachwitz. Her relationship with her mother had reached rock bottom. She stayed in contact with her father by letter, but formed the closest relationship with her governess. In fact Richard would often visit his daughter, and took a whole series of photographs in 1932 showing a happy, smiling teenager. Meanwhile as Richard confided to his mother-in-law in Berlin, Eva was to develop a close relationship with his widowed sister Lene, whom she was later to confirm as being the one person she regarded as being perfectly able to understand all the marital difficulties that had beset her brother's wife. Whether Lene did sympathise with her passionate and somewhat emotional sister-in-law is debatable, but it must have given Eva some comfort to believe she had a female confidante.

During the early years of the 1930s, Eva would spend many of her days in Dresden. Her daughter was away at school in Geneva, her husband was out all day in the factory in Sebnitz and was frequently away for long periods on business trips abroad. She never learned to drive, so it was quite probable that Braun the chauffeur would have taken her into the city for shopping, sightseeing or visiting galleries. As a 'big-city' girl she seemed to love the art and architecture of Dresden: the famous *Zwinger*, designed by Pepelmann in very ornate rococo style; the square with its castle belonging to the royal house of Saxony; the river Elbe flowing nearby with its beautiful bridges; the delightful architecture of the *Frauenkirche*, the baroque church of Our Lady. She thought it was a wonderful town and its old, narrow and cobbled streets very pleasant. She would later tell people that she lived a 'retired' life at this time, but that she had a lot of friends and sang often. She thought her life was quite 'gay' in that she had a beautiful house and enormous garden.

This impression could not have been the whole truth. With the departure of Ursula to go to school abroad, there must have been very little of the marriage to cement the relationship between Richard and Eva. Perhaps that was one of the reasons he spent so much time overseas. Another letter from Waldmann five years previously showed that the flame of passion was burning ardently between him and Eva, and seemed likely to have gone on burning despite the difficulties it caused to Eva's marriage.

One of the sad things about Eva's relationship with Emil Waldmann was not merely that he was also married with two sons of his own; he was a man who was in very bad health, and who seemed to suffer from bouts of bronchial illness. In a letter written late in the summer of 1926 after he had been ill, he wrote with passion and then some considerable impatience. The letter also shows that not only did they use various hotels for their secret assignations, but also used the villa in the Uhlandstrasse as a kind of poste restante or 'box number' at which to communicate with each other.

'My beloved darling!' he wrote. 'You see I'm up again—in fact I've been up for two hours, and have taken a walk in the garden as it's not raining any more. I wanted to write a greeting to you before Hilken [his secretary] comes for dictation. Of course I'm feeling a little bit shaky, but if I can see you again in a fortnight nothing else will have mattered. Come here, lie in my arms and let me kiss you—think of me and love your beloved. Oh how I'm longing for you! Where can I meet you in two weeks? Dresden is no good, but you could come to Berlin, couldn't you?' He went on to suggest meeting at the Kaiserhof, one of Berlin's most prestigious hotels and probably one of the locations of their secret assignations. The rest of his letter expressed a passion that could only exist between lovers.

> I love you passionately [he continued] and I kiss you all over. I love you so much—d'you love me the same? Have a good trip and think lovingly of me. I kiss your eyes and take your beloved being in my hands, lovingly and tenderly. I'm always thinking of you and of our utterly beautiful and blessed moments together, and also of the times when we've just sat quietly next to each other and I've sat silently stroking your arm, and felt so good, so tender, so loving. O my beloved creature, my love. I kiss you—we'll see each other soon.' The letter finished, 'Be well, God bless you and our life. You are the pride of my heart—ever renewed.*

It was not known if Waldmann's wife Minerva was as aware of her husband's straying from marital fidelity as Richard Vollmann was of his wife's. But events were to take a very different turn. By 1933 a momentous happening was taking place in Germany that was to change the course of Eva's life irrevocably: the rise to power of Adolf Hitler.

From the very start of the Fascist era, Richard Vollmann was to have scant regard for the Nazi regime. He would refer to Hitler in the most

* This last sentence was written in Italian, and in some letters Waldmann would quote poetry in French and English—so between the two of them Eva and her lover would write in four languages.

derogatory of terms as *'dieser verdammte Oberkellner!'* ('this damned jumped-up waiter'). His widowed sister Lene in Sebnitz, however, believed that after all the iniquities of the Treaty of Versailles and the terrible problems faced by the German economy, Adolf Hitler was the most wonderful person to arrive into her life, and she was to become quite enamoured of the Fuehrer. While Ursula was still quite safe in neutral Switzerland, her younger cousin Gila had become a *Küken* ('young chick') in her first year of schooling in Sebnitz, while she was still only six years old. This benevolent title, rather equivalent to the Brownies, hid a sinister intent. It was the first step on the road to the complete indoctrination of the young, which at its worst level encouraged children to spy on their parents. Once the girls had reached their teenage years, they would then be made to join the *Mädchenbund* (League of Girls), which was the movement where blonde-plaited, blue-eyed girls were held up as the flower of German womanhood and the future mothers of the 'pure' race of Aryans. The three cousins—Lene's son Ulli and Walter's two boys Christian and Dieter, all of them perfectly blond, blue-eyed specimens of German adolescence—together with their classmates would all be recruited into the Hitler Youth.

Despite Lene's obviously Nazi leanings, Eva always maintained that she still had a close and warm-hearted relationship with her sister-in-law.

Ironically, one of the first casualties of the Nazi fervour sweeping across Germany was Magnus Hirschfeld's Institute of Sexology, attended so unwillingly some eight years previously by Richard Vollmann. In all the future newsreel footage to emerge out of Germany from the Nazi period, the image of bands of youthful fanatics creating enormous bonfires and hurling books into the flames is taken from the time when Hirschfeld's library was set on fire. Luckily for Magnus Hirschfeld he was out of the country on a speaking tour at the time, and never returned to Germany. He was to die in exile in Nice in 1935. Berlin became the focus of the National Socialists' determination to cleanse the city's libraries of 'un-German' material. The crowd of students, backed by members of the SA (Storm Troopers) and a marching band, had stormed the institute's offices. The ensuing conflagration consumed over ten thousands books, articles and research material. As a final insult, a sculpted bust of Hirschfeld was carried in a torchlight procession by the Nazis and tossed on top of the bonfire in Opera Square. This was to mark the beginning of the Nazi determination to eradicate all traces of homosexual emancipation from every level of German society.

Hirschfeld's colleague Dr Schapiro had become medical director of the institute. As soon as the Nazis had plundered and closed the building, Schapiro as a Swiss citizen was fortunately able to leave with his wife and four children and return to Zurich. Within months he had set up a successful medical practice.

An even more famous citizen to disappear from Germany at that time was Albert Einstein. The world-famous physicist, whose 50th birthday in March 1929 was celebrated with congratulations and presents from all over the world, had spent all his savings on having his beloved summer house constructed in Caputh* (where Eva had spent most of the war years with her young daughter Ursula). From that time until Hitler's rise to power, his popularity remained unbroken and he received invitations from all over the world to hold lectures on his latest scientific theories at the most prestigious universities, and to receive awards. For him, however, it was the seclusion of his house in Caputh that was to offer him the peace and tranquillity he so desired, where he could pursue his thoughts on matters physical (including quantum physics and the beginning of a unified field theory). During his time in Berlin he was a member of the Prussian Academy of Sciences, and professor at the Friedrich Wilhelm University. He was also head of the newly founded Kaiser Wilhelm Institute of Physics and had succeeded Max Planck as president of the German Physics Society.

All these honours and elevated posts were to come crumbling around his ears as the Nazis came to power. The public burning of 'un-German' writing, organised by Goebbels, included works by Albert Einstein. Even before Hitler's accession to power in April 1933, the leadership of the National Socialist Workers Party was demanding a national boycott on Jews. Albert Einstein became the focus of the Nazis' hostility towards Jews, and his summer house was searched by Nazis under the supposition that it was hiding a cache of weapons for the Communists. In the summer of 1933 Einstein lost his German citizenship and his whole fortune was seized. By 1935 Einstein's beloved summer house would be confiscated and handed over to the state of Prussia.

Einstein's reaction was to resign from the Prussian Academy of Sciences, renounce his German citizenship, and to cut off all contact with every German institution he had ever dealt with. After a spell in Europe he was to spend the rest of his days in the United States, never setting foot again on German soil. He said at the time, 'As long as it is possible for me I will only stay in a country in which political freedom, tolerance and the equality of all citizens are stated in law ... None of these

* Einstein's summer house is in the process of being restored, as it was the first commission for a student of the famous Bauhaus movement called Konrad Wachsmann and as such had been considered by the town of Caputh a listed building.

conditions are being fulfilled in Germany today.'

In Dresden, despite being married to a 'true' German (who was still blond and definitely blue-eyed), Eva was soon to experience the hostility felt by many fellow Jews. Her cook, for one, proved her allegiance to be completely pro-Nazi and turned even more against her mistress. In the city itself whole families began to disappear. The Jews made up the intellectual class of the city, such as the Bondis who ran one of the banks and the Wolfs who ran the local press, as well as the legal stratum of judges and lawyers. Many eminent professionals were to commit suicide, while the local branch of the Rothschild family escaped to Paris.

For the Steinthals in Berlin, things were no easier. After 62 years of faithful service to Deutsche Bank, Max Steinthal finally agreed to resign 'voluntarily' so as to prevent any 'unpleasantness' for the other members of the board. He had moved to the bank's supervisory board in 1905, in his 55th year, and by invitation had served as its chairman from the age of 73 until his 82nd birthday. He had been instrumental in funding the construction of the electrified railway and subway in Berlin, and had transformed the Mannesmann business into a joint-stock company. Beyond the business world Max Steinthal's interests spread far and wide. As a member of various cultural and artistic institutions, he was the joint donor as far back as 1897 of Jean François Millet's 'November' to the *Nationalgalerie* in Berlin. From that time onwards he was a friend of the great museum director Wilhelm von Bode, who would have advised Max on his collection of paintings. Amongst his treasured possessions, apart from his favourite Sorolla, were the names Millet, Picasso, Munch, Lovis Corinth, Segantini and Pissarro.

Despite all these achievements, the other members of the board of Deutsche Bank felt that in the current political climate, they would have to sever all connections with Max Steinthal. The truth was that for the sake of expediency, as soon as Hitler had come to power, Deutsche Bank 'got into bed' with the new Nazi regime, with many of its employees joining up as 'brown-shirt' members of the SA. Over the ensuing years Max also had to resign all his memberships and chairmanships of various boards, including the Mannesmann Company that he had served so faithfully for decades. Even with all his years of experience, this must have been a truly bitter blow.

12

Enemy of the State

The advent of Hitler and the Nazis was to have far-reaching repercussions in all branches connected directly or indirectly to Eva's family—even to her lover, who was ostensibly as 'Aryan' as Richard Vollmann. And yet, as if ignoring the political events taking place around them, in 1933 Eva accompanied Richard on a business trip to New York, while Ursula, aged 18, was still at her school in Geneva. They sailed across the Atlantic by steamer, and spent several days together in the lively city. Much to Richard's astonishment, however, Eva insisted on taking the return steamer back to Europe a week before they were actually due to leave. She was later to explain the circumstances in a letter written to Richard the following year while Eva was in Geneva visiting Ursula. This followed after a previous explanation she had offered when Ursula was first sent to Geneva at around 17 (precisely for the reason of escaping the poisonous atmosphere at home):

> It hurts me so immensely that you regard me as having completely betrayed you. That is wrong, completely falsely judged, even though I can understand your point of view. Of course I was in those places and with those people that I told you about, but it became completely impossible for me to tell you to your face, when and where I met my friend [lover], either before or afterwards. The lies arose out of this predicament.
>
> Now that the relationship is going to become extinct, you yourself will see that there can be no more lying. Every accusation in your so utterly irreconcilable letter has hit me directly in the heart. I'm paying a heavy price for my mistakes; we're living apart now and I've told you that I will do everything in my power to enable you finally to find happiness and peace.

In every letter amassed by Richard, Eva seemed to be apologising for the hurt she had caused her husband and assuring him that she was just about to break off the relationship with her lover. But nothing concrete in that intent seemed to happen. Using the changing political situation as an excuse, she wrote in 1934:

> I travelled back a week before you from New York, in order to break off my relationship with him, because I considered it unfair that you should be burdened with a Jewish wife during the Hitler regime, a wife moreover who had a lover. I've already told you the reason why I was incapable of finding a solution at that time. Today I'm leaving him for other reasons … and these are because I cannot maintain a liaison with him as long as I know how much pain and insult I have caused you.

This was perhaps not the entire truth. Hitler's incipient anti-Semitism must have caused problems from Emil Waldmann's point of view, and there is evidence to suggest that Eva's lover might not have proved such a staunch defender of his mistress's lineage as she might have supposed. Of course he had his own wife and two boys to think of, not to mention his position as director of the Kunsthalle in Bremen, a post that was very much in the public eye. Years later Richard was to remark somewhat bitterly in a letter to his mother-in-law Fanny that he almost felt sorry for Eva. He told Fanny in a rather laconic tone of voice, that the very man who had been so happy to maintain an elegant mistress without a thought for other members of his family, had only once made the slightest attempt to divorce his wife in order to be able to marry Eva.

By the winter of 1933 Eva had changed her mind again: she told Richard that she was unable to break off her relationship with Emil Waldmann because he was too ill. This statement must have been the final straw, and Richard finally lost patience with his errant and insubordinate wife. He pleaded with her that they should live separate lives. Eva was aghast at the very idea, but her husband was adamant and after many arguments she finally agreed to a trial separation. After a lot of discussion it was agreed that Eva would go on living in Wachwitz, but that Richard would build a small house in Sebnitz for himself and Ursula. Eva seemed to spend weeks at a time in Geneva, although it is quite probable that Ursula's governess would have created as many obstacles as possible to prevent the mother seeing her daughter.

Eva wrote again to Richard during the summer of 1934, 'Yes, I have made grave mistakes, but now there should be no more obstacles on your road to happiness and contentment. In fact, you might take fresh courage and believe that things are looking up.' And again in the same letter she wrote, 'Today I'm seeing Waldmann, who's travelling home from Venice. This is therefore my chance to take the first steps to break off this relationship. You'll probably think I'm doing this out of some kind of Jewish opportunism. But if that were indeed the case, then I wouldn't be racking my brain for ways in which I could at least begin to rectify the wrongs I've done you.'

Nothing was to come of the separation, and Eva suggested once again that she should continue living with Richard. He became completely indifferent to the whole situation, even though he knew a year further on that Eva was still in touch with Waldmann. The couple must have been existing as two separate beings in the same house, while Richard was later to state that he ignored the whole affair, 'in case either of them should happen to come into conflict because of the heavy Nuremberg laws and their severe penalties'.

This was no empty sentiment: after the violent events of the 'Night of the Long Knives' in which Roehm, leader of the SA, was assassinated, Himmler had gained immense power. He turned the Gestapo into an arm of his terrifying security system, augmented with Heydrich's SD (*Sicherheitsdienst* or Security Service). Himmler was the most influential figure in changing the face of Nazi terror. Unlike Roehm, whose brown-shirted SA troops had had the reputation for thuggish behaviour, he disliked obvious violence. His well-organised system of control was largely covert, and therefore much more insidious. And in the deeply ingrained sense of injustice felt by normal Germans, it was a deceptively simple task to get thousands of people to accept and aid the Nazis in their quest for total conformity. One later wartime file was to report that the Gestapo employed more than 60,000 agents and over 100,000 informers, not including the millions of people who spied, reported and informed of their own volition, or worked as part-time agents. Some of these were motivated by self-interest, or possibly self-preservation. By showing loyalty to the state they sought their own promotion. Some may have concocted evidence to settle old scores; others were genuinely motivated by Nazi ideology. The whole stage was set for the persecution of all 'un-German' elements in Hitler's totalitarian state: socialists, communists, Catholics, homosexuals, gypsies, the disabled, Jehovah's Witnesses, Freemasons and most of all Jews.

As if in defiance of all these troubling events, both at home and in the wider political arena, Richard and Eva somehow set aside their differences to take Ursula to Austria on a skiing holiday in the winter of 1934. Ursula was 20 and was in her last year of finishing school in Geneva. This show of togetherness did not last, however, and much to Eva's disgust Richard then disappeared—by this time she was probably aware, however unconsciously, of her husband's 'other interests'. To Ursula's delight, nonetheless, Eva then phoned the Reichenheims and invited 17-year-old Gisèle to come on holiday with her cousin. Gisèle was later to recall vividly the excitement of travelling on her own by train from Berlin to Austria. Throughout the long journey she was chased by Nazi officers, not once because they were aware of her Jewish roots but only because of her attractive blonde hair. She had always been able to pass herself off as 'Aryan'. Gisèle did not ski herself, but had great fun at the dances held in the evening at the hotel. Being a very curious and forthright girl, she kept asking Eva when her uncle Richard would come back to the snow-covered village. All Eva could do was fob her niece off with non-committal answers. At the same time, Ursula was being hopelessly pursued by a lovelorn boy called Utz Thüner whom she knew from Dresden. Gisèle regarded the lad as Ursula's first real 'flame' but the feeling was, alas, not reciprocated. Undeterred by her aloofness towards him, Utz spent one evening dancing with Ursula. Gisèle watched in rapt fascination and so was completely oblivious to the lateness of the hour, until her aunt Eva came bursting onto the dance floor just before midnight. She had thrown her sable fur coat over her nightdress, and her face was absolutely thunderous. Both girls were forbidden any more dances.

In autumn of the next year Eva and Richard once again made a show of 'togetherness' in front of their daughter, and the three of them undertook a fairly adventurous journey to the Middle East. Departing from Hamburg in the steamship *Milwaukee*, they sailed through the Bay of Biscay, round Portugal and southern Spain, through the Straits of Gibraltar and then all along the Mediterranean as far as Beirut in Lebanon. From there they visited Palestine and Egypt, for which Richard had secured temporary visas for all three of them. It is probable that Richard's consular status would have granted him access to most destinations, but already two years of the administration of the Third Reich were reflected in personal documents. Richard's passport for 1935, which originated in Dresden, was stamped with a Nazi swastika and was valid for five years and for journeys to and from Austria. It stated Richard's occupation as 'Factory Owner and Royal Belgian Consul', with 'hair blond; eyes blue'. Ursula's passport was issued in the same year at the German Consulate in Geneva, and was also stamped with the Nazi swastika.

Frequent travelling was certainly a way of life for the Vollmanns, a fact that was reflected in all three passports. Richard's business principally involved the expansion of foreign markets, and there were several stamps issued by the Department of Trade and Industry in Dresden for business visits to France, England, the USA and Canada. Each foreign visit required the appropriate visa, and each time money was exchanged it had to be noted in the passport. Once Ursula had started her studies in London, she would come home for almost every holiday, returning to England in term-time. She usually travelled by ship to the ports of Harwich, Dover and Southampton, but there was one entry showing that on a trip to Venice she went by air. Eva meanwhile travelled frequently to Switzerland to visit her daughter while she was at the finishing school in Geneva, but also engaged in various trips to Austria and France. In 1937 the Vollmanns went on a cruise to Norway, possibly to experience the splendour of the fjords. In October of the same year, Richard took his daughter with him to France to attend the international exhibition in Paris.

It was at the annual rally of the NSDAP in Nuremberg in 1935 that a special Reichstag session was held, in which the Reich Citizenship Law and the 'Law for the Protection of German Blood and German Honour' were passed. In the first law, citizenship of Germany could only be granted to a national of 'German or kindred blood'. In the second law, all Jews were defined as 'not of German blood'. Oddly the definition of Jewishness was based upon the religion, rather than the race, of the grandparents and parents, but this contradiction did nothing to faze the Nazis. Marriage between Jews and German 'nationals' was strictly forbidden, as were sexual relations between the two 'races' outside marriage. Most importantly of all, Jews were to be excluded from all aspects of German life: they were without citizenship, without rights and without recourse to the law. Goebbels was delighted that racial anti-Semitism had now been given fully legal and legitimate expression.*

In autumn of the same year, shortly before her 21st birthday, Ursula moved from Switzerland to London and began her studying at the Courtauld Institute of Art for a diploma in art and architecture. It was probably the safest place for her to be: out of the reaches of the Nazi state, and away from the unpleasant atmosphere at her home in Wachwitz.

One of the most vicious attacks on the Jews happened on the night of 9—10 November 1938. *Kristallnacht* was to become synonymous with anti-Semitism, but it was very much in keeping with earlier measures. Made to look like a 'spontaneous' reprisal for the murder of a German diplomat by a Jewish youth in Paris, the pogrom had in fact been planned in detail by Goebbels together with local officials. The police president Count von Hellendorf ensured that Jewish buildings were isolated and that gas and electricity supplies were cut off. The fire

* Richie, *Faust's Metropolis*, p. 429.

brigade was on full alert to prevent damage to neighbouring 'Aryan' property.

At 2 a.m. hundreds of Nazis, who had been loitering in the streets, began to smash up shop windows and set fire to Jewish property. Out of the twelve large Berlin synagogues nine were plundered and destroyed, including the beautiful synagogue on Oranienburger Strasse, which was engulfed in flames as the fire fighters simply stood by and watched. At daybreak hordes of Berliners ran through the streets, beating Jews and looting their property. Glass lay in thousands of shards all over the pavements and the streets; hence the name coined for that fateful night. Over 20,000 Jews were loaded onto trucks like cattle and hauled off to Buchenwald, Dachau or Oranienburg.

At no small risk to his own safety, Richard Vollmann had sought security arrangements through his former drinking buddy Stauss—he was still employed at Deutsche Bank and had become a staunch member of the SA. All night long, two brown-shirted guards stood on sentry duty at the impressive villa and grounds of his parents-in-law in the Uhlandstrasse. The house remained unharmed, but by then the process had already begun that was to result in all seven children of Max and Fanny Steinthal having to emigrate for good from the country of their birth.

Some members of the Steinthal family, however, stayed resolutely defiant throughout this period. Ursula's cousin Gisèle, Daisy's daughter, went out with a Jewish girlfriend and attended one day of the Berlin Olympics in 1936. She was just 19 at the time. When the entire German crowd rose as one and shot out their arms in salute to Hitler standing on the podium, the girls sat with their arms folded across their chests, refusing to shout *'Heil Hitler!'*. It could have been an arrestable offence, but in the excitement of the occasion their indiscretion was luckily overlooked.

At the beginning of the fateful year for Jews that was highlighted by the Nuremberg Rally, Fanny wrote a brief but touching note addressed to her seven children, stating her last wishes.

> Beloved Children, I wish that over my coffin no words about me be spoken. I simply wish that a 'person of courage'—no Jewish minister—read the verses about Love, where it says: *Love suffereth not and is kind; Love envieth not, Love vaunteth not itself, is not puffed up. Love beareth all things, believeth all things, hopeth all things, endureth all things. Love never faileth.*[*] Through these

[*] 1 Corinthians 13, New Testament, King James Bible.

beautiful words I'll be able to speak to you all once more, and ask you to think of me in love, and to hold love, which is the greatest sentiment in man's life, as just as important a factor in your own lives, in everything you strive for in your lives. Your *Mutting*.

While the political situation in Germany was becoming increasingly threatening for Jewish families—even those with considerable personal wealth like the Steinthals—Ursula was well set up in London. She was living in a comfortable apartment in Chelsea—no doubt paid for by her father—and enjoying her studies at the Courtauld Institute. One of her tutors was a young man by the name of Anthony Blunt who at that time was one of the most distinguished art lecturers of his generation. He would go on to become a personal adviser to the Royal Family, including the Queen, on all matters concerning art. His infamy, as a member of the 'Cambridge Five' and his consequent uncovering as a spy, would only arise decades later. As far as Ursula was concerned, Anthony Blunt was just one of a series of lecturers at the Institute, who also included Nicholas Pevsner, helping advance her knowledge of art and architecture. She was to find that her education, first in Cannes (which she had found very difficult in French) and then in Geneva, was of definite benefit. Unlike her English fellow students, she found little difficulty learning all the Italian expressions and names relating, for example, to the Renaissance which formed an important part of her course.

For the young Ursula her early twenties were a time of independence and self-discovery, not least in the most intimate sense. She experimented in sex during the course of several liaisons. While she had lived at home in Wachwitz, she had frequently complained to her mother that her legs were too fat and that she was not pretty. Her mother always considered that her daughter had a lovely figure, with a 'tightly modelled little bottom'. This was certainly true from the photographs taken at the time, where the fashion was for long skirts and short jackets that emphasised the waist and hips. Then again, Eva herself always thought that she was too short to have a perfect figure, and had always been jealous of her elder sister Daisy and her supposed 'great beauty'. In the less restrictive atmosphere of London, Ursula must have discovered a much greater level of freedom. Steadily gaining in confidence, she would soon learn how to emphasise her own attributes.

Ursula was also to become much more politically aware—not because of the events in Germany, but through a branch of the family who had fled to England as political refugees. Some of Richard's South American cousins, the Ferreyros, had been expelled from Peru in the early 1930s by the Peruvian government of the time, for purely political reasons. They had even suffered incarceration, subsequently escaping prison by paying 'cartloads' of money to the current government. They ended up in Liverpool, where Ursula was able to visit her cousins, without really understanding what it meant for them to be political refugees. The family had been running a coffee export business. Ursula was to meet Tia Ana, the mother of Richard's cousin Anita. Tia Ana was a tiny woman, a half-caste, but these were an 'upper-class' kind of refugee. Ursula was initiated into the mysteries of how to make Peruvian cakes, the recipe for which included lots of condensed milk. Following the inevitable coup in that turbulent country, there was a change of president in Peru. Much to their relief, the Ferreyros family were able to return home to their hacienda.

At this time, around 1936, Richard Vollmann was still making frequent business trips to Paris and London. As far as he was concerned, the City of London was the most secure place in which to invest money, and he considered the British economy one of the most solid in the world. He had a bank account in London and conducted much of his business with City traders. One of his business colleagues in London was a merchant by the name of Harman, who ran an import business for artificial flowers called Artiflora. He had two sons, the younger one of whom would become Lord Mayor. Edward Harman, the older boy, was born around 1908 and had been educated at public school. It was probably Richard Vollmann who introduced his daughter to the good-natured, somewhat awkward and shy young man.

Teddy was invited over to visit the Vollmanns in Wachwitz on several occasions, and Eva took an instant liking to this typical young Englishman. He would be dressed in a sober tweed suit and brogues, making Eva regard him with affection as a perfectly 'proper' and well brought-up young man. The Harmans were entirely happy for their son to be associated with Ursula, whom they realised came from a family with considerable money. Richard, as perhaps the most far-sighted member of the family, could sense the gathering clouds of war. From his point of view, the safest place for his daughter in the teeth of the Nazi regime was to marry an Englishman and live in England. During the summer of 1938 the young couple announced their engagement, much to the satisfaction of both families. The official notice was given in the *Daily Telegraph* in London. The photos taken at the time show the 'happy couple' relaxing on the terrace of the villa in Wachwitz, while Eva looks on contentedly.

Later on that year, as if attempting to maintain a sense of normality, Richard took his family on a cruise through the Caribbean. They visited

Havana in Cuba as well as several other islands, and travelled in great style and luxury. Several photos were taken of Eva during this time, where she looks dazzlingly beautiful. Dressed in an elegant black chiffon evening dress, she has a double string of pearls round her neck and two diamond rings on her fingers. She smiles directly into the camera, and her carefree look belies not only the turmoil of her personal and political situation, but also her 45 years.

In July 1939 Ursula graduated from the Courtauld Institute with a diploma in art and architecture. She had flown back to London from Berlin on 1 July, in order to receive her results. Her visa, which was 'granted under instructions' by His Majesty's Consul, permitted her only three months' stay in Britain. Just over a month later, on 17 August, Ruth Ursula Vollmann married Edward Clarence Valentine Harman at Notting Hill registry office, only six weeks before her 25th birthday. He was 31. Ursula was later to confess that she was never passionate about Teddy, but she was certainly very fond of him. The wedding was attended by Mr and Mrs Harman on one side and Eva on the other. Ursula's marriage to Ted meant that from that date she could apply for a British passport. The couple had a very brief honeymoon in Salisbury and by the seaside.

At the beginning of September Eva was on the train to Liverpool. She would not see her daughter again for almost ten years.

By 1938 Max Steinthal was in his 88th year, while his devoted wife Fanny was 72. With heavy hearts, they realised that the political situation was becoming untenable for all Jewish families. By this time all Jews were forced to bear the name 'Sarah' for women and 'Israel' for men in their passports and all documents of identification, while having to wear the yellow Star of David on their sleeves. It is not known if this indignity was forced upon the Steinthals as well, but they knew that their seven children would have to emigrate if they were to escape the fate that had already befallen thousands of their contemporaries. What is certain is that each one of them had the red 'J' stamped into all their personal documents. Despite all Max's efforts at assimilation into German society, the Nazi regime regarded all the Steinthals as 'non-German'.

The oldest son Erich had experienced the greatest problems because of the metal plate in his head (arising from that first automobile accident in the early 1900s). He decided that as the oldest child, he should be responsible for his parents' welfare, despite the considerable danger to himself (all physically or mentally damaged citizens were regarded as 'disabled' by the Nazi authorities, and therefore candidates for the death camps). Max was in his late eighties, but even so during 1938 Fanny was to suffer the indignity of being arrested for some minor financial infraction, and incarcerated for eight days in a Gestapo prison.

Even though Werner and Peter had both worked for their father in minor positions at Deutsche Bank (in the twenties and thirties), they had shown themselves to have a far greater liking for gambling and living the 'high life' than for hard work. None of the boys demonstrated any tendency to follow in their father's footsteps: rather, their somewhat indulged upbringing, despite their shared experiences of the horrors of war, had resulted in several failed business ventures and no clarity of ambition. This lack of purpose did not apply to Erich, however, who had often spent time in Montmartre in Paris, amongst the artists and booksellers. He was proud of his collection of rare books, for which he had commissioned contemporary artists to add illustrations. These included Picasso and Corinth.

The threat of deportation for Jews was growing ever more real in Hitler's Germany. By now all those designated 'Jew' were denied full German citizenship, but to ensure his family's safe passage out of Germany Max had to spend a considerable proportion of his wealth and hand over either gold coin or diamonds to the Nazi authorities. All Jewish assets had to be declared in full, and alarmingly complete files were kept on every Jew by the Gestapo.

Neither Erich nor Peter was married at this time, but while Erich decided to stay with his parents his youngest brother attempted to get to England. Of the five remaining children, only Ruth would stay married to her first husband. Werner had already divorced his wife Helene in 1932, but now his childhood polio was beginning to have a marked effect on his physical abilities. He walked with a pronounced limp, which could have led to his immediate arrest as both a disabled person and a 'non-German'. Happily he had met Barbara, whom he intended to marry, but they both knew they would have to leave Germany because she was a full-blooded 'Aryan'. As she battled bravely with the authorities against Werner's imminent house arrest, the situation seemed hopeless.

Eduard had also divorced his wife Gabriele by the mid thirties. In August 1938 the Gestapo seized Eduard's flat in Düsseldorf where he had been living, and closed the bank account that was intended to fund his emigration. With the help of his father's payment of around half a million Reichsmarks to the Gestapo, he was able to get to Paris.

In late 1936 had Gisèle spent a wonderful year in Italy studying sculpture with her uncle Julius and aunt Ruth. Mussolini's alliance with Hutler and the threat of war, however, was to put a cruel end to what could have been a promising career as a sculptress. Gisèle returned home to Berlin, while Julius managed to take Ruth to London with their ten-year-old son Peter.

Daisy was left on her own in Berlin, with three young people under 24 to think about. Her husband Lutz Reichenheim was to play an extremely cruel trick on the family. All through their marriage he had lived in comfort off his wealthy wife's generous allowance. In fact, although officially designated an 'engineer', he spent most of his time at his club, gambling his money and frittering his time away. By now well aware of the impending political situation, he took a steamer from Hamburg to New York in order to secure American visas for his whole family. When he came home, however, he had brought only one visa back with him: for himself. After finalising their inevitable divorce, he returned to the United States with his latest mistress, but without his family, basically sealing them to their fate. Gisèle was never able to forgive her father for this appalling behaviour.

In early 1939 Richard told Eva that he would have to divorce her, because of the draconian Nuremberg laws. Despite all the past difficulties of their married life, Eva truly believed that this would be a temporary measure, and that when the threat of war was over the whole family would be able to get together again. She thought she would be able to spend the war with her daughter in England. Both Ursula and Richard had other ideas, however. Ursula thought that her mother's German accent, far stronger than her own, would cause unnecessary problems, mainly with the English authorities but especially with her Harman in-laws. Richard added to the force of this argument by stating that Eva would be nothing but an embarrassment to their newly Anglicised daughter.

The divorce documents were drawn up, and were expressed in the meanest of terms. Not only was Eva blamed outright for the divorce, but she also had to pay all the costs of the legal process. It stated furthermore that because she had 'voluntarily' left Germany, she had renounced all rights to her German citizenship and to a German marriage. The actual divorce went through in November of 1939, after Eva had left Europe, but to all intents and purposes the marriage between Eva and Richard was finished by March of that year. On all the documentation, Eva was referred to as 'the un-German female enemy of the State'.

Since 1934 the house at Wachwitzhöhe had been used as the Belgian consulate, and Richard himself was able to use the title of consul. It was probably this position that gave him the authority to persuade his Nazi friend Stauss to organise the two guards to protect the house of his parents-in-law during *Kristallnacht*. Because Eva needed an address abroad, both for the purposes of the divorce and also because of her impending exile, Richard used his connections in the consulate. A small apartment was found for her in Brussels. Again by paying vast sums of money to the authorities, Jews leaving Germany were permitted to take one load of furniture out with them. Many of Eva's possessions were sent in trunks to the apartment in Brussels.

With his usual great powers of persuasion, Richard assured Eva that the safest place for her under the threat of war was to be on the other side of the world, in South America. He himself would not be able to leave Germany, he told her, because he needed to stay to look after the factory. This was not the case with other such mixed marriages: many 'men of honour' decided to emigrate with their Jewish wives, so as not to become separated from their loved ones. Eva, however, believed everything that Richard told her, and reluctantly agreed to take the steamer across the Atlantic to Peru. Her only tenuous links with South America were Richard's Gaffron and Ferreyros cousins, whom she had never met.

The daughter of the chairman of Deutsche Bank was being expelled from her homeland, to travel on her own halfway across the world. Her enforced journey was destined to take her to a country she did not know and a culture that was completely unfamiliar to her. She did not speak a word of Spanish.

Eva's staff

Eva rock-climbing in Arolla (1923)

Eva with mountain guide (1923)

Eva by a Junker, Zurich Airfield (1923)

Eva in Italy (1924)

Young Ursula skiing

Ursula and Grandfather Vollmann

The Steinthals' summer house at Neumuehle

A Vollmann Party at Wachwitz (1920s)

Ursula with setter (aged around 15)

Ursula and Eva in deer park (around 1930s)

Portrait of Max (Board of Mannesmann)

Portrait of Richard by Slevogt

Max on his 80th birthday at Deutsche Bank (1930)

Another Vollmann party (1930s)

Ursula and her governess in the south of France (1932)

View from the Vollmann villa over the Elbe

The village of Wachwitz on the Elbe

Richard's 'exotic' collection in the sitting room

Photographic portrait of Eva aged 45

Portrait of Professor Emil Waldmann
by Leo von König

Ursula & Teddy at Wachwitz (1938)

Ursula & Teddy's wedding (London, August 1939)

Part 2: Peru

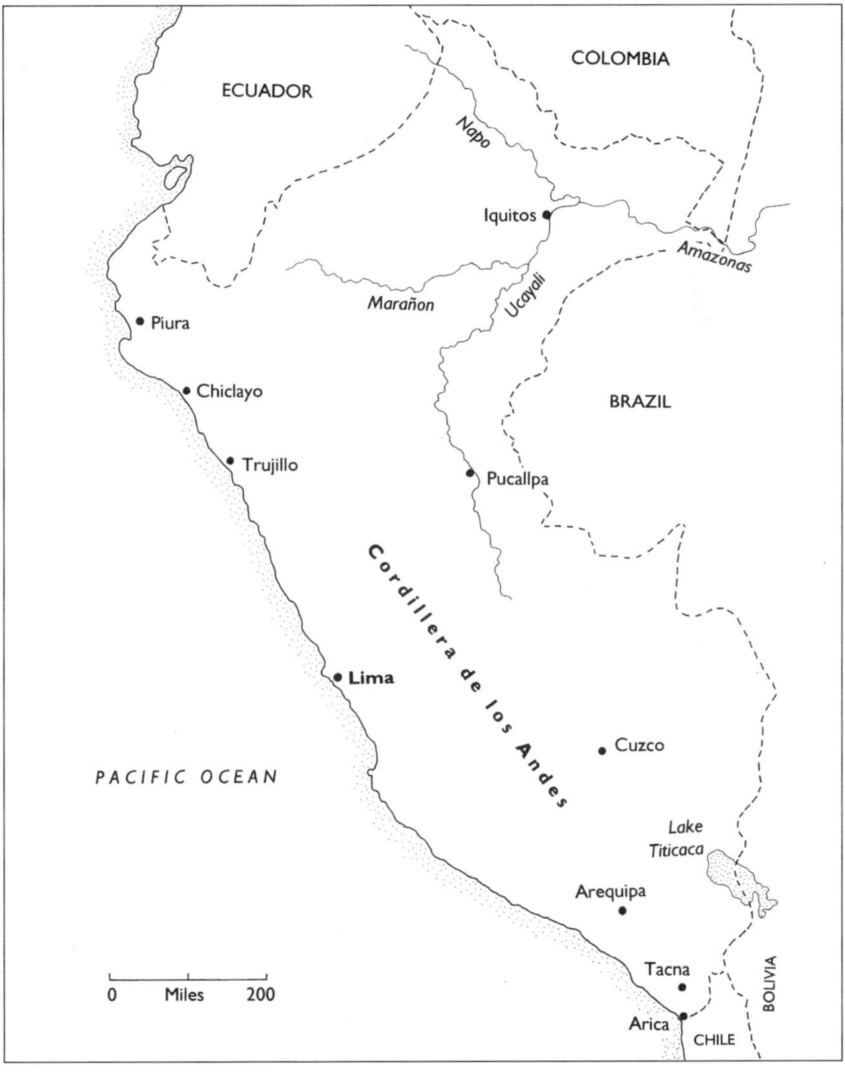

Map 4 Peru.

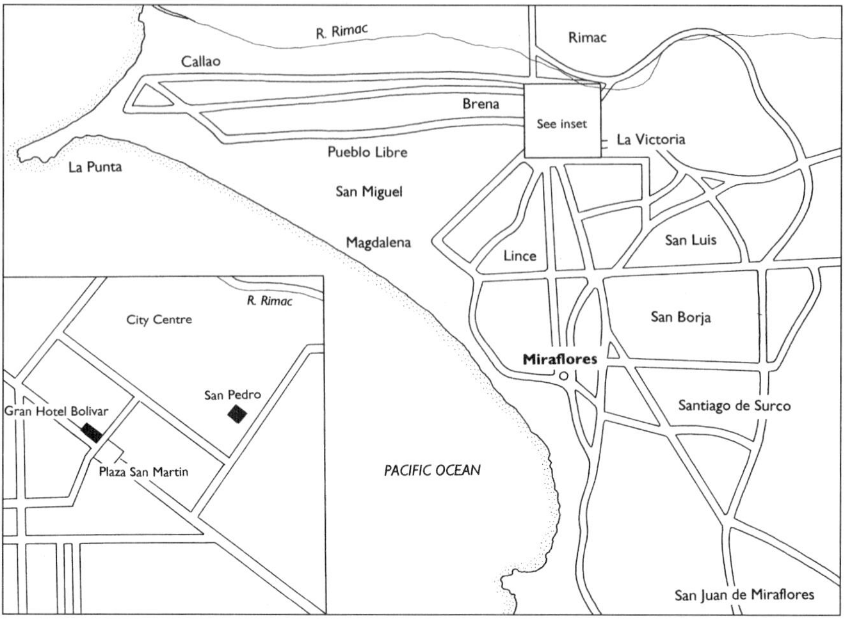

Map 5 Lima, showing central area and Miraflores.

Map 6 The river Ucayali, showing Pucallpa and Iquitos.

13

Wolf Packs

Somewhere in the North Atlantic
3rd September 1939

On the afternoon that war was declared, a young *Oberleutnant* was patrolling the seas off the north-west coast of Ireland in U-30. Proud of his first command of this modern submarine, Fritz-Julius Lemp was on the look-out for legitimate targets. Three wireless messages had been sent to all vessels in the *Kriegsmarine* to indicate that a state of war was in force, that attacks on enemy shipping were to commence and that vessels should feel free to begin hostilities without awaiting provocation. Taking care to absorb these instructions, Lemp spotted a ship on the horizon heading away from the jagged shores of the west coast of Scotland in a north-westerly direction. Ordering U-30 to dive to periscope depth, he took a look at the ship and was able to observe that the vessel was blacked out, was zigzagging, and appeared to be carrying guns on her deck. These were all indications that she was an armed merchantman or auxiliary cruiser and therefore a legitimate target.

On his command two torpedoes were fired; one struck its target squarely amidships, the other misfired. He immediately ordered U-30 to dive, in order to avoid the imminent danger of the defective torpedo circling back towards the U-boat. Surfacing once more, he noticed that the ship did not appear to be sinking, and so fired a third torpedo. This one missed as well. Close enough by now to observe the ship's silhouette, Lemp compared this to his Lloyd's Register and became aware at once of his mistake. The ship he had fired on was the *Athenia*, a 13,500-ton passenger liner en route from Glasgow to Montreal and carrying 1,103 civilians. These included more than 300 Americans hurrying home under the clouds of war.

Lemp did not take the opportunity to make a report at the time, even though the *Athenia*'s distress calls had eliminated the need to conceal his position. Fully aware of the magnitude of his blunder, he chose to maintain wireless silence until a full eleven days later. He then reported damage received in confrontation with two destroyers following the sinking of a British freighter, while requesting permission to disembark a wounded man in Iceland for medical attention. He still made no mention of the *Athenia* nor did he aid the survivors. He had probably observed a Norwegian boat in the area earlier that evening, and might have thought that her crew would come to the aid of the stricken passengers in the lifeboats. He no doubt also believed that departing the scene was the wisest course of action, before further attention could be focused on his cherished U-30.

The attack on the *Athenia* caused widespread repercussions. The rescue operation was indeed aided by the Norwegian ship, as well as by two merchant ships and three British destroyers. In total 118 passengers and crew died as a result of the initial explosion, or later as the ship sank. Berlin was only to learn of the sinking from news broadcast by the BBC in London. There was nationwide outrage at this first casualty of the war, but even greater despair in Germany. The years of effort to erase the memory of unrestricted submarine warfare in the First World War had been cancelled out in an instant, in the very first few hours of the war. With the phantom of the *Lusitania** rising up before him, Hitler decreed that all accusations would be met with categorical denial. In the Propaganda Ministry Goebbels spread the story that the British had torpedoed the liner themselves, in a scurrilous attempt to bring the United States into the war.

For the passengers waiting anxiously at the docks in Liverpool, news of the Athenia affair created an atmosphere of fear and trepidation. Having taken the train from London up to Liverpool, Eva spent the night in the Adelphi Hotel before embarking in the SS *Orduña*. It was the first time in her life that she had eaten in a restaurant by herself. She was so unused to this process that she left without paying the bill, expecting a non-existent male companion to take care of those sorts of mundane matters for her.

It had been a terrible wrench to leave Germany, even though she had

* The *Lusitania* was a passenger liner sailing from New York to Britain. On board were 1,257 civilians and, controversially, a cargo of arms that included rifle cartridges, shells and fuses. She was also rumoured to have a fortune in gold bullion on board. Just after 2 p.m. on 7 May 1915, she was torpedoed by U-20 8 miles off the coast of Kinsale, Ireland, and sank in 18 minutes. 1,198 people died, leaving only 59 survivors. The German U-boat captain Schwieger was condemned as a war criminal, but even though 128 Americans were amongst the dead, including a Vanderbilt heir, President Woodrow Wilson would not be drawn into a European war at that time. He was bitterly reviled as a coward. The British Admiralty blamed the *Lusitania*'s master for ignoring the danger of U-boats.

her daughter's wedding to look forward to. More than anything, she was utterly heartbroken at having to leave her dogs behind. Robin had been her favourite Irish setter, while his son Kai had won several prizes. The dogs stayed with Richard in Wachwitz. Eva had 'inherited' another dog from a visiting American couple a few months before, a 'scruffy little thing' called Betty. The dog had not particularly taken to Eva herself, but had shown inordinate affection towards her sister-in-law Lene every time she came to visit. When Eva was forced to leave her home, her lady's maid Helena took care of Betty. Her departure from Germany was further complicated by an interim period in Brussels, where Eva rented the apartment that had been acquired through Richard's efforts as Belgian consul. As with her siblings, an inordinate amount of money had to be paid to the Nazi authorities in the form of *Reichsfluchtsteuer* ('Reich exile tax'), which once again her father had been forced to provide. It is debatable whether there was even time for a quick trip to Berlin in order to say farewell to her parents. With her father approaching his 89th birthday, Eva knew she was unlikely ever to see him again.

Eva was due to leave on 3 September. Departure was delayed by 24 hours, however, because of the *Athenia* affair. It was now considered so dangerous to cross the Atlantic that the captain would sail only in convoy. On 4 September they finally departed, but almost immediately lay up in a bay for three days while they waited for the convoy to form. As part of the Pacific Steam Navigation Company, the ship had been a former Royal Mail Steamer but now plied regularly between Liverpool, Panama and Valparaíso in Chile. She was just over 15,500 tons and had one funnel, two masts, a triple screw and a top speed of 14 knots.

In the ship's manifest, Eva's name was entered as 'Vollmann Eva Karola, age 46, first class, not accompanied by husband'. Her address was given as 11 Princes House, Kensington Park Road, W11 (Ted and Ursula's address in London), while her intended country of residence was put as Belgium, and it was stated that she was a German citizen. Her passport would have been stamped with the intrusive red 'J' for 'Jew'. Even though she was travelling first class, her cabin accommodation was very cramped. She soon found that the dresses she had packed so carefully into her trunk were rather unsuitable, and that there was very little room to hang anything up.

To compound Eva's immense sense of loneliness, isolation and abandonment, she found that on board ship nobody wanted to speak to a woman who was travelling without her husband. In the strictly regulated social sphere in which she had been brought up, a married woman on her own was of absolutely no interest, and without formal introductions she found it almost impossible to strike up a conversation with any of the other passengers on the ship.

After three days, twelve or thirteen similar ships had gathered together in what was most likely Conwy Bay. With an escort of two or three RAF planes, they finally weighed anchor for the first part of their journey across the Atlantic.

On board ship there were some 80 'aliens' and around 175 British passengers. Their destinations were many and varied: first of all Bermuda, and then in the Caribbean, Nassau and other ports in the Bahamas, Cuba and Jamaica—from where some passengers were going to the USA; in the Central Americas: El Salvador, Guatemala, Cristobal in Costa Rica, and Colombia; down the Pacific Coast: Ecuador, Paita and Arica in Peru, and finally Iquique in Chile. Eva's journey had been booked as far as Callao in Lima, Peru.

Some of the 'alien' passengers were designated 'stateless' (meaning Jews or other 'undesirables' who had been thrown out of their countries like Eva). Others were Cuban, German, Peruvian, Spanish, Chilean, Costa Rican, Lithuanian, Swiss, Hungarian, Austrian, French, Polish and American.

In first class there were some ten such 'alien' families and some 60 British families. All the other passengers were in second and third class. In total there were 42 children up to the age of 12, and a total of 283 passengers as well as 67 Board of Trade passengers. The occupations given included: the consul-general to Chile, a bacteriologist, a mill owner, engineers, nurses, missionaries, a stenographer, a seamstress, a pattern cutter, chemists, British diplomats going to Peru, a cricket professional going to Bermuda, a Baptist minister travelling to Nassau, a film producer called Max Bernstein going to Chile, bakers, teachers, professors, housewives, a Cuban artist from the Empire Theatre in Glasgow and several government officers. Eva was not listed as having any sort of occupation.

Ever mindful of the danger of the 'wolf-packs' of U-boats already patrolling the Atlantic, the Master, H. B. Reece, issued orders that any porthole had to be completely blacked out by all passengers without exception from 6 p.m. to 6 a.m. The first part of the voyage followed the same zigzag pattern as that adopted by the ill-fated *Athenia.* After steaming down the Irish Channel they passed the southern tip of Ireland, and then proceeded in what appeared to the passengers to be fits and starts towards the Azores. It took eleven days to reach the south-westerly tip of these islands.

A whole battery of unfamiliar sensations were assaulting Eva all at once, making this voyage into the unknown particularly unpleasant, not to say frightening for her. For the first time in her 46 years she was utterly on her own. From the day of her birth in Berlin she had been surrounded by siblings, parents, relatives, and particularly servants. Even during the difficult times of the Great War, she had been able to retain a nursery nurse or a maid to help look after her young daughter Ursula. And then in Wachwitz her household had been almost as sizeable as that of her mother in the Uhlandstrasse. She had a lady's maid to do her hair and help her dress, a housekeeper to run the household, a cook to provide all the meals, a gardener to maintain the extensive gardens and a chauffeur to drive her into the city of Dresden. Growing up in Berlin, she had lived the life of a 'high society' girl, and once she was married and they were living near Dresden, she had attempted to instil her Berlin values into her lifestyle at the villa in Wachwitz.

No doubt Eva's housekeeper would have taken care of the daily shopping, or else goods would have been delivered to their door. While Richard was away at the factory in Sebnitz or abroad on business, Eva had her dogs to keep her company. Once Ursula had been sent away to school, she too had to be chaperoned, and she had retained the company of her governess Fräulein Franke until almost the age of 21, when she graduated from her school in Geneva to take up her studies at the Courtauld Institute in London. If Eva needed to buy a dress for some particular social occasion, she would have been driven into the city centre of Dresden by Braun the chauffeur, possibly accompanied by her lady's maid Helena. In between visits to art galleries, museums and concerts, frequent gatherings of the Vollmann clan in Wachwitz as well as meetings for coffee with her friends, Eva had the added excitement of clandestine assignations with her lover Professor Emil Waldmann.

It was the first time in her life that Eva had to make her own decisions, and somehow find a way to survive the next few gruelling weeks. She had left behind an indulged, comfortable lifestyle, a house full of treasured possessions, her beloved dogs and a marriage of over 25 years' duration. Her aged parents had been left alone in Berlin—her father was coming up to his 89th birthday and was becoming increasingly frail. Her mother was 73. Six of the seven Steinthal children, as well as five grandchildren, had been forced to emigrate. There was absolutely no guarantee that any of them was safe. For Eva, travelling by ship was even more terrible, because the conditions were nothing like those she and her husband Richard had enjoyed for example on their cruise round the Caribbean the previous year, never mind on the world's most luxurious liner, the *Queen Mary*, in which they had crossed the Atlantic to New York.

Even though the *Orduña* had originally been built with accommodation for over 1,100, once Eva and her fellow passengers had boarded the boat with such trepidation in Liverpool, the conditions soon became extremely cramped. Many sections of the ship had been completely cut off, such as the gymnasium that was to remain out of bounds and closed for the whole voyage. Compared to the better appointed liners, this was a relatively small ship. Because the captain and crew had to be so much more concerned with the dangers of German U-boats than with the needs of the passengers, service on board, even for those in first class, was kept to a minimum. For the first part of the voyage there was no fresh food at all, and Eva had to become used to eating tinned food.

Worse than anything must have been the fact that Eva now had a daughter who had married an Englishman, and whose marriage was also destined to be doomed before it had hardly started by the advent of hostilities. She now had her immediate family split between England and Germany, who politically were of course on absolutely opposing sides. While part of her yearned for nothing more than all her familiar belongings round her in her home in Wachwitz, her heart wanted to be with her daughter in England.

To alleviate some of these almost unbearable sufferings, Eva spent her days sitting on deck during the hours of daylight, typing letters. At sundown all the passengers had to stay in their rooms, with the portholes blacked out for fully twelve hours until daybreak the next morning. For Eva one of the worst things to endure was the level of noise on board ship, and the fact that there was nowhere she could go to escape the frequent cacophony around her of yelling children and blaring gramophones.

It is debatable whether Ursula bothered to write to her mother at all during the first days of the war, or even during the first weeks of her mother's voyage over the Atlantic. She had been living her own life since the mid thirties, although from the tone of some of Eva's letters to her daughter she still seemed to be treating her as a child. This did not change even after her daughter was married. In a letter dated January 1938, when Ursula had obviously just returned from Christmas in Germany to her studies at the Courtauld Institute, Eva wrote to her daughter in a tone of voice that seemed to be ticking her off like a naughty child for not writing sooner. Eva was always very keen about letter-writing as a means of communication. This had two distinct consequences: it probably caused resentment in a daughter who was much more concerned about having fun and living her own life, and it was to give Richard 'ammunition' in later letters about his former wife's love affair. In this particular letter, Eva is trying to be light-hearted and 'newsy', while at the same time obviously playing down the very probable tensions existing in her home at the time.

> My beloved child [she wrote]. So there you are back in London [at the Courtauld Institute], and I still haven't received a single word to say that you've arrived safely. Meanwhile your dear mother is sitting here with nothing to do, because for the first days without you it's always so difficult to find oneself completely alone again.* I could clear out loads of cupboards and other such delightful things but I've got absolutely no desire to do that, mostly because I'm feeling so tired. Last night I don't think I managed even a full half-hour of unbroken sleep and it was simply ghastly. Even so I intend to go out today just in case I manage to get a ticket for *Aida*, because at the moment it's a big help if I can find an excuse to get to bed really late. The blackbird is annoying me because it's sitting there, fat and cheeky, and chasing away the little birds that in this 2C of cold and snowy east wind would also like something to eat. I went for a long walk with the dogs—I've got to make a special fuss of Robin who still won't believe me that you've gone away yet again.

Once Ursula was married, her mother regarded her new son-in-law Teddy as one of her children as well, and would frequently refer to the two of them (aged at the beginning of the war 31 and nearly 25 respectively) as 'my children' or 'the children'. Because of the immediate British Government appointment of a letter-censor, Eva decided to write her letters to her daughter in English. Interestingly, her facility in that language was not nearly as comprehensive as in French.

In her first letter written on board the boat, Eva tried to make light of her situation by describing some of her fellow passengers. It was clear that at this stage quite a bit of social snobbery was coming to the fore. She also kept making reference to 'Pop' (Ursula's name for her father), as if they were still married and her daughter was quite ignorant of the fact that her mother had been forced to divorce her father. At the same time it was of course forbidden to make any mention of the conditions on board ship or the route they were taking. So Eva appeared to be sitting on the deck and playing 'poor little me', while making rather snide observations about her fellow passengers.

> Well this first day on board boat has been particularly uneventful.

* By 'alone' Eva meant in the company of all the staff but without her daughter.

> Luckily the sea has been perfectly calm, and up to now I haven't felt at all bad. That is one good point about this boat, that she is said to be very stable. You can't imagine how different it is to travel on a ship like this, not for pleasure but simply as an essential trip. The passengers on board are quite different to what we've been accustomed to. As it turns out, most of them are British, which surprised me because I had thought they would be mostly South American. As it is I'm sitting next to a civil servant, who is going back to Jamaica and who is a very pleasant fellow—old of course! He is just as worried as I am, because he has left his wife all on her own and can therefore understand how I'm feeling about you. And about Ted as well, because his boy is also in the Territorials. On my other side there is the wife of the postmaster of Bermuda. She is also experiencing a lot of bother, because she has taken her young boy on this trip against her husband's advice. Of course now with all this *Athenia* business, she is very nervous. On the deckchair next to me sits a mother taking her daughter back to Guatemala, where the husband is a railway manager of some sort.

In her second letter, written a week into the voyage and therefore probably about halfway between Ireland and the Azores, although Eva is attempting to put a brave face on her situation, the depth of her anguish can really be felt, especially at everything she has left behind in Germany. She also appears to be telling Ursula that all the things that used to matter to them as a family—good food, pretty clothes, frequent hairdressing, and an indulged life—have probably changed forever. She is trying to be brave in admitting that there are thousands of others in a similar or worse situation, but nevertheless Eva does appear to be finding it extremely difficult to cope with her new circumstances without complaint.

> My trip will take me about 5 weeks—can you imagine what this means to me? Well anyway I must be grateful if we get there safely. Up to now the sea has not been too rough, another thing to be thankful for. But only last night I had to leave dinner and run to my cabin, because I felt my tummy turning upside down. How I am going to get over 4 more weeks of this, I am really quite unable to see. It is such a nuisance that I always feel so tired out and so absolutely worn out on board boat. Even reading is beyond me! But at least I have been able to exchange my cabin for a much larger one and that is a blessing.

All the portholes are tightly closed at night and not a breath of air is allowed to come in. Of course sleep is rather difficult under such circumstances, but I bear this with fortitude, as there are only too many who can't sleep either! I only feel extremely lonely—I have made a vow, that should I ever return safely from this journey, I will never make such a long trip again. I am really not fond of travelling; I only like short little trips like going to Sienna, or to the mountains, or being taken on a drive through pleasant countryside. What I really pine for is my home-life, to be allowed to live quietly with my family and in my own four walls! I am nowhere near recovering from all the changes I have had to undergo over the last few months. I long for everything and anything: Pop—he may believe it or not—my family, my children, my home and my quiet garden with its cherished atmosphere, my animals, everything and every single person. I woke up this morning talking with Lene, and I simply couldn't understand where I was. Well I'll have to get through it though it is not easy, and I can't imagine today how I ever will. But every one of us has so much to go through that nobody has the right to complain, as long as I survive and the hope exists that one day we may be happier again.

I am constantly thinking about what you may be doing. There is nothing to take one's mind off one's sad thoughts as there are no games or cinema or entertainment of any kind. I daresay nobody feels in the mood for it. And so it happens that this journey is just full of anguish and anxiety, of homesickness and sorrow of all kinds. One has also to get used to the food. Of course I don't look in the least 'pretty', but that does not matter anyway, as there's not a soul to take the slightest interest in me. But don't think that I'm only thinking of myself all the time. On the contrary, my constant thoughts are with my beloved and dear ones at home.

Back in England Ursula was experiencing emotional problems of her own, and it is very likely that the fate of her mother, or even the fact that she was travelling in such hazardous conditions to the other side of the world, was the last thing on her mind.

After their register office wedding in Notting Hill, Ted and Ursula spent their first night in a little hotel in Stockbridge, just outside Salisbury. Only a week after her honeymoon, around 25 August, Ted was called up for active service. This was not the same as in the First World War, where most of the 'flower of English youth' had volunteered. In the battle to fight Hitler and Fascism, the government made sure that all men of appropriate age would be called up to serve their country, unless they could give very good reasons not to.

From the Territorials, Ted started off as an NCO in searchlights. The young couple would spend their first winter of married life—the period of the so-called 'phoney war'—in Fleetwood in Lancashire, which Ursula was later to describe as 'horrible'. A year later Ted would be sent to Shrivenham to train as an officer. He later rose to the rank of lieutenant, and Ursula had to survive being with the 'awful' colonel's wife. By the end of 1940 Ted would be posted overseas to Cairo and Ursula would find herself feeling completely bereft. On one occasion she was invited to stay with Christine in Cheltenham, a lively lady with whom she had struck up a warm friendship during her time at the Courtauld in London. Already distraught, she managed to lose all her luggage on the train journey. Ted came back for another month and then Ursula had to go through all the trauma of saying goodbye yet again. Even though she was not passionate about him and was to confess later that he really was 'not very good in bed', she was very fond of Ted. He obviously adored her, and it must have been a terrible wrench for him to have to leave his wife behind in England, living with relative strangers.

While Ted was away overseas in Egypt, Ursula lived with his captain's wife. Both the captain and his wife were Irish, and the wife especially had scant regard for Ursula, who spoke English with a very strong German accent. In England at that time most people had travelled abroad so little and were so unused to foreigners that they would not have been able to distinguish between, say, a Polish or a French or a German accent. Foreigners in England were only looked at askance if, for example, they were caught in breach of the strict black-out regulations.

Meanwhile, in Germany, Richard's factory was almost immediately requisitioned by the Nazi authorities. It was turned over to the production of buttons for soldiers' uniforms. Richard was 56 years old on the day that war was declared, and therefore too old to be called up for a second time. He probably would have refused to fight anyway, but it is doubtful whether the draconian system of the Third Reich would have tolerated such disobedience. For his siblings, however, there was the added stress of their children being called up into Hitler's army. Although inordinately proud of her only son, Richard's widowed sister Lene felt her heart wrench as she watched Ulli leaving by train in his smart new uniform. At much the same time, her brother Walter's two boys were also called up into the army. All three boys would fight on the Russian front, just as the Steinthal boys had done in the 'war to end all wars'. As far as

Lene was concerned, the Fuehrer's aggressive foreign policy was absolutely right: more than anything she believed that her son and his cousins would be fighting the evils of communism.

Eva meanwhile remained quite unaware of these developments. She and her fellow passengers had to endure a news black-out until the ship reached their first port of call, Bermuda.

In the first week of sailing, the crew carried out four lifeboat drills, which the passengers got so used to that most of them slept with their most precious belongings under their pillow. There were to be a further six such drills during the voyage to Peru, but this was the only form of exercise that the passengers were able to take. As they sailed away from the Azores and towards Bermuda, the temperatures rose and conditions on board became increasingly difficult to bear.

On the thirteenth day after leaving Liverpool the *Orduña* steamed into the port of Hamilton, the capital of Bermuda. It was 17 September and the first time that the passengers were allowed off the boat. Eva woke as if from a terrible, dark nightmare. Without even making a conscious decision, she found herself taking a ride in a horse-drawn buggy. Looking with delight at the pink-and-white houses of the town of Hamilton sparkling in bright sunshine, she stared in wonder at the scarlet-red hibiscus draped nonchalantly over so many of the hedgerows. A sudden tropical downpour drenched her to the skin, but she did not care in the least. She breathed in great lungfuls of the heady scents of semi-tropical flowers, and was only sad to leave the island after too short a break, to be entombed into the restrictive confines of the ship once more.

The waters of the Caribbean were to prove quite choppy, and Eva spent the next two days being seasick. It was a pointless exercise thinking back to the New Year she had spent in Havana less than two years before, with both Richard and Ursula. Such memories were simply too painful.

In the next five days they sailed first of all to the Bahamas, where most of the American passengers disembarked to change ships to sail to Miami, and possibly from there on to New York. By 25 September, after calling at Havana on Cuba where they deposited passengers destined for the various countries in Central America, they had reached Kingston, Jamaica. Their course next day took them south-west of the island of Haiti and San Domingo, from where they sailed due south towards the Panama Canal. In the days before 1912 ships would sail from Southampton across the Atlantic, and all the way south to Terra del Fuego, negotiating the narrow straits round the Horn and then heading north up the Pacific Coast of South America. Once the Panama Canal had been opened ships would ply regularly between Southampton, Panama and Callao in Peru.

Temperatures had risen to tropical levels as the *Orduña* chugged slowly through the narrow confines of the Panama Canal. Before then, by the time they had reached the Azores they had lost their RAF escort and the other members of the convoy, and had been sailing alone. The short break at Bermuda had caused morale amongst the bedraggled passengers to rise dramatically, and several of them believed that they must now be well out of the danger zone. However, news from the captain was extremely hard to come by, and there was still a high degree of anxiety prevalent amongst the remaining passengers.

In her final letter written to Ursula on the boat, and without having received a single word about the fate of her family back in Europe, Eva was feeling her isolation more keenly than ever. Now she wrote, 'It's still such a new and very unfamiliar sensation to be perfectly alone. I was aware of it beforehand, but now know better than ever what awful snobs most people are. If you are a woman travelling alone who doesn't possess the character of constantly showing off her own dazzling qualities, they will talk to you only if they've got bored with everybody else. If however somebody then happens to appear, whom they believe to be more worthy of their attention—and that is anybody they regard as either wealthier or of a higher social standing—then they'll just turn their backs on you and completely ignore you.'

14

An Alien in a Foreign Land

In the week of 4 October 1939 the ship sailed into the port of Callao. The whole journey from Liverpool had taken almost five weeks. Two weeks into the journey Eva had realised that her daughter was coming up to her 25th birthday at the end of September, and that she would be completely unable to send her anything but a letter. Sadly there was also no guarantee, at that early stage in the war, that any post would get through to England. She was still trying to compare her former life with her experiences on the ship, and to make light of her sense of desolation.

> I haven't got the faintest idea how long this letter will take to get to you, but as it is 17 September today at least I will think of your birthday—the first lonely and sad one in your whole life! Let us wish most fervently that it will turn out to be the only one of its kind, and that all the horrible worry and anxiety you have to go through now will be over before your next birthday. I am so sorry I can't send you the slightest gift. I would so much have liked to organise a pleasant day to celebrate the 29th but we must take things as they come. That means for this present year having to face whatever comes head on. I know there's nothing I can do to change the situation. Anyway you can be sure there's somebody here sharing all your unhappiness—of course this doesn't add up to much but it does mean something! I have made a particularly disturbing discovery during my trip: it is quite frankly a very solitary thing not to have a soul to talk to.
>
> Last night we were all invited to a so-called 'carnival dinner'. I found the entire evening so very odd because there was nothing to drink but water, the menu hadn't been altered in the slightest, but consisted of the same old sirloin of beef with horseradish sauce that's been served every day, and the whole affair lasted just one hour! If you compare this to our own traditions it's rather comical, isn't it?

In a previous letter written just five days before, Eva had suddenly appeared to become obsessed with her possessions, and even more fixated on the possibility that she would soon be able to obtain a visa to return to England. This seems to have been an utterly fanciful idea, given the circumstances. Not only would it have been exceedingly dangerous to make a return journey across the Atlantic—there was no way that Eva as a German Jew would have been granted any sort of domiciliary rights in England, whether her daughter was married to an Englishman or not.

She further asked that Ursula should take care of her crate of furniture, which she had been allowed to have shipped over from Germany via Belgium before leaving her homeland for good, in exchange for an absolutely huge sum of Reichsmarks, shares and gold. Ursula, however, had enough problems of her own to deal with, and probably wanted to have nothing whatever to do with her mother's affairs. Again, there was no guarantee that any of Eva's letters from the ship actually reached her daughter.

The last part of the journey was particularly gruelling for Eva. Even after spending the month of September on board ship, surrounded by hundreds of people, it was nevertheless still such a new and very unfamiliar sensation to be utterly alone. She truly could not imagine how she was going to survive without anyone to help her, and could only hold onto the hope that her cousins-in-law would take pity on her and offer her some comfort. It took a whole two weeks to get through the Panama Canal and then for the ship to make its way down the Pacific Coast of South America. Once against they were beset by rough weather, and Eva spent most of that time curled up miserably in her cabin, feeling particularly sorry for herself.

Then the weather calmed down, and she would spend long hours standing on the deck, gazing at the coastline. At this stage she cared little that the whole coast of Peru measures over 1,500 miles (about 2,400 kilometres), and that it contains some of the driest desert in the world. The very first strip of Peruvian soil she saw would have been right up in the north, near the northern port of Paita, close to the Ecuadorian border. Her heart felt as heavy as lead, as she gazed out at this alien country. All she could make out were primitive huts constructed of nothing but mud and reeds, whose walls were completely bowed and crooked. Surrounding these miserable indications of human habitation she could see tumbling, barren rocks without any sort of vegetation—not even the smallest blade of grass. These first glimpses combined to form a hotchpotch impression of grinding poverty, oppressive heat and neglect. At that particular moment she felt then as if all the desolation in her heart had been transformed into the concrete manifestation of a nightmare landscape, as remote and bleak as the moon.

The temperature was rising into the high thirties as the *Orduña* steamed into Callao, chief port of Lima, the capital of Peru. The passengers stood crowded together on the deck, staring at the forest of derricks and cranes in front of them, outlined against a backdrop of wharves, factories, plants and dry-docks. They could see bales of goods being loaded into waiting ships, and crates being unloaded from other ships. The port seemed busy and bustling, but as far as Eva was concerned her first view of the place where she knew she was destined to stay did nothing to lift her quailing spirits. After almost five weeks on board boat in cramped, noisy, uncomfortable conditions, she felt unwashed, unkempt and completely uncared for. With a deep sigh she joined the throng of people as they staggered down the gangplank in the bright sunshine. She had spent the whole of the previous day packing her one trunk, making sure her precious photos of her daughter and her erstwhile husband were safely stowed amongst her dresses. She clutched her passport in her hand, and felt beads of sweat gathering in a most unladylike fashion above her eyebrows.

As Eva stood gazing at the unfamiliar surroundings of the busy port, she pulled at her dress, which was sagging round her waist. She had definitely lost weight in the past couple of weeks, not just because of the monotony of the ship's catering but mostly because of the days she had spent being miserably seasick. The air was filled with the voices of the dockworkers: nut-brown, black-haired, squat-shaped men who trotted backwards and forwards between the cranes and derricks along the quayside, shouting to each other in an unintelligible language. The air smelled of the salty tang of the sea combined with the heady fumes of diesel. As in every port in the world, flocks of whirling seagulls squabbled and fought over scraps of fish near the dockside.

After the interminable customs formalities had finally been completed, Eva found herself in an unbelievably ancient taxi, being driven with alarming insouciance by a smiling, nodding driver whose mouth sparkled with an array of gold teeth. Eva, who had hardly got used to the level feeling of the ground after weeks away at sea, began to feel the onset of seasickness again, and clutched the door-handle as the impressive colonial façades of Lima's buildings sped past. The driver had looked at her in wry amusement when she had mentioned the Hotel Bolívar, but he agreed to take her there as soon as she had shown him the American dollars that had been so carefully stashed in her purse and kept for weeks on end under her pillow in her cramped little cabin on board ship.

Hoping that the hotel would turn out to be quite modest, for she had no idea how long her money would be able to last in this unknown land, Eva felt a frisson of apprehension as the taxi lurched to a stop in front of the white façade of an imposingly tall edifice.

'Hotel Bolívar?' she queried, as she clambered wearily out of the taxi.

'*Si, si*, Hotel Bolívar!' grinned the taxi driver, dragging her heavy trunk out of the boot of his battered car. He waved vaguely round his head. 'Plaza San Martín!' he said, and then cheerfully pocketing his handful of dollars he left her standing on the marble steps of what she was later to learn was Lima's premier hotel.

She stood for a moment in the square in the setting sun, travel-stained and covered in dust. Starlike streets led from the square in all directions. In the centre of the Plaza, San Martín—the Liberator—rode on horseback in marble dignity. It was only much later that she was to read about his exploits. Some disrespectful urchin had stuck a red geranium into his stony hat. Horns hooted and people shouted on all sides. Surprisingly elegant motor cars sped by in a continuous stream, and even the taxis looked beautiful, differing from private cars only by the addition of small numbers on the doors. Wireless music drifted up to her from almost every one of them. And all the women looked surprisingly and stunningly well dressed. Even in her tired state, she could see sophisticated ladies on whom Fortune smiled and for whom the stately hall-porter opened their carriage door. Further down the street, she was vaguely aware of gangs of working girls flooding into the street out of the stores; it must have been closing time.

Eva felt increasingly uncomfortable as she stumbled through the front door of the hotel, dragging her trunk and looking for a porter. This hotel, she was later to discover, enjoyed an impeccable international reputation. It had all the latest amenities and the most fashionable lobby. Here chic women bedecked in the most expensive blue-and-silver fox furs, sables and other stylish accoutrements of fashion would meet for tea and cocktails. Haughty as a butler, the hotel lifted its six floors superciliously above the crowds in the square.

Swaggering along the crest of the roof were swirling curls made of heavy plaster, and a dozen snow-white spires. There was even a baroque seashell. The vulnerability, however, of such exaggerated decoration—or so she was to discover—had become apparent just a few years before her arrival. During a severe earthquake, the violent tremors caused the plaster embellishments to break away from their solid base and plummet down on top of a luxurious automobile parked outside. This was promptly transformed into a pancake.

Eva's immediate concern, however, was how she would be able to afford to pay for such luxurious accommodation. All her travel arrangements had been made by an agency in London, just before Ursula's wedding, and it must have been assumed that she would require first-class accommodation as well as her first-class ticket on the boat. Before she had time to ruminate any further, she was being asked yet again to show her passport and fill in endless forms. She was then shown up to her room by a somewhat superior-mannered bellboy, whose sideways glance at her dishevelled appearance obviously did nothing to increase his expectation of a generous tip. But then the delight of a long, hot and luxuriously bubbled bath swept away her immediate concerns, and she was finally able to scrub away the filth of weeks of travel.

Eva spent the next couple of days in virtual isolation, being unable to raise any enthusiasm about this strange country on whose shores she had been washed up like some piece of flotsam. She would stare out of her window for hours, looking at her surroundings without really seeing anything. She was only dimly aware of the outlines of church domes and flat roofs, visible beyond the flushed crowns of the trees. Black vultures soared above and the melancholy chirrup of the ubiquitous flocks of sparrows vibrated incessantly through the air. Far away, when she did focus, she could make out a hazy blue smoke-line on the distant horizon: was that the fabled Cordillera? Every morning she would blink at the bright sun flooding the Plaza San Martín below. All around the square grew crepe myrtle trees, each dressed in a thick halo of rose-pink blossoms. This was the first oddity she had to get used to: it was October—the beginning of spring in this new world below the Equator.

After a few days in her new and still unfamiliar surroundings, Eva plucked up courage and went to call on Richard's relatives. The Gaffrons, close relatives of Richard's mother, were a family of German settlers who had gone to Peru at the beginning of the twentieth century to become *hacienderos* or plantation owners. Herman, brother to the original settler, was a philanthropic eye-doctor who had treated many of the native *Indios* in the Andes on the same terms as the upper-class 'whites'. Peruvian society was very strictly delineated, with a clear line drawn between the *criollos* (mostly living in Lima), who could trace their bloodlines back to the Spanish conquest, and the *mestizos* who had a mix of Amerindian and European heritage. Anyone living in the rural hinterlands but assuming Western dress was usually referred to as *mestizo* or sometimes *cholo*.

Herman Gaffron's brother, the original settler from Germany, had married a local *chola*, much to the consternation of the family back home in Germany. The daughters they produced, however, were to become beauty queens in Peru as they were all extremely fine-looking. One of these girls, Anita, married Alfredo Ferreyros, who was of Spanish descent. Long before Eva had arrived in Peru, this part of the family had become completely indigenised, adopting the Catholic faith with enthusiasm and living a much more Spanish lifestyle.

Eva was soon to find that her former husband's Peruvian family had very little time for their European 'relative'. Without showing it overtly they nevertheless disapproved of her very much—not because she was Jewish, but because she was divorced. As Peru was to remain a neutral country throughout the war, it is quite possible that even amongst the intelligentsia of Lima their view of the war was somewhat clouded because of their country's non-involvement. They can have had little understanding of the dangers that had befallen Eva and her family through the Steinthals' Jewish ancestry. Eva was used to being invited to tea in order to meet people, and she would never have dared instigate a new acquaintance without first being introduced, either in person or by the exchange of visiting cards. Throughout her stay in Peru she was to encounter problems with the 'family' that she never really resolved. The biggest obstacle, however, to Eva's advance with new people was learning Spanish.

In her first letter from Peru, written just over a month after her arrival in Lima, Eva tells Ursula that she has moved from the exorbitantly expensive Hotel Bolívar into a nice *pension*, run by an American, which would probably be somewhere between 'furnished rooms' and a 'boarding house' in England. It was in the Avenida da Brazil, quite near the Ferreyros' house. She wrote to Ursula, 'I share this house with a young engineer, whom I never see as he is always out when I am in, and in this way we get on fine. The food is extremely good and the place is clean and up to now it has not given me a single flea.'

She also wrote, with some self-effacement, that 'if an earthquake starts, I can be out of my room in a jiff, because between myself and the garden there is only one small door, as the building in which I live consists only of two rooms and a bath and has only one floor.' In other words it was a typical one-storey bungalow, no doubt built in Spanish colonial style with a red-tiled roof, arched doorways and tiled floors to keep the inside of the building cool.

Much of the letter seemed to be complaining at or about her family back home. And yet how could she have known what problems her daughter was facing in England, and especially what conditions were like in Nazi Germany during the first weeks of the war? Obviously all communication between England and Germany had been cut off, and there would have been no way that Ursula could have kept in contact with her father in Dresden or her grandparents in Sebnitz, never mind her Jewish grandparents in Berlin. Daisy did manage to write to her sister, not long after the ship had left Liverpool for its hazardous journey over the Atlantic. She must have addressed the letter to the Ferreyros in Lima, and it took just over a month to reach Eva. Fanny as well had managed to get two letters to her daughter in Peru, but Eva was to tell her own daughter in a grudging tone of voice that she had heard nothing either from her sister-in-law Lene or from Richard's mother. It seems very odd that she should consider they would either want or be able to stay in contact with her, since to all intents and purposes Eva and Richard had been divorced since March that year. Apart from anything else, airmail letters were extremely expensive to send.

What Eva griped about more than anything was the attitude of her family 'back home' towards her status in Peru. Daisy appeared to be envious of Eva's 'good fortune', while Eva thought Daisy should rejoice in the fact that she was together with her daughter. Eva was quite unaware of the dangers that Daisy had faced and was continuing to encounter, and how close she had come to not being able to get an exit visa out of Germany. Acquaintances of hers working in Berlin's film industry had taken pity on her plight, after her husband had so cruelly abandoned the family. Connected to them was a Dutchman by the name of Hemmes, who agreed to marry her in order for Daisy to be granted an immediate Dutch passport. It was a particularly generous gesture, as the man in question was a self-confessed homosexual. They were never to spend any time together as man and wife (he lived in Amsterdam with his sister), but with the correct papers as a Dutch citizen Daisy was able to escape through Belgium and Luxemburg. And then when she had finally survived the perilous journey to France, her daughter Gisèle, who still had her German passport stamped with its red 'J', was to spend time in a concentration camp high up in the Pyrenees.* From Eva's point of view, this would have been an unimaginable fate for her own daughter.

Eva was very fortunate in that to start off with Richard had been sending her money through his contacts in New York. And even though by her standards she was living in very straightened circumstances and had to watch every penny, this could not even begin to compare with the conditions being imposed by all the European governments involved in the war in the form of rationing that affected every citizen. Petrol was

* This was a camp at Gurs, which had been set up in the Pyrenees in 1936 for the internment of escapees from the Spanish Civil War. Gisèle, aged only 22, was destined to spend six months there.

one of the first commodities to be rationed, which meant a severe restriction on movement.

Meanwhile Eva had been filling her days with visiting all the museums in Lima, together with a good selection of *huacas* (ruins or temples). She soon got to know the old parts of Lima, and made herself familiar with its many Catholic churches and the Palace of Government. Her first impression was that Peru was a 'weird and unusual country'. This opinion was hers alone, as in her solitary state she was of course compelled to undertake most of these initial visits on her own. She wrote in the letter to Ursula that 'of course it would have made things very much easier for me if Anita had invited me to tea in order to acquaint me with her and Alfredo's family, but she gets so wretchedly tired with all her parties and the demands of the children, that she hasn't felt up to it.' Eva maintained she could understand this attitude, while at the same time telling her daughter 'if you've been imagining me as being surrounded by loving family—you are very much mistaken. I have now got quite used to being nearly always on my own. All those stories they tell, of how delighted people would be to see you more than once, are just fairytales and only apply to "other people". Up to now and very much to my regret I have not been able to wear any of the nice, elegant dresses I brought with me so pointlessly. All this business of getting to know people is a slow one and depends entirely on being well acquainted with the language. I'm doing my best in that regard and it is with Spanish that I'm filling up my empty hours.' Later in the same letter she stated, 'I cannot imagine what Lene or any of the family would do in my place, but I keep busy as best I can. If there is nothing else to do, there are always heaps of stockings to mend.'

Despite all her protestations to her daughter, Eva was eventually invited to tea, and here at her cousins' house she had her first encounter with the Peruvian concept of a patio. This was no 'courtyard' as it was translated in Eva's dictionary nor was it a square; it was a living room in the open air. Round about this patio were situated all the other rooms and while the din of the streets continued beyond the walls, here she found blessed silence falling soothingly on her jangled nerves. To the visitor, the house appeared to turn its face away from the crowds outside and focus on the individual. A slender thread of water was trickling lazily into a fountain made of ancient Spanish tiles, while a profusion of colourful plants in flowerpots of all sizes overflowed onto the sun-baked flagstones. The first patio led to a second and then to a third—before long one had entered a different world. The house, looking so narrow from the outside, opened up in depth. From the exterior it seemed to be just one amongst innumerable others. Inside it was a haven amidst the rushing hustle and bustle of urban life: it had air and space, a vista and a garden, and was concealed from all intruding glances by high forbidding walls.

It would be another year before Eva could experience the full extent of her cousin Anita's prowess as a hostess. This was on the occasion of the festival of *Señor de los Milagros* (Lord of the Miracles), a magnificent annual procession celebrating Lima's patron saint where all the participants dress up in purple. On that occasion, as Eva walked up the stairs to a room opening onto a rickety wooden balcony, she felt quite overcome on seeing so many other visitors there. The ladies were very pretty and very charmingly attired. All this impressed her far less than the tea table that attracted her eyes like a magnet. An arrangement of Venetian lace, orchids and candles decorated the table, which was laden with dozens of little dishes. Every single one was filled with a different kind of sweet, cake or confectionery; candy, biscuits, varieties of sweet and salty almonds; hot and cold sandwiches and titbits; chocolates; yellow, violet and pink dainties ... She was quite overwhelmed when she counted at a first glance 42 different kinds of teatime dish.

She was later to learn that this incredible opulence in entertainment looked back upon a long tradition. Young girls learned in their childhood, long before they left school, *hacer dulces*—to prepare sweets. Before a large reception, a cocktail-party or tea—or 'chocolate' as it was often called—the whole family would be kept busy for days, including mothers and in-laws, cousins and aunts. Although this was her first experience, Eva learned that such parties were given almost daily during the season. She was amazed how the Limanian ladies manage to remain so slender.

Less than two months into her stay in Lima, Eva was to go on her first excursion into the hinterland of Peru. Although she had written that she could not regard her enforced stay in South America as a 'pleasure trip', she nevertheless gradually came round to the view that she should take advantage of the opportunity of travelling when it was presented to her. For a while she was able to forget all about her principal and overriding concern: getting a visa to return to England.

15

Ups and Downs

As the mountains rose higher and higher, a glacier appeared to be stretching down in front of them almost as far as the road. The driver drove the valiant old Ford with astonishing skill and speed through the hundreds of turnings; and each hairpin bend uncovered a new and varied kind of landscape. The whole area was barren and arid, with only a few herds of llama to be seen—no birds, no other living thing, only rocks in shades of vivid red, copper, grey and green. At 16,000 feet (4,835 metres) they had reached the top of the pass. Eva was very proud of herself because with the exception of some rapid heart-beating she felt no ill effect whatsoever and, unlike other less fortunate travellers, did not succumb to the dreaded *Soroche*, or mountain sickness.*

She had become acquainted with a young American couple in her *pension* and when they told her they were going to the Chanchamayo and asked if she wanted to come along, Eva suddenly lost all her indecision and sense of isolation. It took her only a moment to make up her mind, and she accepted the invitation gratefully. To reach the valley of the Chanchamayo it was necessary to traverse the Cordillera, which was the first difficulty, for many people were not able then (and are not able now) to tolerate the enormous altitude. They left on a Saturday morning and drove up and up for what seemed like hours. The winding road led them past the barren and pitiless mountains that surrounded Lima, through Tamboraque (where many people experienced severe difficulties in breathing), out of the sunshine and into the clouds of the Cordillera.

As they descended over the other side of the pass, three large lakes extended before them, one below the other, the first steel-grey, the next deep green and the lowest one aquamarine blue. A few scanty little

* As a comparison, the highest mountain in Western Europe is Mont Blanc (4,808 metres or 15,774 feet), while the highest point accessible by mountain train is the Jungfraujoch (3,700 m. or 11,500 ft), known as the 'Roof of Europe' and now a World Heritage Site.

dwellings gradually appeared here and there, dotted over the hillsides, as well as some small trees. Eva's party could see *Serrana*-women herding their llamas or sheep or donkeys, walking around them and spinning as they walked. Then a green shimmer of life and fertility appeared on the sides of the massive mountains. After another two hours they were driving through a backdrop of reddish earth covered with eucalyptus trees, where pink houses clung to the hillsides between gurgling streams and *Indios* rode on mules and packhorses. It was a landscape blessed by rain, in complete contrast to the dry and dusty countryside of Lima. By the time they had reached Tarma, the little town at 3,000 metres where they were to spend the night, they were absolutely aching from sitting in a creaky car, grinding round the thousands of hairpin bends through which the winding, narrow road had led them.

In contrast to their expectations of this sparsely populated mountain region, their hotel turned out to be quite impressive. The first thing Eva noticed, however, was a rather odd noise emanating from her ceiling, which brought to mind all the stories of rats that Richard used to tell her about in such lurid detail when recounting tales of his trips to Peru. Despite her initial fears, she was extremely relieved to discover that these creatures were perfectly harmless cats, gambolling and playing about on the canvas covering the room. It was as cold as in a mountain hut, but with the added luxury of electric light. Eva found it a bit of a chore having to clean her teeth in bottled mineral water, but she did not dare use the natural water there.

After a fairly peaceful night's sleep, they continued on their journey early next morning. The two young Americans were as astonished as Eva was by the topography that was to greet them. It was at once alarming and thrilling to travel on a road that teetered over terrifying abysses, a road so narrow that they often had the feeling they were just about to fall over the edge. Hundreds of feet below them flowed the river Tarma. Every so often the driver would gleefully point out the wrecks of cars that had been incautious enough to tumble headlong over the precipice. Eva could well imagine (in different circumstances) how delighted Richard would have been to take part in this exciting adventure, given his erstwhile predilection for rock-climbing up vertical cliff-faces.

All at once the road became quite beautiful. They were getting into real jungle country, complete with men wielding machetes and surrounded by tree ferns, air-roots and orchids. Eva gasped as she saw giant blue butterflies flapping about, living versions of the ones Richard had amassed during his travels and which now lay preserved under glass in Wachwitz. Her only disappointment was the lack of parrots and monkeys. The heat was becoming oppressive and, after the icy cold air of the mountains, a shock to the system for the three travellers. They passed though tunnels and over laughably narrow bridges, which were just wide enough to let the car go across by advancing with extreme caution—otherwise they might have suffered the same fate as those other less fortunate travellers now languishing at the bottom of the river.

Finally they arrived at La Merced, a jungle town of 'unbelievable heat and filth'. Despite this, Eva found exploring the market there an enjoyable experience. And it was here that she had her first encounter with the native Indians called *Chunchus*, who were dressed in brown sacks and who painted their faces a muddy red. Eva considered this extremely unattractive. She later discovered that it was the missionaries belonging to an Adventist sect who had taught the Indians to dress themselves, and wear an unbecoming brown sack instead of going naked. Since that time many of them succumbed to the common cold and tuberculosis introduced inadvertently by the well-meaning strangers.

In the heat of noon the travellers returned to Tarma, where they spent another night. Here Eva met a pleasant young man from London, who was out there hunting and collecting birds on behalf of the British Museum. How she wished she could have accompanied him on his expedition, because then she might have seen some real parrots.

Among Eva's principal obsessions during her first few weeks in Peru was in getting two sets of people to sort out her visa. One was Richard's business partner in London, Mr Harman—Teddy's father whom she always addressed as 'Bertie' and who was supposed to be able to sort out her papers from that end while she was on the other side of the world. And the other person was her cousin-by-marriage Alfredo Ferreyros, who was somehow meant to be obtaining a visa for her while she was in Lima. She had also taken the bold step of writing to Richard in Dresden, asking him how long she was expected to live in this foreign country. The whole affair seemed to be quite futile. Surely it was felt on all sides that for the duration of the war, however long that was to last and however it turned out, the safest place Eva could be (given her nationality and status) was in neutral South America? And in Peru she did at least have some contacts.

Another thing that filled her mind completely was her shipment of belongings that had been sent over from Germany via Brussels, and which would eventually be stored in a warehouse in Tottenham in north London. She expected her daughter to bother about her mother's personal effects, while Ursula herself was attempting to survive the first very difficult weeks of her marriage with her husband being frequently absent, and not knowing exactly where they would be sent to live.

She wrote to Ursula in a rather impatient and demanding tone of voice, 'If I should stay here longer than expected, please do not forget to look after my things in storage. You really cannot imagine with what longing I think of all my treasured possessions which are so much a part of my old life and home. Please don't think I've become a "property person" because it's really not the property that I'm attached to, but everything that these belongings stand for. Even if I weren't able to live with them myself, but knew that they were making a home for you, then that would satisfy me. Just don't forget about this, please.'

Meanwhile Eva was still attempting to learn the Spanish language, which she was actually finding quite difficult especially as she kept confusing it with Italian. She would spend at least a couple of hours a day learning the grammar on her own, and then her teacher Celia would come in every day for an hour's conversation. For someone used to the clear accent of 'received' English and the beautifully enunciated French of the *Académie Française*, she found the Spanish intonation very difficult to master, and more especially even harder to understand. Of course this was not Castilian but South American Spanish, but even so it gave her a considerable amount of trouble to get to grips with. Her relatives, in particular Tia Ana, would often completely lose patience with her when she could not follow what they were saying.

By early December she had been in Lima for around two months, and suddenly found herself in the depths of a deep and black depression. She wrote to Ursula without having first received any word from her daughter, and the whole tone of the letter made her sound very sorry for herself.

> Time goes on and on and nothing's been happening at all. So I have nothing of any interest to write to you, except that I have been feeling low and depressed this week. Everything has been problematic and I have had to endure many disagreeable and worry-filled days. Worst of all is the intense waiting and strain on my nerves, from trying to find out whether my business will have a successful outcome, or whether I will have to go through even bigger mountains of uncertainty until I can get back [to England]. It is really very hard to bear all this insecurity. Alfredo on the other hand is doing all he possibly can, and I think he feels that if things don't turn out right, then it's certainly not for want of his efforts. To be perfectly honest I get the impression that he's absolutely fed up with the whole affair. Imagine your father in the same position and then you will readily understand his feelings. On top of all that the family is—as far as I can see—rather fed up

> by my going round so much to their house. But what am I to do? I can't sit in my room from morning till night just learning Spanish. I've been doing this for hours at a time, but towards evening I generally feel the need to hear the sound of my voice or to have the opportunity to hold a decent conversation with somebody else. So I usually go to Anita's house at teatime. Most of the time I don't find anybody in, because Anita is absolutely incapable of remembering to ring me up to tell me that they will be out between 5 and 7. So it often happens that I go round there for nothing at all and just have to go away again, which makes me feel like an unwanted poor relation.

This last assumption was painfully close to the truth. In the same letter she even confessed that she would rather have stayed in Belgium and faced all the unpleasant consequences there, than have to continue in utter isolation and loneliness in Peru.* She also made comments about her landlady, complaining that she was being charged well over the odds, even though by Lima's standards her accommodation was clean and roomy, had a big garden and served good food. Eva was beginning to have real concerns about her precarious financial situation, and then told her daughter that she had finally received a letter from her own mother in Berlin explaining why Eva would be unable to receive any news from either Lene or Richard's mother. Quite naively, Eva professed astonishment that her former mother-in-law dared not write to her for fear of jeopardising her three grandsons' careers in Hitler's army. Given the strict nature of German censorship, this fear seemed very reasonable.

In the New Year Eva eagerly took up an invitation to visit a new paper factory that had recently been built on a hacienda and about which her Spanish language teacher, who was also a professional journalist, had been commissioned to write an article. She had originally planned to start travelling in earnest around the month of April when the temperatures would be receding in severity, but the excursion proved to be a welcome break from the gloomy depression she had encountered over the previous two weeks. It was the first time in her life that she had spent Christmas and New Year without a single member of her close family.

Christmas had indeed been rather a dismal affair. Christmas Eve, the

* This wish would of course have sealed her fate, as by this time Belgium and France were being occupied by the Nazis. Jews were being rounded up and sent off to the concentration camps in cattle trucks. It is extremely unlikely that Eva would have survived.

time when all German families would gather together for their celebratory meal in the evening, was a real disappointment for Eva. She spent the night on her own, as her cousin Anita did not celebrate the occasion in any way except by taking the family to midnight Mass. A few little presents were apparently exchanged, but nothing that would have had any real Christmas feel to them, and even the tree had been only modestly decorated without candles or lights. Despite this she was invited to lunch on Christmas Day and was somewhat surprised when her cousin gave her a very pretty silver photo frame, in which she could display her daughter Ursula's picture on her dressing table. Even more surprising was a rather beautiful gift from a lady Eva hardly knew: a charming little Inca bracelet in silver.

New Year's Eve, however, was to involve her in an unexpected yet unwelcome escapade. Alfredo had gone to bed, Anita had gone to Mass and the children were all attending various parties, leaving Eva completely on her own. So it was that she accepted an invitation to go out on a date with a Portuguese man called da Silva. Her first impressions of him were quite positive, even though he was stone deaf. Yet what started out as a 'jolly' evening turned into something much more intense, and she was later to write that she was lucky to have escaped from the gentleman's clutches and return to her room all in one piece. This undesired and ill-fated romantic interlude caused great resentment in Eva, not least because it shocked her to realise that somebody had thought her attractive enough to be a suitable companion. In her mind she could not visualise what other people thought of a woman like her, who spent her time travelling without any sort of escort.

Eva found it impossible to contemplate making any New Year's resolutions, but she did wish fervently to be able to close the chapter on the previous year of her life that had given her such cause for worry. The first week of 1940 had flung her into an unrelenting and even deeper depression. She was beset with feelings of homesickness, and felt so unhappy that she could not eat or sleep properly. The lack of progress in obtaining her visa was making her feel exhausted and frustrated. At night she was overwhelmed with feelings of futility and the thought that she might have to wait months and months before she could see her daughter again, and at times she really thought she was losing her mind.

This crisis must have made Eva become stronger, for she came to the sudden realisation that nobody could help her, and that she would have to start fighting her battles on her own. Perhaps at that point she was feeling the full effects of the climate, because there were times when the heat was utterly stifling, the sun leaden and the air so stuffy that her body may simply have rebelled at the unfamiliar conditions.

So it was that at the end of the first week of the New Year, Eva found herself travelling northwards out of Lima, in the company of her Spanish language teacher but together with a whole clutch of strangers. As there were only two of them at the start of the journey, the driver stopped off at various addresses to pick up other people to fill the large vehicle, which had room for around ten passengers. This was a new and not exactly pleasant experience for Eva. They drove from town to town, along narrow cobbled streets past stone houses and through muddy villages, in order to seek out those passengers who had booked a seat. These were certainly people, from Eva's point of view, who came from the lower end of the social stratum. Some of them were asleep when the car turned up, and some were eating their breakfast from which they were reluctant to be disturbed. Several of the women were even at the hairdresser's, and the whole company had to wait until they were ready to leave.

She was alarmed to find in their midst two 'bad' women, who from the tone of her letter to her daughter might have been 'ladies of the night'. There was also a man who jumped on board clutching a fighting cock in his lap. Yet Celia her teacher had no qualms whatsoever about her fellow passengers, and took the state of her travelling companions in her stride.

The road winding northwards through the desert followed a precipitous track, high above and parallel to the line of the Pacific Ocean. All along the route they passed cranes and diggers that had to work ceaselessly to keep the sand from overflowing onto the surface of the road. Eva thought the landscape particularly stark and ugly: mountainous sand dunes in all shades of yellow; acres of dry sand; adobe huts that were so dry they seemed about to crumble into dust at any moment. Looking out at the desolate landscape, Eva truly believed that you had to have been born and bred in the harsh environment to love what her Spanish teacher called 'this great country of he-men'.

After a four-hour drive along the Pacific coastline—a journey that would have taken from three in the morning until six in the evening to be completed on horseback—they finally reached Paramonga, a hacienda of sugar cane. Like an oasis in the desert, cotton fields flourished anywhere there was water, with their pretty yellow flowers spreading out in an endless multitude of soft tufts. At the hacienda Celia and Eva were received very hospitably, and they spent the weekend in a guesthouse that had been furnished in the best American style with hot water and netting on all the windows as protection against mosquitoes. All their meals were served in the *casa grande*, and consisted of heavy dishes liberally laced with garlic.

Eva was extremely interested in all the modern facilities that had been introduced to the hacienda. There was a well-equipped maternity ward and a cool, clean day nursery for the babies of the cotton workers. The women, however, were still reluctant to leave their children in the care of strangers, and would often become very anxious if the nurse on duty attempted to bathe their youngsters. Eva noted that in fact all the workers seemed to be afraid of bathing, and discovered that the men could only be induced to do so with the bribe of a cinema ticket. Since the scheme had been introduced the men apparently bathed with delight, although Eva saw no evidence that this was indeed so.

The paper factory itself was interesting because it used molasses or sugar cane to make the paper; in other words the leftovers from sugar production that had previously been simply thrown away. The paper produced was indeed quite good quality; it was not newsprint, but rather wrapping and packaging material. It was very hot in Paramonga, but at sunset Eva enjoyed sitting and listening to the rustle of the wind in the cane, which covered acres of undulating ground like an enormous green sea. They also grew maize in the fields, which made a pleasant swishing sound when the breeze blew through the tall stalks. The hacienda was exactly the same as Eva had previously read about in books, employing 23 people who all lived as one big family.

At Celia's insistence, Eva found herself having to speak Spanish during her entire stay there, which made her very frustrated because she still considered that she could only stumble along in this new language and not talk with any fluency. She was annoyed that her linguistic skills in the language seemed to be advancing so slowly, but she did her best and seemed to get on quite well with the family at the hacienda. It was a step forward, however, in that instead of sitting on her own in Lima she was finally doing something positive to get to know the people of Peru.

16

Packards and High Passes

At the beginning of the year Eva had finally moved out of her 'hotel' in the Avenida Brazil, and after a lot of problems into a much cheaper apartment in a small hotel in the pretty suburb of Miraflores. Despite her misgivings about 'the family' and how they were treating her, she nevertheless seemed to spend much of her time taking notice of what they would think of her and in what living conditions she should exist. It had therefore taken a few weeks of hunting 'high and low' for suitable accommodation to find somewhere that would maintain the high standards expected by the Ferreyros family and yet still cost less. She almost ran herself ragged in the heat of December and January, but was finally successful in uncovering a suitable apartment of the required standard.

Her rooms would consist of a living room, a bedroom with enamelled wood in light green that reminded her of Princes House in Kensington (where Ted and Ursula had lived before being moved out of London), and her very own bathroom—a great luxury since she had had to share the bathroom in her last *pension* with the other guests. Nevertheless it took her some time to get used to her new accommodation, and she was sad to leave her other rooms where she had enjoyed breakfast on the patio with the local dogs. She was also moving from an American establishment to a Peruvian one, which was a 'world of difference'.

Attempting not to feel too daunted by her constantly changing surroundings, Eva set to with energy and managed to find herself a cupboard and a lamp with which to furnish her new rooms. She could order distilled water and her meals* when she wanted them, and was very pleasantly surprised when she returned from her weekend trip to the paper factory to find that her floor had been polished in her absence. The only drawback was the tremendous noise of the neighbourhood, for the

* Throughout her stay in Peru Eva learned neither to drive nor to cook for herself. She was therefore always at the mercy of others to provide her with these essential needs. The standards of both necessities of course varied enormously.

apartment lay on the best but busiest avenue of Miraflores.

Eva had also decided to take matters in hand and effect her own introductions to people, although this was something that her cousin Anita definitely disapproved of. She did at least have introductions to the staff at the American embassy. She had been well acquainted with Mrs Dreyfus, when that lady's husband was American consul in Dresden. Eva had even had calling cards made and dropped them 'all over the place', including at the house of the Belgian chargé d'affaires.

By April, after a good deal of pointless correspondence and worrying about her possessions in the depository in London, Eva decided to 'give her head a chance to think of something different'. This time she went to the *Callejón de Huaylas*, Peru's famous Alpine region that boasts some of the highest mountains in the Western hemisphere.

With her head now getting used to organising excursions, she had fixed up with a local Peruvian writer called Señor Eguren that she would pay to share his car, on the off-chance that he was travelling to that particular region. After a ten-day period of endless talk and telephoning, one fine day the gentleman actually turned up on her doorstep. Eva had been advised to be ready at six in the morning (during her marriage she had been well trained by Richard in how important punctuality was). She stood around in front of her 'hotel' in Miraflores until 7.30, when the writer in question cheerfully drove up with his enormous Packard stuffed full of children. For all the money she had paid in advance, Eva had only half a seat. After stopping to replenish the petrol, oil and tyres they were finally on their way. The children, with whom Eva was already acquainted, were pleasant and well behaved. She had babysat for the family on a number of occasions, but now found herself sitting in front in somewhat cramped conditions, squashed right up against the steering wheel.

Within a very short space of time Eva learned that the driver was an inexperienced teenage boy from the coast who had never been to the Cordillera in his life; that he had never driven this heavy Packard before and was terrified to do so now; that he was equally terrified of the mountains where he had never been; and worst of all that he was even more terrified of *Soroche*, the infamous mountain-sickness. Eva felt a little uncomfortable on apprising herself of these facts, but she certainly could not insult Señor Eguren's hospitality by trying to duck out of the whole expedition at this late stage. As they were well on their way by now there was nothing she could about it. They drove slowly, because the enormous Packard was far too wide for the steep, narrow, winding roads they would encounter, writhing ahead of them in endless zigzags up the mountains.

The heat was beating down mercilessly as they drove into Pativilca, which was still situated on the coast. There they stopped to take breakfast at a small dwelling that served as a shop. When Eva asked to 'wash her hands' the woman led her to her bedroom, where she offered her a silver chamber pot to use, in all seriousness, as no other facilities whatsoever existed there. Then they drove through the hot scrublands at the foot of the *Sierra* where nothing was growing in the arid sand but sticks of cane, along rocky roads and across dry riverbeds, towards the heights of the Cordillera Negra. By midday they had reached a desolate place called Chasquitambo. It consisted of a single hut, the roof of which was covered by a few meagre boards and a mass of cactus leaves. The inside consisted of dirty bare walls covered with tattered cuttings from illustrated magazines. The furniture comprised nothing more than a few old wooden crates. Here they each received a piece of meat of questionable cleanliness to eat. Eva had to make up her mind at that point to take no notice of the flies, and to ignore the state of the kitchen. This was a simple stone fireplace with a hole in the middle—the pans were made of pumpkin shells and the *Serrana*-women were standing there overseeing the cooking, wearing hats from which their hair dangled in long, black plaits.

After the rest, they all felt stronger and carried on and on for several hours. By the time they were approaching the summit, at about 4,000 metres above sea level (over 13,000 feet), a thick fog had spread out in front of them and the rain had begun to drizzle. Already difficult and slippery, the road became nearly invisible and the boy at the steering wheel simply shook with fright. It was gradually growing dark, but they were still in the middle of the Cordillera. By this time the children were all utterly exhausted, and the drizzle had turned into solid sheets of water. Above them loured a dark sky of clouds as thick as black cotton wool, and beside them loomed the precipice that merged into the darkness, but which they knew to be lurking somewhere beneath them.

Despite the immediate danger, the scenery was truly awe-inspiring: wherever the fog lifted Eva was able to catch glimpses of the River Santay winding its way through the abyss thousands of feet below her, while on the other side the Cordillera Blanca lifted its gigantic, needle-sharp, ice-covered peaks into the night sky. The moon came up shining brightly, accompanied by the dazzling sparkle of the great Southern stars. The party became enveloped in an almost eerie silence. By this time they were still hours away from their destination. As it was impossible to continue on their journey with such a timorous chauffeur, Señor Eguren decided they should overnight at a hacienda he knew of in these parts. On and on went the Packard, crawling over tiny bridges which were hardly built to carry such heavy cars, and over tracks made for mules, but not for motorised traffic. In spite of the apparent dangers, they finally reached the hacienda without any mishap.

As they turned to drive through the dilapidated gateway, Eva had to pinch herself hard. Was that an actual coffin she could see in one of the dimly lit rooms? She was thankful that the children were all fast asleep, but it gave her quite a shiver down her back, she later admitted, when she heard that the occupant of the coffin was an unfortunate man who had died of *verruga*, a deadly fever prevalent in those parts of Peru. (She was later to discover that he had contracted the fatal illness in a valley two days' horse-riding distance from the hacienda, and that two men had taken 48 hours on horseback to bring the dead man back to his village.)

The hacienda, which was to shelter the bedraggled group so kindly and generously, consisted simply of a roof over mud walls. A candle was burning in the centre of the room, which was unheated and therefore as cold as ice. Its floor was also made of mud, and the walls had obviously not been whitewashed in ages. Every chair was broken, and apart from these miserable excuses for furniture there was nothing else in the 'room' but the four walls, a dilapidated table and a broken wireless. But the man who welcomed them was most hospitable, and after a short time they were all lying in their allotted beds. Eva shared a room with three Eguren siblings: two girls and their little brother. Nobody undressed at all; it was much too cold for that and besides it was impossible because the place was full of saddles, which would probably be needed by the men at daybreak. Overcome with tiredness, Eva slept well. Even the prospect of catching fleas and lice there did not worry her. She just bound a towel round her head, which was the last act requiring any sort of effort that she was able to perform that night.

Next morning the weather was glorious. Eva woke astonishingly refreshed, and could now see that the dramatic landscape around them had made it all worthwhile staying in this place called Utcuyacu. It was a hacienda embedded at the foot of the high black hills of the Cordillera; and the wonderfully sweet mountain air all around filled her with an unaccustomed feeling of pure joy. There were sheep as far as the eye could see, as the hacienda possessed some four thousand of them. The sun was shining brightly, and the enormous snow-bedecked mountains of the White Cordillera were sparkling in the clear morning light. The sky was filled with the sound of birdsong—which on closer inspection turned out to be emanating from flocks of little yellow and blue finches.

As Eva walked outside with her group, clusters of small *Serrana* children stared at the strangers from the miserably poor and dirty huts surrounding the yard. She watched in fascination as the two men who had brought the corpse got their mules and horses ready again for their ride home. All the saddle things—bridles, saddlecloths and girths—were similar to the ones back home in Richard's South American collection, and the men were all wearing ponchos and big boots as if they had just stepped out of the cinema. She sat on a nearby hillside for a long time, gazing at the deep blue sky and the sheep moving like waves across the green fields.

Despite his fears of the previous day, the Egurens' 17-year-old chauffeur had somehow regained his confidence in driving. On they went in the big Packard to Huaraz, the principal town of the district. The gigantic bulk of Huascarán rose up in front of them—the highest mountain of Peru.* All the surrounding landscape during this rainy season looked as fresh as any in Switzerland. For the remaining three days the whole family lived in the little town. It was a typical *Sierra*-town with hospitable and picturesquely dressed women, all with babies either nestling on their backs or suckling at their voluminous breasts. The vegetation was much the same as in the Chanchamayo, the first place Eva had visited in December. They went on one magnificent excursion to the *Cañon del Patto*, a very impressive gorge formed by the River Santay. Eva learned that it was 1,400 metres from the top of the mountain to the depth of the valley, where the river thundered in foaming torrents. They had to pass through 41 separate tunnels, all built into the rock face of this strangely compelling landscape. Here thousands of men had met their death through a particularly deadly kind of fever-bearing fly.

On their way home from this dramatic excursion, a violent storm broke out right above their heads. As it was late and already rather dark (because most Peruvians could never be persuaded to leave early in the day), in a short time nothing could be seen but blinding lightning. The electrifyingly violent bolts were closer and more powerful than any Eva had ever witnessed in Europe. The water came down in sheer cascades, and within a few minutes the rivers they had to traverse had turned into roaring waterfalls. It was more by luck than judgment that they were able to forge through them before they became impassable, even for the large Packard. The children were all very frightened, with some justification. These mountain roads were prone to collapse under such heavy rainstorms, and if the edge had indeed collapsed under the weight

* 22,200 feet (6,768 metres), the fourth highest peak in the Andes. At only 641 feet higher, Cerro Aconcagua in Argentina is both the highest peak in the Andes and the biggest mountain in the Western hemisphere.

of water, they would have all plunged down into the depths of the abyss.

Despite these inherent dangers, the entire party arrived safely back home in Lima. The only disappointing part was that this storm, followed by another heavy one the next day, prevented Eva from paying a visit to Chancos. Here the profusion of natural hot springs, bubbling up in steaming clouds out of the ground, were said to be a very efficient cure against rheumatism.

By the end of the trip Señor Eguren's large brood of children had come to regard Eva as an extremely curious person. Instead of sharing their combined alarm at the stormy weather, Eva had stood there clapping her hands in delight. But by this time, she been living for so long in Lima's apparently endless period of merciless heat that this explosion of violent weather was of enormous benefit. For her, the cold and rain, the clouds and furious wind provided a blessed relief, and blew all the cobwebs away from her strained and depleted nerves.

Eva's pleasure in her new-found confidence for travelling and exploring was soon to be rudely shattered. In her next letter to Ursula and Ted, written just a few days after her return from her trip to the mountains, she wrote briefly but poignantly about a great difference of opinion that had arisen between her and the family in Lima. By this time, after some six months in Peru, Eva was probably hoping that she had come to be regarded more or less as an acceptable person by Richard's cousins in South America. But the course of the war was to change all that, and in the most cruel way possible. Without any thought of what the Nazis were doing to the Jews, and the difficulties that this was causing Eva's own family, the Ferreyros women especially had decided that as they all had German ancestry, they should show their political allegiance to the German side, and not to the Allies who were fighting despotism and a fanatical dictator. It is uncertain what set the whole episode off. Perhaps Eva was sitting with Tia Ana and Anita and they had insisted on discussing the progress of the war. Whatever it was, it upset her terribly. She nevertheless wrote with considerable self-restraint.

> I have been experiencing some unexpected and distressing differences of opinion with a few members of the family. Tia Ana and Elena and some of the girls not only have different ideas to me, but they have also hurt my feelings extremely cruelly today, because I simply cannot share their point of view. As you know, I would never choose to talk about anything that I might consider a challenging subject. But things suddenly came to a head today, when they insisted that I share their opinions, which because of

their German father are completely unsympathetic to the just cause of the Allies. They have called me names that have really upset me terribly. The worst of it is that I have to go on seeing them, because they are the only relations I have here. I am lonely enough, without quarrelling with the only people I know. It makes me feel as though I am cursed. You have no idea about all the criticisms they have thrown at me. It makes my hair stand on end. I really wonder what blunders I can have made. I have tried so hard to make things go as smoothly as possible under the difficult circumstances, and it is such a blow to me that I have not succeeded in making friends of the family. I am beginning to lose all belief in myself. The energy, which I have contrived with so much pain to use efficiently so as never to be a burden to anybody, is draining out of me because of the shock they gave me today.

It's still summer and the sun has been shining every day. My greatest joy is my daily swim in the ocean, but if I were to live up to the ideals of the family I would have to give up bathing as well. This is all because there is a lady employed by the diplomatic service who frequently joins us on the beach, and whom they consider too 'high up' for me to talk to. It is all quite bizarre. I have never lived in such a small-minded world before. My little town of Sebnitz is much more easy-going than this. Perhaps as well I have never known anyone who would criticise me with such unfeeling and indifferent eyes.

The insult causing Eva such upset was that her family in Peru had accused her of committing *'Rassenschande'*.* This was a particularly horrible expression coined by the Nazis at the time of the Nuremberg laws in 1935. It literally means 'race shame' but refers to illegal sexual relations between an Aryan and a Jew, or as would have been expressed at that time, racial 'contamination' between a German and a 'non-German'. Basically during this particularly acrimonious conversation, Eva's cousins-by-marriage had accused her outright of having contami-

* This was not the only accusation of this type to be levelled at a member of the Steinthal family. During the research I undertook in the Berlin State Archives in early 2006, I was shocked to discover Eduard Steinthal's name amongst very detailed and secret Gestapo files (which would have been kept on all Jews but especially those coming from prominent families). In 1936, a few years after his divorce from Gabriele, Eva's younger brother Eduard was accused of committing *Rassenschande* with a 'full-blooded Aryan' woman because he was a 'non-German'. All his property was later confiscated.

nated pure German blood by marrying their cousin Richard Vollmann, whose mother had been born a Gaffron. It was as if they were condemning Eva for betraying not only the German race, but also the German people by not being in favour of the Fuehrer. It must have shocked her deeply and caused her to retreat into her shell.

As it was, while the whole family had very sporadic news from the seven Steinthal children, the situation for Max and Fanny in Berlin had become extremely difficult. By the first Christmas of the war the Steinthals had been forcibly removed from their home in the Uhlandstrasse, which was requisitioned by the none other than Reichsmarschall Goering for use as an officers' club for the Luftwaffe. The elderly couple were moved to a few rooms in the Hotel Eden in the Budapester Strasse (which ironically Richard had stayed in during the 1920s when he was undergoing his 'treatment' at Magnus Hirschfeld's clinic). In accordance with the laws against Jews, Max was stripped of all his money, his possessions, his stocks and shares and nearly all their furniture. He was 89 years old and had been deprived of every possession he ever owned. Yet despite this parlous situation, Fanny had somehow managed to convey to Eva in Peru that they had 'sold' the house in the Uhlandstrasse and 'bought a small house with eight rooms'. This fanciful impression was further vindicated by Eva's cousin Agathe, who visited the Eden with her teenage daughter. Bärbel would later recall her astonishment at being greeted at the door of the modest hotel by a supercilious butler wearing pristine white gloves, proffering a shiny silver tray on which they were to place their visiting card. Despite the extreme circumstances, Fanny had somehow managed to retain the last vestiges of their former life in the shape of a valet and a lady's maid.

Just before then, in an act of near defiance, Richard Vollmann had arranged for seven crates to be moved from the Uhlandstrasse to his home in Dresden. As each crate was marked with 'Vollmann' and not 'Steinthal', the Nazi authorities let them out of the house without examining them. What Richard had saved from under the noses of Goering's men were 65 of Max's favourite paintings. Sadly Erich was not so fortunate. His entire precious collection of rare books and manuscripts, many of them first editions and some of them illustrated by contemporary artists, was confiscated by the Nazis.

Life at this time for Ursula was also fraught with uncertainties. She and Ted had been moved around the countryside quite frequently while he was on watch, and had faced his infrequent leaves, a very cold winter, increased rationing and the cold and damp conditions of various boarding houses.

In her next letter, Eva seems to have taken herself in hand, given herself a good shake and told herself that there were more important things in life. News of Europe was hard to come by, and probably consisted of sporadic broadcasts from the American news networks if they had a wireless and could tune into them. Even so, news had somehow reached Eva about the disastrous evacuation from Dunkirk and the impending threat of a German invasion of Britain, which eclipsed any hurt she had been feeling about the name-calling from her Peruvian family.

> Of course I am not able to settle down to anything serious, be it Spanish or sewing or whatever it is: one's mind is taken up with intense thoughts, which of course cannot help focusing on anything but the war and you two. I know well enough that I could not be of any use to you at all even if I were there, but the feeling of sharing everything with you would be enough to put me at rest, and to ease my mind a good deal. Even if I were in New York I would feel much nearer to you and would at least consider I lived in the same world. Here in this country everything goes on as usual and women talk about dresses and the winter shopping they have to do. I cannot help watching a little bitterly Elena's joy at being given the huge original drawing of herself in an enormous silver frame, with which she was presented by the editor of the newspaper in which her picture appeared. All this 'Vanity Fair' seems so superficial to me, not because I am personally excluded from this high society life, but because I am constantly thinking of the happenings in your country and worry so deeply about you two and everything in the future.

She continued the letter by joking with her daughter, 'If Ted gets only aggressive every time you feed him on tapioca pudding, you are an extremely lucky girl Ursula dear! I loathe tapioca myself and I promise never to make it should he ever come to my house.' By this time she had even managed to stop fretting about her former possessions. 'I'm not even worrying about my furniture any more, because these things seem so very trifling … A fond kiss to each of you from your Mami.'

17

Letters from a Former Lover

From the beginning of 1940 Eva started receiving letters from Emil Waldmann. She had written to him not long after arriving in Lima, but her first letter dated 27 October took until 23 January to reach him (three months). His reply to her was written in very formal style, because it was typewritten and he had had to dictate it to his secretary. He was writing to Eva as if she were an old friend of the family, telling her about his own situation and expressing his concern that Eva's daughter should have to start out in her married life in such difficult circumstances. He even articulated the wish that should Eva be able to leave Lima any time in the near future and return to Europe—and he commiserated with her that she must be finding Peru's capital somewhat lacking in interest and culture—then he hoped they might even be able to go on another art trip together. Given the circumstances this was of course a very fanciful wish, but it was expressed in such terms because after all he was a professor of art; everything to do with art had been his life-long fascination.

He told her all about the series of winter lectures that he had just given in Bremen. He informed her as well that these had been very well received, despite the black-out conditions. His audience had been just as warm as those in Hamburg or as his clients on board the *Steuben*, the ship on which he had conducted the lectures about the culture of Ancient Greece on its Hellenic cruises around the Mediterranean.

He recalled the trip he had taken with Eva more than 15 years before, or rather when he had accompanied Richard and Eva as a married couple. They had explored the opulence of the Vatican, as well as marvelling at a whole array of Italian art treasures. Perhaps he was looking at the small photograph album that Eva had presented to him at the time, in which she had inscribed, 'To our mentor and patient friend, in happy remembrance of our whistle-stop tour through Italy in October 1924, Eva and Richard Vollmann.' Waldmann's desire then to write a book about Raphael had finally been fulfilled, but only in part. He had been commissioned by a publisher to produce a series of little art books, each with 32 pages of pictures and 16 pages of text.

He also expressed a keen interest in the art of the Incas, and asked if Eva would be able to undertake some research about the Inca inscriptions on certain documents. This was obviously code, knowing the precarious nature of her own predicament (in case his letter was opened by the German censor), for Eva's quest for a visa so that she could return 'home' to England to be with Ursula. As a final note, he told her how bad his health was, but that had been something from which he had suffered for as long as Eva had known him. At the time of writing, Eva was 47 years old and so Emil Waldmann was 59. He signed the letter 'very affectionately E Waldmann', after hoping that 'better times will surely come'.

The next letter from Professor Waldmann was hand-written in his very small and neat handwriting, dated 20 February and received by Eva on 14 March, which meant it took less than a month to reach her. She answered it two days later. He told her of his worries about his one son, who had been an epileptic most of his life but about whom the doctors could not make up their minds whether to operate on or not. Meanwhile it seemed that the boy's business was collapsing because of his ill-health, and his father had to take over his crippling financial burdens, adding to his own level of frailty. At the same time his other son was suffering from a recurrence of asthma, meaning that three out of the four members of the family were ailing. Perhaps his wife Minerva had been responsible for looking after all three of them. Despite a very nasty bout of bronchitis Emil Waldmann got up from his bed and continued his series of lectures, maintaining that people were still hungry for intellectual things. This admirable aim did nothing but result in a setback to his own recovery.

And then in spite of all the gloomy news about bad health, the professor started to refer to the relationship between 'Albert' and 'Pev'. As 'Pev' had always been Eva's pet name (Evchen turned into Pevchen), these names were clearly noms de plume between the two of them, writing to each other as something much more than just correspondents. He said, 'My whole life has been so good to me, despite constant bad health—I've travelled many times, I've seen many things, I've loved writing and working and friendship. But above all else, there was the detailed and intimate exchange of letters twice a week with Pev.'

Alluding again to the relationship between 'Albert' and 'Pev' he wrote, 'There was something quite beautiful about it: happiness and friendship, excitement and passion for beautiful and truly worthwhile things. So it was that Albert was able to be a part of every little thing that delighted Pev. And as far as Pev is concerned, it's certainly true to say that she's experienced as much by way of joy as she has of misfortune. So … let hope for the future be fashioned only from those blessedly happy memories of the past.'

In his final paragraph he again made reference to 'the Inca documents' and wrote, 'How unfortunate that the study of the Inca documents and inscriptions is taking so long. But in the end this misfortune might also lead to the achievement of one's purpose. We hope! My best wishes are always with you and with your endeavours … How envious I am of your daily swim in the Pacific Ocean! Will I ever see the southern ocean [Mediterranean] again, with its palm trees waving in the evening breeze?'

He ended the letter by asking Eva to 'accept my heartfelt good wishes and please write again soon!' and signed the letter 'your Waldmann'.

In May Eva wrote a long letter to Ursula, once again sounding impatient because she had not heard from her or Ted for so long.

> Whitsuntide today! I am sitting as I usually do on Sundays in my little sitting room and enjoying the pleasure I always look forward to during the week: writing to you. The latest letters I've received from you both were the one you wrote on 1 April from Braintree and the one from Ted dated 22 March. So of course I am hankering for news again, as always, especially with the most recent terrible events that have been happening. I really wonder whether you have been able to enjoy that holiday you were looking forward to in the first week of April, and I wonder whether Ted is still stationed at his old place. I wonder how the general feeling is with you two, I wonder about lots of things! Since all these new circumstances have arisen I haven't had a single word from you. I suppose the mail is now much slower than before, so once again I'm feeling completely dazed by so much worry. But I don't want to bore you by always repeating the same things, and it's so important that we all do our utmost to keep courage and spirits up. You should know that I think of not much else but you two, and that my own 'comfort' counts little for me. I wish more than ever I were in the same country as you. But as there is no help and nothing to do about it, I just go on trying to keep body and mind healthy.

She then went on to gripe about a letter she had received from one of the Vollmanns. Instead of rejoicing in that fact, she could only complain to her daughter about the German family's envy of Eva's life in 'lovely Lima'. She wrote, 'I can't tell you how sick I am of receiving these idiotic letters; they seem to think in that tiny village of theirs that I am enjoying the time of my life—of course they don't read my letters properly. They are too lazy in their minds to even consider with how much heartache this "trip" is connected, and with how much loneliness.'

For Eva at that time, life seemed to consist of sewing and learning Spanish, in which she constantly complained of not making sufficient progress. She said her teacher was pleasant but lazy, but that she did not want to change her 'because she is the only reliable person in this town and I am planning to travel with her to Cuzco in the near future'.

By this time as well Eva had experienced two earthquakes, which she admitted were part of the 'humdrum' life of Peru and had to be got used to. The first one had sounded like two cars crashing in front of her window. The shock was short but vehement, rattling her room and cupboards but over in an instant. As she did not realise it had been an earthquake until much later, it did not frighten her at all. The second one was preceded by a deep rumbling noise, like the drone of an aeroplane flying at low level in the far distance. Then all of a sudden the house and walls shook violently; but nothing was damaged and it passed by as rapidly as it had arrived. Once again it all took place so quickly that she had no time to get scared, and she was told that it was just a minor quake. Nevertheless this particular sensation made her think of her daughter and son-in-law now living under the constant threat of bombing from the air. Eva went on to write:

> I've recently come across a sentence in a book written by an old Spanish historian that illustrates very well indeed my experiences here. He says, 'People in this country, thinking only of their own interests, constantly change their minds. Tomorrow they will deny what they promised today. It is for this reason that nobody trusts the word of his fellow-creature, for at the first opportunity it will be broken.' These words written by Cieza de Leòn in the 16th century correspond exactly with what I have personally witnessed in Lima. However, I always exclude Alfredo from this point of view, because I really believe he's doing what he can. He says he has been to see the *ministre des affaires étrangères* this week and that this man has promised to do all he can for me. This of course would be *the* help I need and I go on hoping for a happy resolution to all my troubles.

Waldmann's next letter to Eva was dated towards the end of July, but was received by her only two months later. In a welter of artistic references, some of which might have been cryptic pseudonyms for some former intimate activity between the two of them, he wrote, 'Every letter you send to your erstwhile teacher is a gift gratefully received'. And then while expressing his joy that Eva should be attending lectures in Lima, given by people Waldmann referred to as 'his colleagues' (in other words contemporary professors of art), he also made reference to her 'mane of hair' and wondered what colour it was. He asked at the end of the letter, 'Please write another of your very interesting yet sympathetic letters. Please!' He finished by talking about something very intimate. 'When I get up I find myself thinking of all sorts of themes—a look in the mirror, an unconscious movement ... the beautiful fur coat and the skin underneath it.' This sounded very much like a lover's caress.

Eva was to receive three more letters from 'her' Professor Emil Waldmann between the end of 1940 and the beginning of 1941, each of them getting more familiar in tone. Although he did not say as much to Eva, he was experiencing his own severe difficulties at the hands of the Nazi authorities. By this time, they had been vilifying many renowned art galleries and museums throughout Germany, if they considered their content was 'too French' or 'too foreign'. In a letter dated 1 December, but which Eva replied to almost two months later, he boasted about the amount of new art he had managed to purchase on a 'shopping trip'. He worried greatly about his own personal health, as well as that of his children and his wife. He also asked that Eva and he write to each other as *'du'* (the familiar form of address in German), which seems very odd if they had previously been on such intimate terms. But then again, it must have been very difficult to maintain any kind of continuity in correspondence because of the long periods it took for the post to arrive either in Germany or in Lima. He wrote:

> In a fortnight from today I'll be 60 years old, and it is my wish for my birthday and for Christmas that from now on we address each other as *du*. You were my best student and as far as any debate went you were always my best audience. It's quite right to say that this is not just a long-standing relationship between teacher and student, but also a personal one between two people. Without wishing to annoy you, I'll send you a kiss and likewise you'll send one back to me. Agreed? How courageous and rational you have managed to stay in the face of all obstacles. How else would you have been able to prepare the notes for your book, or write such a beautiful account of your travels including expensive photos? Quite the contrary. Every one of your letters is a joy to me and I'm already looking forward to the next account of your journeys. You write so well and so vividly, and even if you're not always

> surrounded by nice people, they must still be extremely interesting. So write and tell me about yourself, because rest assured I'll definitely be thinking about you over Christmas.

By this time Eva, who had been corresponding principally with her daughter, had also been writing up a journal of her travels so as to keep her mind occupied. She had managed to bring a Zeiss 'Box Tengor'* camera with her from Germany, with which she was taking quite competent black-and-white photographs (although probably very anxious about the high cost of having the films developed).

Emil Waldmann had again referred to the 'troublesome Inca document', obviously his covert reference for the problems that Eva was apparently still encountering in getting a visa to return back to Europe. It was something that seemed to prey on her mind most of the time. Interestingly, however, the next letter was somewhat repetitive in content, but as these letters were hand-written Waldmann probably did not bother to keep copies, and despite the high cost of sending airmail letters he wrote again about his recent purchases of Dutch art, as well as his continuing bad health:

> I haven't heard from you in ages. You will have been lonely these past few days. I'm also quite on my own. I don't want to be there [at his home] over Christmas because of my gloominess about disturbing the others. And I would do so—how well you know and can judge the soft-heartedness of your friend. I always have to think of my lung disease and the 'house arrest' that goes with it. My intention is to stay in Bramsberg for a week, even if by then the lights are no longer illuminated on the Christmas tree. Then my lectures and seminars start in the Northern [German] High Schools, which not only provide me with work but which I also greatly enjoy. You know yourself how much I like imparting knowledge to others. How sad that you'll be alone on Christmas Eve—but not quite: in your secret self you'll be able to sense that there's someone sitting in Bremen who wishes you well.
>
> When I returned [from Holland] after my birthday (No. 60—that's how old your friend is!), I was presented with a great big golden plaque for Art and Science, in honour of Bremen and the Reich—the highest honour my native city can bestow.

* This was an inexpensive, box-shaped camera made in Dresden by Zeiss in the 1930s.

This last sentence is somewhat equivocal, in that Waldmann seems to be delighted to receive an honour in the name of art, but at the same time equally pleased that it is in the name of the Reich. He was then invited to a reception at the home of Leo von Koenig, a very well known contemporary artist who had been commissioned to paint a portrait of Waldmann, which to this day hangs in the *Kunsthalle* in Bremen.

At the end of the letter it seemed very odd for Waldmann to tell Eva that his wife Minerva sent her warmest wishes (as if both these women were good family friends), and then he mentioned a 'half Chilean' young girl who immediately made him think of South America and therefore of Eva. It was almost as if he always wanted to have his cake and eat it. He apparently found it quite natural to flirt with young girls and conduct an affair with his mistress, while remaining firmly married to his wife and maintaining his status as a staunch family man.

The last letter in the Waldmann 'collection' was written at the end of January 1941 in response to a letter Eva had written to him two weeks before Christmas. The interesting thing is that she made no reference to her own parents. In fact, in all the letters both to Waldmann and to Ursula with Ted, she only ever talked about her mother, or sometimes 'my parents', but never about her father. His health must have been failing fast all through the upsets of 1940, but she never mentioned it.

It was also a time of increasing hardship in England, following the Battle of Britain over the southern skies that had played out all through the summer. And then there was the shocking impact of the firebombing of Coventry in November 1940, the first city to be bombed by the Luftwaffe as a specifically identified civilian target. The London Blitz would follow soon after, and Eva would have had no idea where Ursula was living: huddled terrified in some dusty bomb shelter or safe outside the city.

Meanwhile in Germany, six weeks before Christmas Max Steinthal fell down the steps at the Eden Hotel. He was taken to hospital where he lay in a semi-conscious state for the next few weeks. Just seven days before his 90th birthday, Max Steinthal died. Four years previously, when Max submitted the annual 'declaration of assets' demanded of all Jews by the Nazi regime, his entire fortune has been valued at 20 million Reichsmarks.* On the day of his death, the man who had been instru-

* The currently accepted formula for converting the value of Reichsmarks into modern equivalents is to multiply by 10 to get Deutschmarks, and then divide by three in order to get pounds sterling. Using this rough formula means that at the end of the 1930s Max was worth something in the region of £70 million.

mental in the success of the banking movement, not only for Berlin but also for the whole German nation, left this world without a penny to his name. He had been stripped of his title of Privy Counsellor of the City; of all his possessions including his home; of all the wealth that encompassed domestic and industrial property, stocks, shares, gold, paintings and other valuables; and of his status. His widow Fanny was 74 years old. Her only contact with her scattered family, apart from her oldest son Erich, was through her former son-in-law Richard Vollmann.

Waldmann was still concerned about his own health and that of his immediate family, while focusing on matters of art. He again finished his letter by asking Eva if she would address him using the informal *'du'*.

> The day before yesterday, I wrote to you thanking you for the charming birthday present of the description of your journey I received on that day. Then I received your letter of 15 December, for which I thank you very much. You know that everything I receive from you gives me such joy, even when there is gloomy news such as the failing health of elderly people whom nobody round me knows how to help ... I remember that our friend Albert never offered her any money, when Pev helped him with the Chevalier and the Altdorfer [the cataloguing of two particular paintings]—that's how it goes between lovers in this country. But he did give her a beautiful gift, something which women love, like perfume. You haven't given a reply in your letter to my request to use *du*. At 60 years of age I can ask that of my favourite student. You'd never be so high and mighty as to ignore this request. So I'm asking you again, please can we use *du*, and please receive a kiss from me in your mind. If you really don't like that then I won't offer it to you on your eyes, or under your chinchilla-fur coat, but on your hand. There you go. I hope you receive good news from the two children.

Waldmann's reference to 'kissing Eva in his mind' was particularly poignant. He was obviously extremely fond of her. The following batch of letters that were to be exchanged, mostly between Eva and her widowed mother Fanny, must have utterly eradicated the benefit of any feelings of affection Eva might have received across the Atlantic from her former lover.

The next news to arrive from Europe would hit her with all the force of a thunderbolt.

18

The War of Words

By April 1941 Eva had been living in Peru for a year and a half. She had finally moved from the living quarters she had originally been so pleased to find, but which turned out to be a 'horrible hotel'. This was the very *pension* she had taken so much trouble to search for, after being forced to leave the 'American' accommodation because it had become much too expensive. Her second or third landlady had been a Yugoslav woman, who had apparently used 'second-hand' or poor grade cooking oil in all her cuisine. In the end Eva suffered from an acute inflammation of her stomach because of the bad standard of cooking, and was forced to move on the recommendation of the doctor—a diagnosis that cost her dearly both in pocket and in health. Yet, despite this bad experience, she still remained firmly attached to the social norms with which she had been indoctrinated by her Prussian upbringing. Nothing then would have induced her even to consider learning how to cook for herself. After a good deal of frustrated searching, she eventually found a very pleasant apartment, still in Miraflores but of a much higher standard. Eva was to remain there for the rest of her time in Lima.

During all this time Eva had been mentally buoyed up by three distinct factors: that her cousin Alfredo would finally achieve a breakthrough in the bureaucratic yet delicate intricacy of the South American legal system, and thus obtain a visa for her to return to Europe; that her 'children' (Ursula and Ted) would survive their present difficulties and she would be able to see them again very soon; and that, despite all evidence to the contrary, as soon as the war was over she would be able to get back together again with Richard and resume her former life.

She could not have been more wrong. At the end of March 1941, after only three months as a widow, Fanny wrote what must have been a blithely bubbling letter. 'Poor and lonely' Richard had solved all his family problems by getting married again the previous November. Eva's mother cannot have had the slightest idea what huge shockwaves this would send through her daughter, and to what extent Eva was managing to endure her situation in Peru only because of her daily fixation on the romantic ideal of her former home life. In fact, after her husband Max's death in such sad circumstances following 51 years of happy marriage, Fanny, who was now nearing 75, would have relied more and more on Richard for advice. As the only 'Aryan' in her immediate family, he had been made executor to her will because under the Third Reich this function was forbidden to any Jew. By law he was entitled to one-fifth of her estate.

Eva's reply to her mother, written on 19 April, was full of such grief and anger that the words seem to jump off the page. She was almost beside herself with anguish. From her mother's point of view, she who must have had some inkling about all the years of problems in Eva's marriage, the fact that Richard should seek further female companionship was absolutely understandable. For Eva, however, the distress of such news seemed to have driven her almost to the contemplation of suicide.

> Your letters of 23 and 24 March arrived only yesterday. Since then I've been sitting here and holding them in my hand. You've been telling me I should write to you regularly and without deliberation or pretence. This is exactly why, just for once in this absolutely appalling time, I'm not going to wait for weeks on end before facing up to this terrible insult, nor wait until the worst effect of the initial shock has subsided. Why on earth should I always have to keep my emotions under control? I've been doing this my whole life long and it's served me damned little purpose, and only caused people to consider me hard or cold, which has made me suffer more burdens than any other woman I know. I have no words to tell you my grief; my heart is so broken I'm simply stunned.
>
> Is this really possible? It's absolutely staggering. I've been forced to make so many sacrifices. I've had to give up *every* hope, *every* single thing at home that I've cherished and all that is so unutterably dear to me. I'll *never ever* be able to have any of that back again—that's what none of you can comprehend or even measure the tiniest part of, or even begin to understand how much any of this means for me. You say that Dick has been so very lonely. Mother, what does he know of loneliness! A fine house in his native land, a mass of treasured belongings especially the garden, the dogs, the people he's grown up with all around him, the work he's loved, his friends, his family—what on earth has he had to do without? He's got *everything*—and what have I got? What has he known of my unbearable solitude wandering the streets in a foreign land, where nobody and nothing is waiting for me—which, oh Mother, none of you can even imagine. I'm only

> a simple woman, but for all that a person who needs a little goodness and love in her life! 26 years of my existence have been utterly extinguished, as if I were dead.

She then went on to wish that the good Lord had struck her dead in 1937, rather than let her suffer in this terrible way. She was referring to an episode of blood poisoning when she became gravely ill. For her, this news of Richard's remarriage was like torture. 'And now I'm forgotten,' she wrote, 'replaced, more than replaced.' She continued:

> My mind is so utterly confused that I can't even begin to describe it on paper, because it's like a storm crashing around inside my head. How can anyone have to bear so much—the deep and persistent worries over Ursele that daily loom like some dark menace before my very eyes; the calamitous loss of my precious things, on which the reconstruction of my shattered existence was to depend, and which has now been made impossible; being left to survive completely on my own; the rising toll of bitter events and the dozens of disappointments here—why should all this happen to me?

Her last sentence was most telling of all. 'How can I possibly go on living—what can I ever hope for?'

The very next day Eva seemed to have come slightly to her senses, and was feeling that despite her own state of shock it would not serve any purpose to cause her mother more worry than necessary. But she did admit that she would have been quite happy to lie in bed and let a passing earthquake do its worst, rather than make her escape out of the house as usual.

'I'll do what you ask and take care to swallow whatever food is put in front of me,' she wrote. 'That much will keep me alive. And from now on I'll make sure I take suitable precautions—for your sake as well—by jolting myself awake the next time there's an earthquake. We've just had two; a very strong one during the day and another one last night. I didn't even bother to get up because I thought the roof could happily fall on my head and that would have suited me just fine—at least then it would have put an end to this whole horrible business.'

Her anger against Richard ('Dick') was almost palpable. What seemed to strike Eva more than anything was that by marrying this Ilse Schmidt, he had discarded 26 years of marriage to Eva as if they had never happened. Suddenly her eyes had been opened; she accused him not only of having been unfaithful to her during the marriage, but also of abandoning her 'just when I became an inconvenience to him'. This was a reference to their divorce, and completely ignored the problems caused by her being of Jewish origin in a Nazi regime. She almost screamed at her mother in the letter about how much suffering Dick had caused her, and how he personally had been responsible for taking away every single thing that was precious to her in her life. The only thing keeping her sane, Eva wrote, was her love for her daughter. Interestingly she seemed to have latched onto Lene, Richard's sister, as her own ally, rather than imagining for one moment that Lene would more likely take her brother's side.

Then she was suddenly struck with morbid curiosity, and wanted to know from her mother how her erstwhile husband had met his new wife, suspecting she might be a nurse working for a certain consultant ophthalmologist that Richard used to visit in Cologne. In truth, the shock of the marriage had knocked Richard off the pedestal on which Eva had placed her husband all through their married life. Suddenly certain things were making sense to her, situations that in her trusting naivety she had completely ignored. 'But from now on don't think of him as God Almighty,' she warned her mother, 'as I did throughout my entire life; don't forget that he was unfaithful to your daughter during our life together. And don't blindly believe every word he says: that my separation was "an absolute necessity" is simply not true … because he abandoned me just at that moment when I was becoming an inconvenience for him.' The letter continued with an outpouring of bitterness, punctuated by deeply sarcastic and rhetorical questions.

> For all those countless years, in which I was the very antithesis of a 'hindrance', I was good enough to construct an entire lifestyle for him. And for this I'm being attacked in the most vicious way. So the poor man was transplanted by force to Wachwitz, was he? He didn't belong there and he was totally unhappy there and that elegant high life for which I was specifically picked out was anathema to his soul, was it? But now? Now he's ripped away each and every thing that brought me joy in my life. *He* did that, not some other superior being. *He alone*. And by getting rid of me, he's been free to replace me with a new person who is living with my things, *my* dogs, *my* staff trained by me, my house—while he left me nothing more than a shabby roof over my head and just about enough to eat. And absolutely *nothing else*. He's taken everything, *everything*, and has totally and utterly abused my spirit.

The next letter was to cause the greatest number of problems in this very acrimonious correspondence. Eva wrote to her sister-in-law Lene in the frankest and most open manner, personally accusing her ex-husband of never having loved her. She sent a copy to her mother, adding a note at the bottom that once Fanny had read it, she should destroy the letter. For whatever reason, Fanny chose not to obey her daughter's wishes and kept all the letters together in a batch, which she bundled together with their envelopes and tied in a ribbon.

There is no letter from Lene in the collection. It would have been very interesting to gauge her reaction at having her brother accused by his former wife of neglect, abandonment, sadism, celibacy, impotence and finally infidelity. Eva also vehemently denied that she had ever been unfaithful, and stated firmly that her 'relationship' with Waldmann was nothing more than a platonic friendship.

'Yesterday evening the meaning of the words suddenly became as clear to me as if the scales had fallen from my eyes,' she wrote to her sister-in-law, 'and it's only now that I've realised—you'll tell me how very late that is—how this hopelessly tangled mess came about. It can be expressed in very few words: I believe that Dick never loved me.' She told Lene in the strongest possible terms what this meant: the total collapse of her life. Having expressed herself so forcefully, Eva then allowed the floodgates to be opened and all the pent-up miseries inside her to come pouring out. Considering that Lene must have been worried sick about her only son fighting on the Russian Front, it is no wonder that she was to give this letter to her brother to read, thus providing him with all the ammunition he needed to respond to the accusations.

> Remember how quickly he neglected me; we hadn't even been married a year and I was expecting my first child in extreme pain and discomfort. How often he left me alone at that time. I'd never thought of that until this moment, but now I can bring it all to mind again, of how angry he became when his Uncle Otto interfered and wrote to me that it would be better if he stopped all his travelling. For that's when he was away all the time, even though I was suffering so much. But when he was at home, that's when we had to run about in the heat of summer in Hochbusch. How often I cried there. And then war broke out, and we were forced to move house to Berlin and from there to Caputh. You know too well how badly he treated me at that time. You can probably remember more details about that time than I can. That's when he started drinking so much together with that Stauss. A happy young man wouldn't have needed to drink—why should he

> seek oblivion in alcohol? I think he was already unhappy with me. And then the neglect became so bad that in the end he had to go to a psychiatrist.
>
> After 1919 I stayed faithful through seven long and difficult years. Seven years is a long time for a young woman. I know that nobody will believe me when I say I waited seven years—but nevertheless it's true. In those unhappy years everything that occurred was a direct cause for what's happening now. He never loved me.

Eva went on to admit that when Lene had voiced her suspicions about Ursula's governess Fräulein Franke in 1934, she had simply refused to believe her. When the housekeeper, Marga, had also written Eva a letter accusing the governess of being far too close to her employer Richard, Eva had simply thrown it in the bin as a pack of lies. 'And then misfortune reared its ugly head in the shape of Franke,' she told her sister-in-law, 'who not only stirred up animosity against me, but also spied on me and reported every single conversation, criticised every action, and goaded him and spoke to him against me in the most spiteful manner, saying that I was carrying on with Waldmann at a time when that was the furthest thing on my mind.'

Given the passionate exchange of letters that had occurred between Eva and Emil Waldmann, she did seem to be protesting her innocence a little too much. And from her lonely position across the other side of the world, she had completely forgotten about the letters she had written to Richard, asking him to forgive her behaviour. Towards the end of the letter to Lene she finally admitted her actions, which she claimed she undertook because she assumed Richard to be impotent (although never using 'that horrible word' in front of him). 'Finally when I couldn't stand my nun's existence any longer,' she confessed in her letter, 'I can state with absolute justification: with doubt in my heart I finally took a lover. But I will say it again: even then I waited months and months before I decided to take such a drastic step. It never entered my head that I was "betraying" Dick—that simply wasn't the question. I assumed right from the start that he knew about my actions and understood them, because he himself wasn't capable.'

She soon realised that she had made an extremely serious miscalculation; she had assumed things that simply were not true. She thought he knew and understood everything—whereas at that time, she realised now, he was developing a hatred for everything to do with her. But it had never occurred to her at the time to think even the slightest bad thought about him. To her, Richard her husband was simply sacrosanct.

It was now that Eva realised how much this 'person' had held the power in her house and over her child. She had begged Richard so often to let Fräulein Franke go 'because she was unbearable', and every time he had insisted that she was too important for Ursula's upbringing. In Eva's 'laughable trust' in him, as she put it, she found it so sweet of him that he should 'burden' himself with the governess on a trip to Italy. She found nothing odd about the fact that he should want to travel to Rome without his wife 'to meet a certain business man', until it turned out that Franke had been travelling with him the whole time. As she was writing this, she confessed to Lene, she could not understand how a woman could possibly be as stupid as she had been. 'This was no misunderstanding,' she wrote. 'He never loved me—and that's all. I have absolutely no idea how I can even begin to save the hopeless shipwreck of my life. All my self-belief and all my confidence have been utterly destroyed.' The one thing that gave her a reason to live was her child, but for Eva what Richard had done by marrying again was the most unforgivable betrayal.

'Of course I'd counted steadfastly on staying on with him,' she told her sister-in-law. 'A woman alone in a foreign country, without the slightest clue or advice on how to survive on her own—I think you've all got such poor powers of imagination that you can't possibly conceive how unendingly difficult it has been for me. But even this feeling of anxiety of living alone for the rest of my life is nothing, but nothing, compared to the knowledge that Dick has so inexplicably betrayed me. I am simply unable to grasp the reason why. Why, for God's sake, didn't he tell me the truth?'

The next letter that Eva wrote to her mother was dated at the end of May, and was in response to four letters she had received from Fanny and which had taken around a month to reach her. Her mother seemed to be relating all the latest gossip about Eva's 'affair' (or rather unfaithfulness throughout her marriage), which was being propagated by somebody she called 'Mrs Scandalmonger'. Rather oddly, Eva chose to use a third person technique to tell her mother what must have been her own personal story. She referred to her 'friend Eva' and told her story as if she were a close friend. Once again she begged her mother to destroy this particular letter once she had read it, and most importantly not to show it to 'Eva's husband'. And once again Fanny chose her own reasons to refrain from carrying out either wish. She was probably leaning on Richard more than ever, now that she was a widow without means living on her own in the Hotel Eden.

Eva's next letter to her mother was written only three days later, again referring to her 'friend Eva'. Her main concern seemed to be that despite her warnings, Fanny was still 'receiving' Richard into her home. But much worse this time was the fact that he had brought his new wife with him to Berlin to visit his former mother-in-law. Eva seemed to feel not only had she been cruelly betrayed by Richard, but that she had also been abandoned by her family (i.e. her mother) who had simply not been able to grasp the depth of Eva's pain throughout this whole sorry affair. She appeared to have forgotten that her mother was in exactly the same position as her 'betrayed' daughter: she was a woman surviving on her own, made a widow after 51 years of marriage (twice the length of Eva's), and with no male counsellor other than her former son-in-law on whom she must have relied frequently for advice. And yet Eva accused her of lack of understanding, when she herself had railed against her family for not recognising her own state of solitude.

'I find it absolutely outrageous that he should visit you with his wife,' she thundered in her letter. And then she continued in the third person, 'The husband knows everything. He's very clever. And to prevent Eva from starting up any accusations against him, he's been to the old lady [Fanny] and with consummate skill he's beguiled her completely. Because he's so skilful, this lonely old lady has been so delighted to have a friend and ally that she's completely fallen under his spell. She's been quite incapable of realising that it was he who, unbeknown to her, had imposed his will on her in such an utterly self-centred and ice-cold manner.'

Once again, Eva begged her mother to destroy the letter once she had read it, and not to allow it to fall into Richard's hands. 'You won't believe with how much exertion and trouble and heartache for me these letters about the whole affair are connected,' she wrote. This last statement contained more than an element of truth in it. Almost overnight, the shock of hearing about Richard's remarriage had turned Eva's beautiful dark hair completely white. She was not even 50 years old.

In his first letter to Fanny, Richard wrote very clearly, coherently and concisely in a reassuring tone of voice, designed to put Fanny at ease about her daughter's apparent financial predicament. He also managed to imply that Eva was basically making a mountain out of a molehill, and that her situation was not nearly as precarious as she would have her family believe. He portrayed himself very much as the dutiful son-in-law who was still concerned about his former wife's state of affairs.

'I have steadfastly told both you and Pev that I will always remain the same good friend that I have always been,' he wrote. 'I think I have proved this and if today I concern myself with your needs, then I do so because it is my duty to help you as much as I can, but more than anything so that I can salvage as much regarding Pev as there is to salvage. You can rest assured that Pev has a very particular place in my affairs. As for my heart, that's another matter and you really can't expect anything other from me after Pev—through the liaison, about which you have been fully aware—quite deliberately embittered my heart and went on doing so for years. This has all been well established, but as far as I'm concerned there's absolutely nothing more to say about the matter.'

The next three letters in the batch were all from Eva, dated towards the end of June, the first one written on her return from another trip. Amongst the continued discussion about her almost unbearable situation, she lets slip some details about life going on in the rest of the world. By this time Ted had been posted overseas and was to spend the rest of the war attached to the signals section of his regiment in Egypt. Ursula was destined to be without her husband until almost the end of the war. Meanwhile the Blitz that battered London over the first months of 1941 had finally put paid to the last vestiges of Eva's hold on the past: the depository in Tottenham, in which all her remaining belongings had been stored after great import difficulties, suffered a direct hit. Everything was destroyed.

However, she still could not hide the bitterness of her emotions when writing to her mother. 'What I'm asking for today, quite frankly, Mother, is to be able to express a very practical opinion. But it just so happens that this opinion will unfortunately be thought of as defamation of character on my part. I've also received a letter from Muttel [Dick's mother], in which she says again that 'I loved another [person] more than Richard'—of course this is what her son told her to exonerate his own guilt. Look how shamefully I've been betrayed, if people have to sink to the level of washing their dirty laundry in public.' And then she confessed her deepest feelings to Fanny. 'It's quite incredible: up until now I wouldn't have been able to find it in my heart to condemn Dick. But the wretchedness of the last letter has for the first time evoked a feeling in me I've never experienced in my life before: utter contempt.' And then she admitted further, 'If I sound very bitter about all this, it's because another person is making herself at home with all my lovely things and is being served by my Helene, happily living in the ambience created by me.'

Eva's suspicions held more than an element of truth: when Richard married Ilse, she brought her own mother to live with the couple in the house in Wachwitz. As Richard's new relative, this woman was always known as '*Schwiemu*', which is short for *Schwiegermutter* or 'mother-in-law'. It is unlikely that Eva's faithful maid Helene thought much of the new domestic arrangements, but she was always loyal to her employer.

The anger in this exchange of letters, despite the drawbacks of time and space between them, was like a palpable force in the midst of the war. Yet even more striking was that while Waldmann's letters to Eva in Peru were never touched by the censor, every single one of these latest letters were opened by German Army HQ and stamped several times over with the Nazi swastika.

The last letter in the batch collected and kept by Fanny was written on 7 July 1941 and was a long epistle, in which Richard offered full and final proof to his mother-in-law of her daughter's long-term affair. He was, however, very clever in that he made no mention of his own infidelities. Richard obviously felt that Eva's letter to his sister Lene was the last straw, and that he had been unjustifiably accused and vilified in public. His letter was a masterpiece of carefully composed logic, with all the proof of Eva's infidelities enclosed. He was still finding the whole matter quite distasteful, even though by now he had been remarried for eight months.

> Since Pev decided to write the letter to Lene, of which copies were sent to you and Agathe and I don't know whom else, I find it necessary to be able to clarify to you, in my eyes at least, how our marriage played out from the time of the First World War. Perhaps this will cause you pain and anguish, but I'd like to portray everything as I found it then and as I still find it today. I'll attempt to back up the facts I'm telling you with extracts from Pev's letters, while leaving out those sections where she keeps vowing that she loves only Ursel and me and that everything else is just another story altogether. My feelings and my understanding about the whole thing stand, as they always have, diametrically opposite to those of Pev. As I have proved my friendship to Pev despite the rift all these years, and which I will continue to prove to her, you will see that today I'm thinking quite calmly, so to speak, about these things.

After giving his own version of their relationship from the beginning, Richard wrote, 'In late summer of 1933 Pev told me that she had separated from her lover, because during that summer he had handled himself badly with regard to the Jewish question. I actually felt sorry for her: from Waldmann's point of view it was perhaps understandable. He had to take care of his family and his whole existence centred around playing a game, much of which was probably exemplified by the character of a man who was very happy and ready to keep an elegant mistress for many years at the cost of others, but who (not once during the first year of the liaison) made only the slightest attempt to divorce his wife [Minerva] in order to be able to marry Pev.' He continued:

> Nothing came from our separation: Pev suggested that she stay with me. I know precisely that Pev was still in contact with Waldmann in August 1935: I simply didn't bother with the matter any more, partly out of indifference and partly because I didn't want to get caught up in the affair, in case either of them should happen to come into conflict because of the heavy Nuremberg laws and their severe penalties. The last time I heard of Waldmann was in August 1939. I flew from London to Brussels to pack up all the trunks that Pev had left in the flat, and send them on to London. On her writing desk lay her personal post which had arrived in the meantime; on top was a book that Waldmann had sent her, labelled with precisely the right address of the *Résidence* in Brussels. Since I certainly hadn't given it to him, it must have been Pev who probably did so. Now I wish to draw a closing line under the bitterest chapter of my life, to which I give the title: *Waldmann—My Wife*.

In his last paragraph Richard seemed to regard Eva's attitude to the whole matter with resignation at her lack of understanding. 'Sadly Pev does indeed appear to have very little appreciation of the realitics of this world, and above all not to notice when somebody tries, out of pure friendship, to behave in a gentlemanly fashion towards her. Just as an example, she complained bitterly to Lene at the time that the divorce would have to be carried out because of the Nuremberg laws. She didn't even consider that I was only doing this in order to spare her. Perhaps she might have suggested that I wash her dirty laundry, including that of her splendid beau (see above), in public at Court.'

19

From Jew to Peruvian

The irony in all this vitriolic exchange of letters was that Richard Vollmann had indeed married his mistress. Ilse Schmidt was the daughter of an apothecary in Hanover, whom he had met several years before as a *Tennisliebchen.* These were single girls who used tennis clubs as venues in which to meet eligible young men, the younger and richer the better. Richard of course was married, and very considerably older than she was, but that did nothing to deter Ilse from her determination to get her claws into him. Richard would visit Bad Kissingen once a year and that was where they met for the first time. From a very early stage in their relationship she plotted to get Richard to divorce his wife Eva, whom she referred to as 'your little Jewess'. While a flood of morally upstanding Germans married to Jews emigrated with their Jewish spouses, it had been Ilse who had persuaded Richard to stay behind in Germany. Quite unaware of this, as she would later confess in her letters from South America, Eva believed every reason he gave for her immediate and necessary deportation. Ilse meanwhile, delighted that her 'competition' had been exiled to the other side of the world, did not experience a single qualm when the Vollmanns' large and thriving artificial flower factory was requisitioned by the Nazi authorities for the production of buttons for military uniforms. All she cared about was securing her status of being connected to a wealthy and influential property owner.

When Richard married Ilse in November 1940, he was 57 and she was 37—a full 20 years younger than him and only 11 years older than Ursula. Eva would have taken scant pleasure in the fact that in their wedding photo, both of them look much older than their stated age. Ursula would not come face to face with her stepmother until many years later.

As far as Eva was concerned, the very last remnants of her former life ended during 1941. Her only connection to the old world was her daughter in England. Just ten months after the death of Max Steinthal, Fanny died in Berlin in her 77th year. Although unbeknown to the rest of the family at the time, her death was in fact a blessed release. If she had survived just another couple of months, she would have been forced to join the remaining Jews who were being rounded up and shovelled without ceremony into the cattle trucks leading eastwards out of Berlin. Without doubt she would have died in extreme circumstances in Auschwitz.

The financial situation soon become precarious for Eva. In December 1941, after the unprovoked attack on Pearl Harbor by the Japanese, America finally entered the war. This meant that Richard could no longer transfer dollars from his New York account, and to all intents and purposes Eva was cut off and would have to learn to survive on her own. She was certainly loath to ask for money from her 'family' in Peru, but already the angry exchange of letters about Richard's remarriage and Eva's former love-life must have served as some sort of catalyst. By the time Richard Vollmann was writing to his mother-in-law from his home in Wachwitz in June of that year, Eva was already rejecting her past and had changed her nationality.

Although no mention is made of it in any of her letters to her daughter, Eva's cousin-by-marriage Alfredo must have been able to offer some assistance regarding her affairs and domicile in Peru. Giving up on the impossible pursuit of obtaining a visa back to England, he had managed to complete the paperwork for Eva Vollmann to become a Peruvian citizen. She had probably also been fired up to forget her German past, because of all the upset caused by her cousins declaring themselves in favour of the Axis powers and therefore against the Allies (and by association pro-Nazi). She had been travelling all this time with a passport in which the red 'J' for 'Jew' was stamped very clearly inside, and in which her name was given as 'Eva Carola *Sarah* Vollmann', an imposition by the Nazi regime so that all Jews were immediately recognisable by the authorities. All her brothers had been forced to have the name 'Israel' added to their passports. In order to speed up the process of naturalisation, Eva actually lied on the forms. She put her age at six years older, claiming that she had married in 1907. The lie worked. By mid 1941 Eva had become a Peruvian citizen.

Through the exchange of letters with her mother, Eva seemed to reach some life-altering decision. She had made her mind up to go travelling, while writing about her experiences. Obviously the events stirred up by the letters would have preyed on her mind, and this must have been her way to forget the past. The various jottings that Eva completed at the end of each journey were eventually to be turned into a lengthy book. She would spend months compiling this detailed account of all her experiences in Peru.

At the same time Eva was also still attending university, not only to learn Spanish but also to immerse herself in the history and culture of the Inca civilisation. She matriculated from the course, without really knowing what she could do with the knowledge she had gained. Much of this learning would eventually end up in Eva's book, the final draft of which consisted of around a quarter of a million words and some wonderful black-and-white photographs.

Approaching her 49th birthday, Eva decided that she would have to survive on her own wits. Already feeling abandoned by her supposed 'family' in Peru, she turned to another German family. By offering her services as a teacher of English, Eva managed to find work as a governess with a wealthy family of German merchants, colonists originating from Hamburg called the Gildermeisters. The family ran coffee plantations and belonged to the higher echelons of *hacienderos* or plantation owners. After the war the family would be forced move to the USA, because the future Peruvian government was destined to nationalise most of the plantations.

Eva offered babysitting services to the family, and she enjoyed looking after several of the children. They were utterly German and had not been indigenised in the slightest (unlike the Gaffrons who had married into the Ferreyros family). One of the Gildemeister girls, Sabine, had been sent to a German boarding school to be educated in the ways and virtues of being a good German *Hausfrau*.

With no hope of learning of the progress of the war, and beginning to feel like a fully-fledged Peruvian, Eva decided to travel as much as possible in order to forget her past life. At first she seemed to throw caution to the winds, setting out on the most dangerous sort of journeys that put her friends in Lima into a frenzy of horror. Limanians loved their home comforts and could not possibly begin to understand Eva's restlessness, and especially her apparent abandonment of her own personal comforts. By this time Eva had a charming Peruvian friend, also called Anita, who was just as puzzled by her German friend's wanderlust. But Eva was determined to learn as much as possible about her adoptive home. Another reason for her frequent travels was the uncomfortable climate unique to Lima. Six months of rainless heat would be followed by six months of energy-sapping grey fog called *garua*, which rolled in off the Pacific Ocean and covered the city in a muffled damp blanket. During the foggy season, most Limanians would escape to their villas nestling high above the city in the hills. Eva, however, used this time of year to explore much further afield.

Less than two years later she was writing three long letters to Ursula in England, describing her trip to Satipo in the depths of the jungle. It was material that she was later to use in her book, which ended up being written in German. The text was subsequently translated into English, most improbably by a local priest whose native language was Spanish. Whereas her first journeys had been conducted in chauffeur-driven cars (such as the Packard in which she first explored the mountains), by this time she was well used to travelling in considerable discomfort by truck. And gone was the hesitant, self-effacing woman whose only point of contact was through yearned-for invitations, which never arrived from her 'family'. She was now perfectly capable of commandeering all the necessary transport and determining herself how to travel to her desired destinations.

Eva now had no close family left with whom she could communicate regularly. Both parents had died, and six of the seven siblings were scattered over the world. Out of duty to his aged parents, Erich had come home from France in order to look after them at the Hotel Eden. This put his own life in considerable danger, as the after-effects of his childhood automobile accident had left him physically and mentally frail. After the traumatic deaths of his parents he was immediately labelled 'disabled' by the local Gestapo, and was incarcerated for eighteen months in a mental institution. From there his life was saved in a quite extraordinary fashion, by a man whose story was somewhat akin to that of Schindler's in the Sudentenland. A well-respected colonist was returning to the Reich from German South-West Africa, and in exchange for his specialist 'services rendered' to the Nazi regime, he insisted on being allowed to grant ten inmates of this particularly notorious 'mad' hospital visas to neutral Sweden. By this time Bernadotte was allowing Jewish refugees into his country, and in 1944 Erich did indeed end up in Sweden. Meanwhile his youngest brother Peter had managed to escape to Sussex in England. Ruth was in London with her sculptor husband Uli Nimptsch, together with their son Peter. And thanks to the valiant efforts of his fiancée Barbara, Werner had been granted a visa to leave Germany and was now living north of London in Chalfont St Peters. All three men had been interned for several months on the Isle of Man. Married by this time to Barbara, Werner shared his house with her sister Plinter, where they kept chickens and dug potatoes 'for victory'.

Eduard's boys had been sent to school in Switzerland, from where they went to England with their mother and where Michael was to take up British citizenship by joining the army on his eighteenth birthday. His younger brother Frank ended up in Canada. Meanwhile, by staying in Paris their father Eduard sealed his own fate.

He had met an unmarried French girl called Marie Bonneville, who had been ostracised by her Jewish family because of her 'loose morals' that had produced a son who would never know his father. Touched by their plight, Eduard offered to marry Marie and adopt her 11-year-old son Claude. This generous gesture was to be his downfall. It was 1942 and the Gestapo were everywhere in the occupied city. Faced with a 'Sophie's choice' when questioned by the forbidding, black-uniformed officers, Marie was compelled to save her child by betraying her new husband. He was captured on the train on his way out of the city and taken immediately to the infamous camp at Drancy, where Klaus Barbie would carry out his hideous experiments on children. Eduard's papers would have identified him immediately as 'Jewish'. In August of that year all the detainees in the overcrowded camp were loaded onto cattle trucks bound eastwards out of France. Their destination was Auschwitz. Eduard died either on the way there, or soon after his arrival. He was the first of the seven children of Max and Fanny Steinthal to fall victim not just to Nazi persecution, but also to the Holocaust. Eva would not hear of her brother's death until years later.

Daisy had managed to escape with Gisèle via Belgium and Luxembourg to France, just eight days before the start of the war; now mother and daughter were living somewhat precariously in Nice. Her other two children had ended up in the Americas. Monica arrived in New York, where she married the first person she could find to gain American citizenship. Her choice of husband, however, was particularly unfortunate and she ended up with an actual 'axe-murderer'—or at least a man who was crazy enough to attack her with a knife from the kitchen drawer. Escaping by the skin of her teeth, Monica made her way to the other side of the United States, eventually ending in Hollywood. Using her skill with her hands, she earned her living as a dressmaker, creating costumes for the film industry. For her brother John, fate had other ideas in store. Through his acquaintances in the film industry, for whom he had been working in Italy, he managed to secure a last-minute ticket on a boat due to cross the Atlantic from Naples to Rio de Janeiro. Resigned to this change of fortune, he became a Brazilian citizen working coincidentally like his sister in the film industry.

Another member of the family was to suffer the same fate as Eduard. Tante Anna, the elderly widow of Max's older brother Leopold, had to be taken to the station by her own son. He stood helplessly on the platform, as his frail mother was loaded into the cattle trucks by the Gestapo. She died later in the ghetto that was supposed to be a holding camp, at the town of Theresienstadt otherwise known as Terezín.

By 1943 and after numerous journeys, Eva had become a very competent traveller. She knew exactly what clothing and equipment to take, and had become quite self-sufficient, especially in regard to her own medicine chest. Once she had embarked on her first travels, she was to learn by trial and error how to become a seasoned traveller in Peru. Knowing how to equip herself properly for travel became as much a part of her character as her curiosity. She found it amazing, however, once she had taken the plunge and had embarked on her first journeys beyond Lima, how naturally this travelling way of life seemed to suit her. She must have forgotten all about the letter she had written on board boat crossing the Atlantic some four years previously, in which she had stated quite unequivocally how if she were spared 'she would never go on such a long journey again'.

In sharp contrast to her first tentative forays into the Peruvian hinterland, when she had naively assumed that she would be able to buy provisions on the way, now her travel bag always included the same indispensable items. It was obvious that it would be hot in the *Selva* (jungle) and cold in the *Sierra* (mountain region). The first thing she put into her travel bag would be her hot water bottle, followed by her own personal blanket and pillow. As well as these she would include a home-made sleeping bag, concocted most simply of two sheets sewn together, leaving an open space at the top for her to crawl inside. By fastening it at the neck she would feel well protected against contact with any bed linen of doubtful cleanliness. Through experience she had learned that only the landlord of a particular inn could know whether he would be able to give Eva a *cama fria*, a fresh bed, or a *cama caliente*, one that was still warm from the previous occupier. She would also make sure to pack her own towels. The next important thing was a flashlight, because at night weird sounds would abound wherever she went: mice, *cucurachas* (bugs), guinea pigs, bats, mules—there was always a large variety of noise-creators. She found it a great comfort to be able look them squarely in the face. As batteries usually ran out after a few days in the moist rainforest it was safer to take candles and matches along as well, especially if Eva wished to avoid sharing her bed with the ubiquitous flock of chickens that inhabited most countryside inns.

For the *Sierra* a warm coat and woollen clothes were an essential factor; for the *Selva* it was loose-fitting clothing with long sleeves, in spite of the heat. Mosquitoes could take all the fun out of life, as she had discovered on several occasions to her cost. A mosquito net was therefore one of the most important pieces of equipment for the *Selva*, as well as a waterproof raincoat; in the rainforest it usually poured with rain a minimum of once a day, even in the dry season. Whether aiming for mountain or jungle, she would usually never travel anywhere without her trusty poncho, that would protect her from both rain and cold.

A few tins of food were particularly handy for possible emergencies. Whether travelling by truck or by train, there was always the chance of getting stuck. By June the danger of any landslides, so-called *huaicos*, had passed, but one solid downpour could wash an entire bridge away, or the truck itself would frequently fall victim to an array of mechanical breakdowns. An empty stomach made one feel far less stoical than a full one, not to mention the appearance of tasty provisions greatly increasing Eva's popularity in the eyes of her fellow passengers.

As a final precaution, she always had to think of including her personal brand of emergency medical kit. Eva found aspirin an efficient preventative against the dreaded *Soroche*, or mountain sickness. It was then a sensible precaution to include medicine against dysentery, such as Enterovioform. She further put her trust in iodine-based Mercurochrome for small wounds, quinine to protect against malaria and citronella in large quantities against plagues of mosquitoes. Last but not least, a good cream for face and hands was vital, because it was very easy for Eva's skin to dry out in the thin air of the high mountains and in the parching sun. Finally she would pack up some insecticide, either in liquid or powder form. Thus prepared Eva would feel that she had taken all necessary safety measures, and that she could confidently set out on her journeys.

Used as she was to wearing long skirts and blouses or dresses, she soon became accustomed to wearing some kind of baggy trousers, especially in the jungle or when visiting plantations. And as she frequently went on horse-rides on her various visits, she would also wear riding britches with high boots. A suitable hat was indispensable in all weathers.

As a final comment, it might be wondered how a single, middle-aged woman of European extraction could guarantee her safety in such an alien environment, and how she never got attacked. The native Peruvians very rarely show even a grey hair in old age, never mind white hair. In their eyes, the sight of a woman whose head was completely covered in white hair could mean only one thing: she must be very holy. During all her years of travelling in Peru, she was never assaulted or attacked in any way, which led Eva to conclude very fondly that the indigenous Peruvians were an extremely endearing people.

20

The Lake of Fairytales

Eva's trips were to become more and more adventurous. She travelled by train, by car, by truck, by canoe, by steamboat, by Catalina seaplane and sometimes even by horse or donkey or llama. She visited the length and breadth of the country, uncovering the wonders of Inca civilisation in temples and ruins from Cuzco to Machu Picchu. She experienced each of Peru's 'three worlds': the scorching dry heat of the desert coastline; some of the highest peaks in the world (as many of the biggest mountains of the Cordillera rise to over 22,000 feet or 6,800 metres above sea level); and the impenetrable greenery and sweltering temperatures of the virgin forest. Although she loved the favourably clement climate of pretty towns such as Arequipa (situated towards the southernmost border of Peru), she seemed to have a particular hankering for increasingly uncomfortable and audacious trips into the jungle. One such journey was a visit to Satipo.

The point of departure for this particular adventure was Huancayo—a small town in the *Sierra* at about 3,400 metres (over 11,000 feet) above sea level that she had already visited on many occasions. The whole journey seemed doomed from the start, however, because despite hours of fruitless searching, she was completely unable to find any truck travelling in that direction. Luckily during her train journey up to Huancayo she had struck up a conversation with a gentleman sitting opposite her, who was also going to Satipo. Despite the rather dubious reputation enjoyed by this jungle settlement because of its difficult climate, its overabundance of poisonous snakes and the harsh living conditions there, Eva had set her heart on finding out about this remote region hidden in Peru's virgin forest. She had heard several stories of the gorgeous flora to be found so far from any modern development.

Eager to impress this unusual, white-haired lady, her travelling companion in the train had immediately started giving her all sorts of good advice about where to stay in Satipo. Best of all, he also presented her with the address of a certain Señora Rosa who was—or so he enthused—the only innkeeper in that locality to provide edible food and reasonably clean beds.

After two days of frustrating waiting about in the little town of Concepción, a truck finally turned up at four o'clock in the morning. The crew had promised faithfully they would call for her soon after midnight, at one sharp, so this was very punctual by Peruvian standards. An inexplicable feeling of happiness would fill her heart now, every time she set out for some hitherto unfamiliar part of Peru. The Southern Cross was glittering in the night sky as they set off through the undulating landscape. Like an archangel's halo, the white splendour of the moon shimmered above the summits of the mountains. Only a few moments later they were plunging deep into the Cordillera, and were driving steadily upwards in tight and winding curves towards the mountain passes.

Morning was breaking as they came to a halt in Comas, a small but very picturesque village, where the truck unloaded some household goods destined for a policeman and his wife. These seemed to consist mainly of an assortment of petrol cans and sundry boxes, but also somewhat incongruously a white kitten. In a diminutive tavern Eva enjoyed some deliciously strong coffee, sweetened with the customary *chancra* (brown sugar), even though it had been served in a particularly dirty cup. With her stomach well satisfied, she then took a stroll towards the little church—the main centre of attraction of any town in Peru. As she pushed open the creaky wooden door, she encountered a statue of Santa Rosa smiling down at her with a most loveable sweet face. She was wearing a striking black velvet dress, hand-embroidered with golden flowers—and she appeared to be amused. Eva soon found out why: the sacristan was snoring in the vestry, loudly enough to make the whole church shake. Santa Rosa and Eva understood each other perfectly with a single glance. As Eva stepped into the village square again, she said goodbye to the saint, smiling at her as if she were a real person.

From Comas they drove on and on towards the mountain passes; hundreds of metres, perhaps thousands below them, sheer precipices plummeted vertiginously off the edge of the road. They were so deep that they disappeared into blue haziness, obliterating any view of the valley floor below. Their truck, which had been laden with sugar and salt and beer to sell in the jungle, made the small and lightly built wooden bridges that spanned the abyss groan alarmingly under its weight. The ability of these apparently fragile bridges to withstand such heavy freight had only one possible explanation that Eva could see: God really had to be a Peruvian. It grew very cold as they approached the summits and Eva sat huddled in the cab of the shuddering truck, shivering in spite of her woolly jumper, windproof jacket, waterproof coat and heavy poncho.

Any sign of human habitation was very scarce in these mountain regions; here and there they could see a simple grass-hut, its roof consisting solely of the coarse mountain grass called *ichu* that fell all the way down to the ground like long yellow beards. These huts looked as if it had not been human beings who had erected them, but as if Nature herself had fashioned them out of the ground, in exactly the same way as the moss-bedecked stones and the hard, unyielding clods of turf. But once the truck had surmounted the pass flanked by high mountain lagoons, thorny weeds began to climb amongst the massive jumble of rocks and stones. Soon vegetation was covering every inch of the ground. Light green shrubs with spines as soft as larch needles reached ever upwards, reaching into crevices to keep themselves upright. Grasping at the rocks to give them a hold, the bushes spread out in luxuriant clusters. In the chaotic yet almost monochromatic greyness, a single orange-coloured bush would blaze out as suddenly as a tongue of fire, its branches drooping with blooms of wild laburnum; then two or three of them would flare up together. Rows of lilac lupins stood to attention along the edge of the road—and all at once they had reached the ocean of trees.

Gnarled little bushes and stunted thorny trees, all entangled by lichen, stood asphyxiated amidst the dense green carpet. The blue depth was no longer blue—the abyss was now filled with a palette of vibrant greenness in which not a single stone remained bare. Green vegetation clothed every rock and pebble with an opulently verdant pillowcase. The gully swallowed up the road for mile after mile. It was as if they were driving directly into the bowels of the earth; the atmospheric pressure became so intense that their ears turned completely deaf. One after another coats and wrappings were discarded ... shawl, gloves, poncho.

Red fuchsias, yellow snapdragons and pink begonias sprang up amidst the tangled, dripping wet undergrowth. Intertwining webs of silver threads hung in festoons from the trees—air-roots—while waterfalls tore jagged white lines into the green hillsides. Eva watched a single little black butterfly fluttering about, and then a second one which was soon joined by bright yellow and red ones. Eventually the appearance of wonderfully large, flamboyant, metallic-blue butterflies heralded their arrival into the virgin forest once more. And the road carved its way forwards, as dramatically as if it had been sliced through the impenetrable wall of endless green vegetation with a machete.

By now they had left all signs of civilisation far behind. This fact was brutally brought home to Eva by the inn where they stopped for a bite to eat: the food was abominable but the mosquitoes were worse. During their long drive along the steep hillsides of the Cordillera, they had stopped at every tiny hamlet, and in every *choza* (hut); here they sold a sack of sugar, there a crate of *chicha* (corn beer). Every deal was sealed by the obligatory *copita*, the little glass of sugar-brandy distilled in many small haciendas. They had spent all afternoon on these protracted but essential business transactions, and so it was completely dark by the time they reached Satipo.

'Here we are,' announced the driver with a self-satisfied smirk. But Eva could not see anything that came close to resembling a village. Just a few small dots of light—that was all. She clambered wearily out of the lorry, and with her bag clutched in her hands she walked towards the lights. As soon as she approached them, however, they dissolved into nothingness. The 'lights' turned out to be nothing more than glow-worms that she had mistaken for candles or lanterns placed in windows. But the houses did indeed exist in spite of it all—only that their occupants were sitting inside them either without any light on at all, or with candles that proved to emit far less light than the *luciérnagas*. At last, by asking her way from house to house she stumbled through the dark into what was Señora Rosa's 'hotel'.

A big fat woman came out to greet her with the greatest enthusiasm, her rotund face illuminated by a lantern. In her tired state, Eva found it almost impossible not to stare at the incongruous pink ribbon that adorned her closely cropped hair. While her voluminous bosom fell to below her waist, her belly was so ample that it made her look as if she were pregnant—which was quite improbable at her age. The most surprising thing about her, however, was her mouth: it was the widest and most lascivious mouth that Eva had ever seen. And she had painted her lips, moreover, in the brightest red imaginable.

'Goodness,' thought Eva to herself, 'I've apparently ended up in some kind of bawdy house.' But as spending the night out in the street was out of the question, she followed the Señora into the straw-roofed hut and into what was to be her bedroom. As usual the first thing Eva did was to sort out her mosquito net. It was so pitch-black that she could hardly see what her hands were doing—which turned out to be a blessing in disguise. Once her eyes had got used to the dark, what struck her first was a dim and hazy impression of frightful disorder. There were objects lying all over the place, which turned out to be soiled clothes mostly. Empty petrol cans were dangling precariously from pegs nailed into the planks that made up the walls. A jumble of old shoes and bottles, together with piles of unidentified filth, was heaped all over the floor.

As her eyes became accustomed to the gloom, she could see that her room was part of a kind of shed constructed of thin planks, through which both air and mosquitoes could enter with equal ease. The floor was made up of the same wooden slats with gaping holes between them, while the ceiling was composed of a simple sheet of corrugated iron—leaving a large space between the walls and the roof. As if this was all quite normal, the Señora bustled busily about, cheerfully bringing fresh 'linen' for Eva's bed. As far as she was concerned, that was all that mattered.

Eva took her supper in the dining room of the 'hotel' in the company of the three other residents, all of whom were men. But she was happy to recognise her companion from the train, Señor Ponce. With her eyes drooping, she plodded her way back to her little bungalow with a candle and tried to go to bed. This very simple objective was somewhat hampered by a sudden rustling sound. As she gingerly investigated where it was coming from, shining her candle into the corners of the room, she found to her disgust that all the cracks in the wooden walls were teeming with *cucarachas*—huge brown cockroaches. Even worse than that was the alarming discovery of an entire nest of stinging spiders. Quick as a flash Eva dived under her mosquito net, drawing it as tightly as possible around her bed and tucking it into every inch of the mattress.

No sooner had she blown out her candle than a cacophony of eerie sounds seemed to erupt from everywhere at once. She could sense things flying across the room, with the breeze of their flight-path blowing right across her face in small puffs. She did not take long to work out that these must be bats, and by the amount of air they were stirring up she knew at once that they had to be the more sizeable variety—vampire bats. She had heard all sorts of stories of how these beasts would happily suck the blood from your fingers, your feet or even your nose if you gave them the slightest chance. But this was a brand-new mosquito net and by this time she was exhausted. The hissing of the vampires and the high-pitched squeaks of smaller bats were not the only sounds in her room. Right outside her window came the unearthly shriek of an owl. All around her she could sense the rustling of the walls, while dull thuds resounded on the roof above her head. There must have been giant moths bumping their heads continuously against the corrugated iron.

For a while Eva lay rigidly in her bed, her eyes wide with fright. But then she came to the sudden realisation that she had nobody to thank but herself for getting into this seemingly precarious situation in the first place. Stopping her ears up with Oropax, she tried once again to go to sleep. Suddenly the door of her bungalow was flung open, and in came one of her dinner companions.

'*Perdone*, Señora, but aren't you feeling very lonely?' he asked.

Now she knew that the mouth of Señora Rosa had not been lying to her. Eyes or hands may tell lies, she thought to herself, but a mouth will always tell the truth. She sent the man flying, and lay awake for a long time, armed with nothing but the security of her mosquito net and her electric torch, which was the only 'weapon' she possessed. With her heart pounding, the cacophonous assortment of noises all conspired to keep her awake: the acute drilling of the cicadas, the shrill and continuous chirp of the scythe-beetle, the hoot of one of the large owls—which, as she was later to learn, will kill and devour cats. Finally something came plodding towards her door. She could hear approaching footsteps and a loud thump—and then to her enormous relief the mule that had been trying to get to her gave an enormous bray. Feeling that it was utterly ridiculous to keep on being terrified, she finally fell into a deep and dreamless sleep, waking in a surprisingly good mood the next morning.

In complete contrast to the steamy jungle was Eva's trip to Titicaca, the world's highest lake that straddles the Peruvian and Bolivian borders. She would later write vividly about her experiences in her journal. After some time spent on the high plateau of Cuzco, exploring all aspects of its fascinating Inca history, she had been determined to take a trip to the fabled lake. Her friends, as usual, were aghast that she should even think of undertaking such a long journey on her own. And true to form, her mind was made up and she was adamant. With many well-meaning pieces of advice ringing in her ears, all warning her of the perils inherent in such a lengthy trek, she booked herself a ticket on the train leaving Cuzco the very next morning.

She would soon recall these warnings. After hours of uncomfortable jolting, Eva herself was beginning to wonder if she had been crazy to embark on the perilous journey from Cuzco. From the time when the train had left the junction of Juliaca, more than eight hours into the journey, she had been gazing out of the window into the austere landscape of the *altiplano*. She knew that this was the point where the tracks divided. One branch ran back towards the valley of Cuzco, while the other one led to Puno and her final destination: Lake Titicaca. There was hardly any vegetation growing on the bleak slopes of the mountains, nothing but sparse tufts of yellow grass, bending beneath the wind's whip. Not a single path could be seen anywhere. Hundreds of years of the bare or sandalled feet of the *Indios* who inhabited these bleak heights had left not a single mark on the hard soil of the *puna*.

As the long and crowded train clattered and shuddered along its tracks, its plume of smoke catching in the clear air, she caught her first glimpse of the world's highest navigable lake. Or so it was in the popular imagination: other Andean lakes were higher, but Lake Titicaca is at over one hundred miles long the largest lake above 7,000 feet in the whole of South America. It was a sobering thought. The air was so thin and icy at this height of some 12,500 feet above sea level that the landscape appeared to frown. Iridescent waters lapped endlessly against the austere and sallow shoreline. Towards the darkening smudge of the horizon, the mountains of the Cordillera Real rose barren and pitiless, granting in the far distance but a cold glint from their summits of everlasting snow. The highest peaks just across the border in Bolivia exceeded 20,000 feet, or so Eva had read in her guidebook.

An icy gust blew in from the region of eternal snow and Eva wrapped herself up in her warm coat, feeling chilled to the marrow in the thin air of this altitude. While shadows gathered in the crevices and clefts of the hills, a profound solitude surrounded the train, and the atmosphere grew almost uncomfortable. She shivered again, causing a few amused glances from her fellow passengers who were far more used to the rigorous conditions. As Eva watched the unending mountain ranges, flanked by rocks that had tumbled down millions of years ago, the *puna* grew ever darker. Gradually the entire landscape was blacked out by a completely moonless night.

It was late in the evening when the train finally pulled into Puno. Mindful of the instructions she had been given in Cuzco, Eva walked across the pitch-black street and stumbled into Puno's Hotel Ferrocarril, a drab-looking and depressing building.

Forgetting her grumbling stomach, her first thought was for any unwelcome beasts in her bed. And she fussed around with her bedding, spreading sheets of newspaper on the mattress, spraying it all thoroughly with insecticide and finally crawling into her own home-made sleeping bag.

That night, on her hard bed and carefully wrapped up in her sheets, Eva dreamed of the mysteries of Lake Titicaca. Images of ancient temples, peopled by mysterious and shadowy figures, swam before her eyes, and then vanished in waves of fog and snow. Just as the answer was about to be revealed to her, explaining the legend of the birth of the Inca civilisation—rumoured to have begun on the Island of the Sun at the very heart of the huge lake—she woke up. As it turned out she managed to get away from her hotel in Puno completely lice-less. She was much encouraged that she had thus escaped at least one of the horrors about which her friends back in Lima were constantly warning her.

The morning sun was a burnished gold in the limpid blue sky. With a good deal of arguing on Eva's part and after considerably skilful and patient negotiations, she finally found a car for hire. Her driver was a saturnine fellow with the typical nut-brown skin and rather squat features of the people of the region. After some discussion about the route, they finally set out for a drive along the shores of Lake Titicaca. Eva was still clutching her guidebook, together with her precious journal.

It was noon by the time they reached Ilave. As the village possessed only one inn, the driver shoved his way towards it in a determined manner, through the good-natured crowds of locals. Leading her to the only available empty table, he invited Eva to sit down. Groups of chattering *Indios* pushed their way past her, eager to display their beautifully colourful, woven blankets and ponchos. Sunday was market day in Ilave, with the whole population turning out in the riotous colours of their Sunday best, according to ancient and time-honoured tradition. But on weekdays, said the guidebook, it was a very quiet spot.

After a simple meal that nevertheless provided a welcome break, they drove on. At this point it was possible to see how heavily populated the countryside was, with all these villages scattered along the edge of the lake. Time and again they came across large groups of *Indios* driving their flocks of laden llamas along the dusty roads. Crowds of Quechua and Aymara women came trotting along the rocky paths, their babies swaddled on their backs. Families were squatting on the stony beach in the acrid smoke of small fires, made up of dung known as *bosta*. They ate their meal or rested and quietly chewed their coca. Seemingly endless lines of long-suffering donkeys could be seen carrying burdens to and fro, between the towns and villages that lay in an uninterrupted chain all along the shore.

It was October and the farmlands had been tilled and sowed, but the earth was still brown and completely barren. Although by now the sun was burning down, the air was as cold as ice. Reflecting the sky like a gigantic mirror, the massive expanse of water sparkled in a shade of blue as vivid as a sheet of cornflowers. At the town of Yunguyo they had finally reached the frontier between Peru and Bolivia. Here Eva was granted official permission with a special visa that allowed her to spend a day over the border in Bolivia. Soon she was jolting along an extremely bad road peppered with potholes, following the curves of the lake. The sun was setting magnificently as her car trundled into the streets of Copacabana on the Bolivian side of Titicaca. It had taken an entire day to get less than a quarter of the way round the lake.

Eva had expected to overnight in an inn as simple as the one in Ilave. She could hardly believe her eyes therefore when she caught sight of a well-appointed and inviting hotel, situated on the banks of the lake. Casting caution to the winds, she decided to spend her hard-earned cash on a night in comfortable surroundings. A little while later she was gazing spellbound out of her room, as the sun bade a dramatic farewell to a resplendent world, sparkling in a blaze of colours. Allowing her no time to recover from her surprise at finding a hotel equipped to the highest and most modern of standards, the proprietor himself—a silver-haired, rather portly gentleman—knocked at her door. Carrying a pot of steaming coffee in one hand and a plate of little biscuits in the other, he coughed politely and shuffled his feet.

Setting down the coffee and biscuits on the small table, he said shyly, 'I couldn't help noticing, Señora, that your name is Vollmann.' Eva nodded vaguely. His gutteral accent was at once familiar, but somehow it did not register with her. 'Could it be that you're from the same family who come from Dresden?' he continued. Unable to believe her ears, Eva found herself talking in German to a man who had emigrated to Bolivia just before the start of the war, but for whom the name Vollmann was still very familiar. She simply could not believe this extraordinarily fortunate card dealt by fate.

It was long after the sun had gone down, and increasing darkness was invading this remote corner of the world, making any sort of writing almost impossible. Just then the bells clanged, and all at once Eva was drawn to Vespers. There was no electric light in Copacabana; in fact no light at all. When night fell, the local people usually took themselves to bed. In the hotel, as Eva had done, everyone used candles. The village was swathed in utter blackness as she stepped out of the front door of the hotel. Only the waters of lake were irradiating the faintest shimmer, while the Cordillera stood massive and coal-black behind the little houses.

Through the hushed darkness she made her way to the cathedral. She had remembered reading that thousands of pilgrims flock throughout the year to pay homage to the miraculous Virgin of this famous little church. What Eva could just make out of the building made her realise that its exterior could in no way be called attractive. Once inside, however, she appreciated the beauty of the nave that was bathed in the light of hundreds of tapers burning in front of ancient, ornate altars. As she sat herself down in an old and delicately carved pew, a group of eight bare-footed *Indios* entered the church and knelt down in the pew opposite her. Despite the dim light, Eva could see that they were all wearing vermilion ponchos. Placing their large conical hats on the ground, they folded their hands in prayer.

Filled with rapture, their intense and staring eyes set deep into bronze faces glowed in the flickering candlelight. Eva thought they must be the impersonation of some Old Master's saints, or the Wise Men of the East come to life. Then one of them glanced over in her direction, and gasped in surprise. Whispering to his companions, he muttered and pointed towards her. Soon all eight of them were gazing at her in wonder. It was a reaction that she had often met on her travels, because of her unusual white hair.

Some time later, Eva emerged blinking from the cathedral. As she gazed overhead, the sky was a dream vision. Or rather, there was no sky; it was an ocean of stars. The entire firmament scintillated and sparkled, while the whole Milky Way seemed to have flooded the deep indigo-blue vault of heaven.

When she awoke the next morning, Eva could hardly believe that it had not just been a dream. She had to pinch herself to believe she really was in this legendary country. Opening the window of her first-floor room to greet the morning air, she watched the dancing sunbeams that rippled across the surface of the lake. With a sigh, she was just about to turn back into her room when she noticed a white motor-launch moored on the beach not far from the hotel. If only she could have a ride to the islands … but then she noticed a mechanic working down on the shore, tinkering with the boat's engine. Perhaps she could ask him to take her out into the lake.

Casting all thoughts of breakfast aside, she ran downstairs, leaving all her precious belongings in the room. Eva walked a little hesitantly along the beach towards the boat, but before she could hail him the mechanic straightened up and turned in her direction. With his hand brushing his flaxen hair, he suddenly rushed towards her, breathless with excitement.

'Madame,' he exclaimed, 'how are you? Don't you know me, Madame?'

Eva stared at the blond-headed mechanic, as he wiped his oily hands on a rag.

'Madame, it's Hans, don't you recognise me?'

'Hans?' she murmured in a daze, and then gasped in recognition. The young man standing in front of her was none other than the local mechanic they had used in Wachwitz, who regularly used to service Richard's Rover car. Without hesitation he offered to take her across the lake to the fabled *Isla del Sol* and *Isla de la Luna* (Islands of the Sun and the Moon). There she spent such a wonderful day, ensconced amidst the ancient temples of sacred legend, that she was reluctant to leave.

Late in the afternoon, on their way back across the water to Copacabana, a violent wind sprang up. Without warning, a vicious hailstorm followed by lashing rain drenched them to the bone. The motorboat pitched and tossed in the heavy swell, and it took them more than four hours to get back to the town. It was only through the skilful handling of his vessel that Hans succeeded in bringing them back to the safety of the shore. Eva had no time to think about this exciting part of her journey, or even to dry herself off, because she had find her driver and set out immediately on their return to Puno. During the long and jolting drive back along the lake, a host of fleeting impressions filled her mind. The starry sky of Copacabana; the silent, red-clad *Indios* of the cathedral; the unexpected encounter with her former native countrymen; the remote grandeur of the sacred islands—all this merged into the strangest sensation. She felt as if she had been acting out a part in a charming but imaginary fairy-tale.

Another trip, starting again in the Titicaca region, took Eva southwards from Puno to Tacna—ostensibly in search of ostriches. This time, when she tried to hitch a lift with a truck she was faced with a bewildering variety of utterly unsuitable vehicles, each one given a more exaggerated name than the last. There was the sky-blue *Papacito Dulce* (Sweet Little Butterfly) and the *Ayudame a Vivir* (Help Me to Live) painted in bright yellow. The *Paciencia Hermano* (Patience Brother!) had sundry parts of his battered body tied up with tattered bits of string and llama-ropes. For quite some time Eva stood watching the *Señor de Gran Poder* (Lord of Great Power) until the driver and his assistant—without whom no Peruvian truck-driver would dream of travelling—relinquished their laborious efforts of trying to start the engine. The *No Me Apures* (Don't Rush Me) spent hours having its tyres mended; *El Terror de la Pista* (the Terror of the Roads) and *El Guapo del Pueblo* (the Beau of the Village), both of them dilapidated and neglected, bore not the slightest indication of either speed or beauty. Finally with his radiator boiling, his entire motor rattling and wheezing, and with an ear-shattering screeching of his brakes, the *Llegó mi Amor* (Here Comes My Love) turned the corner, to find a place among his fellow veterans. None of these alluring trucks would drive to Tacna, however, and Eva had to be content with a very humble Ford by the name of *Postillón*, which was loading coca. Due to their insubstantial weight, the sacks of leaves had to be piled sky-high. This naturally took an inordinately long time, but even so the men promised to leave at the first sign of dawn, early next morning.

It was the truck-driver himself who turned up in person at Eva's inn and shook her awake at five. Much impressed by this zeal she was ready to leave in no time. But then after the advent of this human alarm clock, nothing whatever happened. When she finally took matters into her own hands and went to find out what was happening, she found her *patrullero* completely deserted and half-loaded, just as she had left it the day before. Undaunted, she then hunted up the driver who she finally discovered having a lively time with a party of friends. In her most pleading voice, she begged him to get going, emphasising her words with a generous tip. He promised to start in a moment, but the 'moment' lasted until noon.

After endless coaxing and cajoling from Eva they did finally get on their way. Yet just a few miles out of Puno, the men declared that they were dying of thirst. It was well past three by the time they pushed on. Just beyond Ilave, the highway ceased to be anything resembling a road and turned into a rough track. In its top-heavy state the lorry pitched and stumbled alarmingly, lurching through potholes filled with water from the latest downpour. Once they had passed by a few haciendas surrounded by great flocks of sheep, from then on the vast and empty vista of the *pampa* stretched out endlessly all around them.

They drove on for hours, and by the time they had reached those heights where vicuñas might browse without fear of humans, night was quickly closing in. Soon they were in total darkness. All Eva's hopes of ever seeing vicuñas and ostriches in the wild were instantly dashed. She felt helpless with indignation. The road now began to writhe in endless zigzags up the steep Cordillera. Shining down on them was the narrow, reddish crescent of the gibbous moon, while blasts of raw wind churned up the dust and sand to such an extent that for miles they seemed to be driving through a thick and swirling fog. Hour after hour went by until finally Señor Fulano, the owner of the freight of coca leaves, proposed that they stop at the next inn and take a short rest.

As soon as the solitary tavern came in sight, they all jumped off the truck. In the pitch-black night they staggered and groped their way to the small hut. The familiar light of a stable lantern illuminated the window, and revealed the presence of several men, seated in the smoke-filled room, who were apparently reaching the climax of some lengthy carousal. Scarcely had they caught a glimpse of the unfamiliar but very female form of Eva standing in the doorway when they rushed up to her, offering her glasses of wine and requesting that she toast this delightful and unexpected encounter. Of course it was something quite out of the ordinary that a lady should stumble into their tavern at that hour of the night. Nevertheless, Eva was not particularly happy about their ministrations.

The driver stood gazing at the rough company of men crowding round Eva for no longer than a few moments. Then he grabbed the glass the men had pressed upon her, dashed its contents to the ground, and muttered, 'Come along, Señora, this is no place for you.' And without waiting for his hot meal or even a well-deserved glass of beer, he escorted her out of the room. His mates all got up without so much as a single murmur, and they all scrambled back into the van, as hungry and thirsty as before, to start out once again on their drive into the

Cordillera night.

Eva was so impressed by this amazingly chivalrous attitude that she completely forgave them her disappointment at the lack of vicuñas and ostriches. They were now driving *en plena sierra*, in the utter desolation of the lonely mountains, through impenetrable darkness. Some time later they stopped in the midst of a wide plateau, where a miserable light promised another hut. Even though it was hardly possible to keep one's eyes open in the whirling gale, they all pushed forward up to the *choza*. Hidden behind a sturdy wall, on a charcoal fire screened from the wind, a delicious smelling *chupe* was bubbling in a thick iron pot. They all sat down close to the particularly welcome and warming blaze of the fire, and eagerly waited their turn for the rich soup made of fish, rice, maize, milk and eggs.

In the lacerated, rugged range of the Andes the truck embodied a little world of its own. It was late and they were tired, but to give way to drowsiness would have been extremely dangerous, as the driver could have fallen asleep. One of the men hummed a Spanish love-song and the others joined in. Eva contributed her share by singing a few German folk songs to the men. In the rattling and jolting van she suddenly felt a poignant sensation. How strange it was to find herself so infinitely far from everything that had previously been her life. There was nothing more to connect her with the past, than the thread of these familiar melodies ringing through the cab of a truck from Puno in a remote region of South America.

After a night spent in an inn at a place called Tarata, where Eva had been too tired to undress, they were back on the road well before sunrise. The little town was still fast asleep; only the truck-drivers were active, those who had to service their lorries for another long day's drive. The surface of the highway grew increasingly bad as soon as they had left the town, but the scenery in the valley was magnificent. Tall, smoke-blue mountains flanked the truck on either side, their steep slopes fusing with the hazy sky, their peaks tinged with crimson in the first light of dawn. Sizeable herds of horses or cows wandered towards their pastures across shady green meadows. Sheep gambolled about or lapped the waters of cool, clear mountain streams. Soon the road ascended steeply again, and its surface grew not only worse than ever but also extremely exposed. Eva was told that a new road was now under construction, but that was little comfort. The cumbersome truck, top-heavy with its bulky cargo, now had to negotiate acute-angled bends so steep that they had to back up every time.

More often than not Eva felt an uneasy sensation in the pit of her stomach, especially when one wheel was dangling in sheer air above the yawning precipice. It was one of those rare moments when she came into conflict with her particular guardian angel, who had sent her driving along the roads of Peru at giddy heights in a battered truck, shivering with cold and on an empty stomach. Distrustfully she watched every inch that separated its tyres from the abyss, while trying desperately to put her confidence in the perspiring and cursing *cholo*. Cigarette in mouth, he heaved the truck impatiently round each curve with a muttered 'Let's see if we can make it!' And it seemed inevitable that at the narrowest and most perilous section of the road, a caravan of *Indios* with their heavily laden donkeys was bound to come trudging along. The resulting chaos was such that Eva dared not breathe, until the last of the beasts had safely passed the truck along the precariously narrow ledge that was keeping them all, man and beast, out of eternity.

Eventually the steep pitch of the nerve-wracking mountain road levelled out, as they neared the coastal desert. A dense sea fog was drifting up towards them from the shoreline. At their feet lay the pretty town of Tacna, a green and inviting oasis in the midst of this particularly dreary, dusty strip of unrelentingly arid desert. And there to greet Eva in the far distance was the infinite, azure-blue line of the Pacific Ocean.

21

In Search of the Amazon

Once Eva had passed her fiftieth birthday, she had been living in Peru for three years. Now a fully-fledged Peruvian citizen, she seemed to have abandoned all thoughts of visas and returning home, and was becoming an inveterate traveller. On the other side of the world, however, the war was taking its toll.

Ursula was working more or less as a Land Girl, living on a farm run by a woman called Brenda, where her job was to chase the chickens in the morning, retrieve eggs from the henhouse, clean out the stables and help with any 'digging for victory'. She had been taught to drive and would act as chauffeur for the owners. She was also responsible for lighting the wood fire in the sitting room, and in the evenings they would assemble round the crackling wireless to listen to the speeches of Mr Churchill. It was a hard but relatively safe life, and photographs taken at the time show her dressed in dungarees and looking like any other wartime English Land Army girl surviving in the country. She was at least able to supplement the dismal fare provided by ration cards with farm food, although at one stage she was to complain vociferously of being forced to eat crow pie, which she found absolutely disgusting. Likc most of the population, she became very slim from all the hard work and rationing. It was her very slight figure, however, that was to attract the attention of a Canadian officer whose army camp had been established nearby. He was tall and dashingly handsome in his greatcoat. Given the unpredictable nature of life during the war, it was scarcely surprising that John and Ursula ultimately engaged in a passionate love affair that would end her marriage.

In Germany, there was more tragic news. After months of fighting on the Russian front, the Vollmann boys were on the long march back through terrible winter conditions after the Siege of Leningrad. With appalling casualties suffered on both sides, Hitler's army—often vaunted by the Nazi High Command as invincible—had been decisively defeated by the Russians. Nevertheless, for the Germans this forced march would always be known as *'der gloriöse Rückkehr'* ('the glorious return journey'). Perhaps weakened by the unrelentingly cruel, sub-zero conditions, both Ulli (Lene's only son) and his cousin Dieter (one of Walter's two sons) were to die on the long trek homewards. Some months later their grandmother Johanna Vollmann, Eva's former mother-in-law, would die of a broken heart. Meanwhile, after Erich had escaped to Sweden, the nightly Allied bombing raids on German cities were to wreak terrible havoc. Amongst the shattered buildings of Berlin stood the Steinthal villa on the Uhlandstrasse. All that remained was a burnt-out shell.

In the mid 1940s, Eva was undertaking more and more adventurous journeys. News of the progress of the war would take months to reach her. The spoilt and much-indulged daughter of one of Germany's richest banking families; whose father had hired entire train carriages just for his family; who was used to travelling in the greatest luxury; whose erstwhile husband had been a seasoned and well-travelled gourmet; and whose every whim was catered for by a bevy of servants—this same woman had now reached a point in her life where all she cared for was learning more and more about the fascinating country of Peru in all its diversity. And the reluctant refugee, who for months had seemed frightened to stand up to her unsympathetic relatives, was now confident enough to commandeer the most rickety of trucks with the roughest of men, and frequently survive on a simple diet of rice and beans. One of her most enterprising journeys was a trip lasting several weeks in search of the mighty Amazon. Her inspiration for even considering such a trip was the opening of the great Pan-American Highway.

The new road linking the Pacific and Atlantic coasts, opened by the president of Peru in 1943, was a miracle of engineering. It crossed high mountain passes at 14,000 feet; rode along the 'roof of the world' of this part of the Andes; tunnelled through rocks; passed through dense vegetation and jungle and foaming torrents; and finally traversed swamps that had swallowed up entire trucks and where the hapless engineers had taken a full four months to construct just nine miles of road. One of its most dramatic features was in the *Cañon del Padre Abad*,* where a bridge was suspended precariously more than a hundred metres above the torrents of the river Yuracyacu, and where high mountains soared up each side of the wild and unruly waters.

Having followed the account in the newspapers of the president's first ride along the new road (taken of course in the comfort of a large limousine), which made it sound a relatively simple journey, Eva set off

* The name Padre Abad means 'Father Abbot'.

in high spirits in a lorry called 'the Triumpher'. It was to take a full two days, however, to reach her first stop in Huánuco, after dozens of delays spent mending the groaning engine. Exhausted from this first part of the journey, her flagging spirits were revived by a visit to her erstwhile Spanish language teacher Celia.

She was living in a tiny cottage far from all the usual hustle and bustle of everyday life. All day long, however, bare-footed *Indios* would plod silently past her simple home, along the merrily bubbling *acequia*, driving their *burros* to market. Washerwomen crouched on the banks amongst the reeds washing their linen. Barelegged children came to fetch water from this ditch, which was also the only washbasin for the entire neighbourhood.

The rooms in Celia's house consisted of whitewashed adobe walls framing beaten earth, their only function being to screen the inhabitants inside from any prying eyes outside. There was no furniture whatever to attract a city-dweller's attention. The room flaunting the title of *sala* (sitting room) was however, in the eyes of its owner, quite adequately furnished with a table and chair, six pigeons, eight chickens and a nest of young birds. Meanwhile an assortment of mongrel dogs and guinea pigs had settled themselves in perfectly harmonious companionship throughout the sleeping quarters. Eva was even happy to see guinea pigs running about a house, as she was quite aware that the traditional Peruvian dish of roast guinea pig was considered a delicacy in the 'big cities'.

Celia's white pony Pedro was treated like a 'spoilt child', as he possessed a stable all of his very own. He was an affectionate animal, and did not care to be excluded from any social activities in the household. While the two women sat in the *sala* he would come in through the front door, rest his head on Celia's shoulder and listen attentively with grave and soulful eyes to their conversation. More than once Eva felt the impulse to apologise for not offering Pedro a chair. Animals were an essential part of this little world, she soon came to realise—personalities in their own right, just as important as humans.

Red coffee berries were ripening in the garden, while fruit trees stood stooped and bowed beneath the weight of oranges and guavas. In a cornfield rustling like starched petticoats, little parrots twittered and wild doves cooed. Celia, Eva's former teacher in Lima, had found a haven of peace in this hermit's existence. The obstacles she had encountered in her personal life had done nothing to break her wings, but rather had merely clipped them. Eva found her friend transformed into a well-balanced, self-possessed figure, quite content with her lot in life and without the slightest ambition for material things.

'What a pity I can't send my newspaper article back to Lima with you,' she remarked thoughtfully one evening. Eva was aware of her friend's financial problems, for the lean wages of a schoolteacher in this remote province scarcely sufficed even for her simple wants.

'Why, haven't you finished it yet?' Eva asked.

'I did,' Celia answered dispassionately, and without a shade of regret in her voice. 'In fact I thought the article turned out quite well. But my puppy chewed it up.'

To possess such a friend in this part of the world, where the acquisition of money was regarded as even more important than in Old Europe, was infinitely refreshing to the spirit. But Eva had to tear herself away from Celia's philosophic attitude to life. Leaving the gentle atmosphere of Huánuco behind her, she set out with renewed determination on her journey to find the Amazon.

Stopping off in Tingo Maria, a town right in the heart of the jungle, Eva was brave enough to take a canoe ride along the river to the renowned 'Cave of Owls'. After a particularly unenthusiastic encounter with 'disgusting' beetles and other creepy-crawlies, she was lucky enough on her return to find a paymaster who would be visiting the engineering camps. This rough and ready construction employee was prepared to offer her a ride in his rugged jeep as far as Pucallpa. It was to be a hair-raising, extremely uncomfortable and tortuous drive through boggy swamps and rushing rivers. They finally arrived, travel-stained and weary, in the jungle town whose name means 'red earth'.

By the time Eva had reached the centre of Pucallpa (some 850 kilometres from Lima), the only inn proved to be completely full. It had been raining consistently over the past few days, and the road was impassable except to the hardiest of jeeps. A large throng of passengers were sitting disconsolately in the fly- and mosquito-infested dining room, enjoying food of a doubtful quality—waiting. She joined them promptly in this stimulating activity. First she waited for a bedroom, which duty she performed meticulously for hours, but without any positive result. Finally in desperation she plucked up courage, walked all the way to the local hospital, and was amazed to be granted a room for the night by its affable and welcoming director.

Over the following days Eva was given ample opportunity to receive further education in the art of waiting. After her first night she succeeded in tracking down an empty cabin, constructed entirely of palm-bark. There, sitting on the edge of her rickety camp bed, she waited for the next downpour to provide her with water for washing. She waited hungrily from one meagre meal to the next, since her appetite was never satisfied. She waited for the freshness of night, and then felt so damp that she waited again for the sun. But most anxiously of all she waited for a ship to Iquitos. Every passenger who was not waiting for a truck was her fellow companion in waiting for the boat.

Days went by, until one afternoon, quite unexpectedly, there was a loud hooting from the river. A ship was approaching and everybody rushed to the landing stage. It was the steamer *Cenepa* on her way to the Blue Goose oil refinery, towing two barges filled with petrol bound for Iquitos. Almost all of these riverboats, plying the 650 miles or so between Pucallpa and Iquitos, towed barges. Eva did not stop to think twice. She hurried to the captain and clearly announced her intentions.

'You are rather brave, Señora!' he said, pulling at his thick black moustache and staring with an expression of surprise at the petite, white-headed woman in front of him.

'Do you think we shall take more than five days to Iquitos?' Eva asked boldly. She had read in books that the trip usually took three days, but using her experience she reckoned on five.

'It is the river that commands,' he answered in his deep voice, with the imperturbable calm of the sailor.

Consequently she registered in high spirits as a passenger of the *Cenepa*, and shoved a sack of oranges underneath her bed to provide drink and food. She waved a last farewell to Pucallpa; looking up towards its clean and tidy market, to the cinema where the projector usually broke down half-a-dozen times during a show, to the pretty citrus groves and to the thick, glossy foliage of the mango trees. The vast sweep of the river soon swallowed up the thatched roofs that lined the banks. And on they glided into an unending landscape of forest and water.

The captain was right: it was the river that commanded. Indeed, it decreed that they were not to travel the usual five days downstream to Iquitos, but ten. Since the Ucayali was very shallow at this time of year in July, they could only travel during the daytime, and had to lie up during the night to avoid the dangers of hidden sandbanks. Hour after hour the captain and the *practico*, the name by which the pilot of the river marine was designated, stood by the wheelhouse and sounded the depth with a plumb line.

The vessel had a small draught of only five feet but the riverbed grew alarmingly shallow from time to time, as the boat was steered across from shore to shore and a navigable track was searched for. The *Cenepa* was an 88-ton steamer belonging to the very grand-sounding *Companía Peruana de Vapores y Dique de Callao*. She had three decks and a large, towering chimneystack that billowed clouds of smoke. Her tow-barges

Morona and *Dondón* were 42 tons each. They carried freight consisting chiefly of drums of oil, but the cargo also included a motley collection of machinery, sacks of sugar, live chickens, bees and pigs, bunches of bananas and bundles of yucca and *barbasco* (a plant used as insecticide). Most importantly of all, the ship itself carried people.

These steamers sailed quite arbitrarily and to no particular schedule. At every landing stage stood crowds of hopeful passengers who had been waiting for weeks, just as Eva had waited in Pucallpa. Nobody was ever refused just because the boat might be overcrowded, and once they had clambered on board people were well used to sorting themselves out. Whoever found no bed on deck slept anywhere, on the floor, on a bench or in a hammock. These were strung from every available fixing around the ship in a profusion of brightly coloured festoons. Hammocks moreover proved extremely useful for their particular owner, as not a single chair was provided anywhere on board.

At the waning of day the deck was transformed into a field of tents, as mosquito nets were put up across every inch of planking. The two cramped and primitive washrooms in the stern could only be reached by stepping across dozens of huddled bodies. These would invariably explode—either into grumbling curses or in wailing shrieks, according to the age of the person trodden on.

Eva was among the elite and favoured passengers who were allotted one of two beds installed in each of the few tiny cabins. The searing heat and ubiquitous mosquitoes, however, made the use of such an apparent luxury quite impractical. She therefore dragged a bench towards the outer rails, spread the straw mattress from her bed upon it, and hung up her mosquito net. Every night she slept, on this unforgettably beautiful journey, in the cool breeze of the tropical night-wind. She later wrote very lyrically of her experiences in her journal.

> I would lie awake for a while, peering through the white muslin of my net into the deep and solemn velvet of the night, into a canopy bubbling with stars. In a sky stained purple, the moon slowly rose. There were nights of great silence and space, wholly tranquil. Their pervasive peace wrapped me in a mantle of content, and I felt absorbed in the delicious scent and muted murmur of night. But towards morning a dense fog screened the world, everything dripped with dew and I shivered despite the heat and nestled in my woollen poncho.
>
> I witnessed the awakening of nature, when the black vault gradually turned grey and the shiver of night passed fragrantly down the river. Hundreds of little birds flitted about in the trees,

> as the first signs of dawn crept up over the treetops and undulating wavelets reflected vermilion tints. Then the limbs of trees were silhouetted a deep black against the glowing sky, and piles of golden clouds peeped just above the horizon. The zenith turned shell pink and finally the sun rose, tearing the last milky mists to shreds. Day awoke, and life flowed back to its familiar rhythm. Sounds and bustle set in and the *Cenepa* took up her journey.

Soon the bell would be clanging throughout the ship, calling the passengers to breakfast. Three times a day they all assembled at the rear of the boat, sharing their communal meal seated in cosy proximity round a long table. With the exception of morning coffee they always ate rice, beans and boiled bananas. But during the national holidays at the end of July the celebrations were marked by opulent menus, for which a whole pig, a couple of chickens or pails of fish would be purchased in some port or other. The food was extremely good, considering the low price of 50 *soles* (about $8) for the ten-day trip.

Since the recent introduction of Peru's national air service, wealthy Peruvians were no longer using these simple and uncomfortable freighters. Eva's fellow passengers consisted of inhabitants of the region, all of them modest, hard-working and well-mannered people. There was an army captain who was returning from his leave—more or less a colleague of Eva's as like her he carried an unpublished manuscript in his pocket. Sundry salesmen were on business trips to villages on the river. Just like their counterparts in other parts of the world, they held animated discussions on the same topics that concerned them all: namely, girls and money. A few clerks and mechanics were travelling to their new posts somewhere in the depth of the virgin forest, places that no map recorded.

The members of a large and noisy family were on their way to a *chacra* (homestead) hidden in the jungle, many days' journey up some forest stream. There were entire households, each with their brood of children. Mothers were taking sick infants to hospital. A little deaf-and-dumb girl was to be handed over to an institution in Iquitos. Other children were being taken to recuperate from anaemia in their grand-parents' orange groves. A teacher with her family of five children had set out from one remote spot deep in the *Selva*, to a similar one where she had been promised a 10-*soles* increase in salary. Every one of the children on board, young or old, was suffering from the typically protruding abdomen caused by hookworm and malnutrition. All of them were fitful and sickly and the 'servants', tattered and filthy little *Chama** boys and girls of around eight or nine years of age, were kept constantly busy at all hours of the night and day, carrying wailing babies from one side of the boat to the other.

Eva was on very good terms with all these people. By now she had had her own personal experience of an old truth: it was far simpler for the less prosperous to be friendly and easy to approach, than it was for the wealthy with all their airs and graces, whose pompous civility often belied a defensive and offhand attitude.

Every so often they would stop at outposts along the river, and the passengers would swarm in all directions in search of something to buy. There was not much. Generally the locals would look with unfriendly eye upon the outsiders. Time and again they had experienced the bickering and haggling that accompanied even the most trivial of sales, depriving them of desperately needed pennies. To every query they would retort with a stolid *'No hay'* (there isn't any), although Eva could see sought-after chickens or bananas with her own eyes.

Every one of these hamlets cultivated some particular speciality: bananas or oranges here; rice, beans, yucca or barbasco there. But one feature was prevalent in all of them: dire poverty. Life here was no easier than that of the *Serranos* in the high Andes, eking out a stark existence in their freezing mountain-huts. It struck Eva forcefully just how extreme was the hardship of life in the *Selva*. Over and again, gazing at the flimsy wooden huts perched on stilts, her thoughts went back to the charming gardens near her apartment in Miraflores; to the luxurious houses of Lima; and to the silver fox-furs in the Hotel Bolívar's lobby. 'Who amongst us ever gives a thought to this remote and almost unknown populace?' she would later write in her journal. It was a rhetorical question, but none the less poignant for that.

The first urban centre they encountered on their journey was Contamaná, the capital of the province of Lower Ucayali. It was inhabited by 4,000 souls and was a sizeable settlement, with straight streets running for more than two miles along the riverbanks. Venerable old orange and lemon trees raised their leafy crowns into the diaphanous air. Overshadowing the dusty plaza were groups of magnificent ancient mango trees, perfume-laden with the heady scent of their luxuriant blossoms. It was 28 July, the most important national holiday in Peru, and everything had stopped to celebrate the Day of Independence. Eva had participated in many fiestas during her travels, but this one ranked

* A local tribe of native Amazonian Indians.

as possibly the hottest.

In temperatures so hot that the iron railings of their boat became sizzling enough to cause instant blisters on those unwary enough to touch them, all the passengers on board the steamboat got dressed up. In that heat it was almost an unbearable effort, but every one of them was eager to participate in the local 'ball'. It was indeed a very pleasant dance—all the ladies were prettily dressed in light silk dresses and they behaved in as polite and old-fashioned a manner as at any ball that Eva had attended as a girl. To the rather primitive but very enthusiastic strains of a native band, complete with guitar, mandolin and flute, they danced the dance currently popular all over the world at the time: the same kind of rumba to every tune.

Next evening, after they had moored up for the night alongside the riverbank, they were invited to another ball taking place at Dos de Mayo. This was a well-appointed yet simply constructed hacienda, open on all sides but with wire netting on the bedroom windows, which in those parts denoted a wealthy and civilised family. The passengers were met with great hospitality: little *copitas* of *pisco* (cane-liquor) were offered as well as bright-green yet refreshing lemonade. With all the farm hands joining in the dancing, it really was an attractive sight. The young girls were barelegged and without shoes, but Eva could see they were scrubbed and presentable, each wearing a light cotton dress and with their long dark tresses well combed.

Ever curious about different customs and cultures, Eva was interested to discover that several of the young men on the dance floor apparently belonged to a better class of worker. Some of them were the sons of the *haciendero*; others worked as administrators on this tropical farm. But they seemed quite content to mix with the *peones* (simple labourers), who danced about happily, as barefoot as the girls. All the young men were very well behaved; nobody got drunk or rowdy, or even amorous with the girls. Of course there was a lot of lovemaking going on behind the scenes, but Eva never noticed it on the dance-floor. This activity would take place outside in the jungle, in some secluded place under the warm, open sky. Morals were somewhat lax in these parts, principally because the women greatly outnumbered the men, who could simply take their pick of the girls. Eva thought them particularly pretty, as many of them had fine features and beautiful eyes. The men on the other hand she usually considered rather unprepossessing, as they were short and squat. (In this particular hacienda, however, it was an exception that there were so many young and attractive-looking boys as well.)

Eva was feeling her age in the heat (even though she was only in her 52nd year), and so she left the dance at a relatively early hour. She walked back to the boat down a muddy track. The tropical night was stiflingly hot, while countless stars twinkled through a misty sky. As she reached the boat through the rising ground mist, her room companion greeted her in a calm voice, but with words that were utterly chilling.

'You had better wash and disinfect yourself thoroughly. Our host has leprosy!'

Eva was almost rigid with shock. Running to the tiny washroom, she used every one of the disinfectants she had brought with her, washed herself at least three times with carbolic soap and poured camphorated spirits all over her naked body. Luckily she had not drunk any *pisco* nor touched anything at the hacienda. Days later, once they had reached Iquitos, Eva was informed that the story of leprosy was just a rumour spread about by the man's enemies. It was hardly very reassuring. The spectre of this dread disease was to haunt her dreams for many nights to come.

Quite apart from the interest of frequent landings and seeing the way of life of townspeople and farms in these utterly remote and isolated parts of the world, the overriding beauty of the whole trip lay in the wonders of nature. There was always some fascinating creature to see. Generally the steamship would set off on its day's journey at around 5.30 in the morning. Waking beneath her wringing-wet mosquito net, Eva would watch the sun rising like a giant pink rose beyond the dark stripes of the banks, and gaze out at the tranquil waters. Millions of little *perequitos* (budgerigars) screeched in the undergrowth, many of them flitting about so close to the boat that she could make out their beautiful emerald-and-sapphire plumage. She could have bought dozens of these enchanting little birds at around 20–30 *centavos* a piece in any of the *caserìos*. In the early morning hours there would always be some other animals visible: what Eva called crocodiles but which were probably caiman would swim around quite near to the boat, and she could often count as many as twenty of those 'nasty beasts' basking on the sun-baked shores.

On some days Eva would watch native fishermen in their fragile canoes, throwing out the *tarafa*, a small round net, which they immediately pulled back in again. Each time the net would be filled with dozens of wriggling fish, large and small. Sometimes a *balsa* would come quietly floating down the river, looking like a small straw hut on tree trunks. The owners could live for weeks in these floating houses until they reached their destination downriver—a *balsa* was only capable of floating without power or oars, and would therefore never travel upstream.

The sun burned down relentlessly, but one day Eva saw a dark cloud and could hear the rushing sounds of an impending storm. Split down to their roots, several hefty trees crashed in splinters down the banks. Looming ahead, a thick yellow dust-cloud threatened to envelop them, and within minutes the steamboat had hurried to the shore to drop anchor. A violent whirlwind whipped up, hurling itself from one bank to the other with the force of a hurricane. The gusting wind was throwing up foam and dust with incredible force. Had the crew not immediately safeguarded their heavy freighters the situation could have become very dangerous, for these kinds of riverboats had only a very shallow draught and could easily be thrown off balance.

Even when it was completely calm, Eva would often watch whirlpools and *moyenas* spinning about on the surface of the water. These were swirling eddies welling up from the bottom of the river that formed circular, spinning vortices. The steamship was large and broad and was therefore able to navigate these obstacles without too much bother. They were a great danger, however, for canoes and *balsas*, because these types of craft were not designed to withstand the strength of the currents. Often a *balsa* would spin around for days without managing to extract itself from this type of whirlpool. Canoes could often be tipped over and would then capsize, because if they could not paddle out of danger, the occupants would be flung into the middle of the whirlpool. Without pity, the churning waters would then suck down boat and humans, leading them inexorably to their fate at the bottom of the river.

On the seventh day of Eva's journey they were travelling along the lush green verges with their heavily loaded *Cenepa* tugging its two freighters, just as they had done on all the previous days. Gradually they were approaching an unpleasant part of the Bajo Ucayali, called Puhinagua. Its notoriety had spread far and wide, due to the prevalence of a certain type of mosquito that bred there like a biblical plague. The *manta blanca*, a tiny insect able to infiltrate the smallest net, was capable of penetrating human hair and stinging people to a dangerous extent. This part of the jungle also had a bad reputation for its shifting waters and dangerous sandbanks. The river would open up with a new current here, a new channel there, and an island could appear all of a sudden where once the river had been deep. Navigation was particularly difficult during the dry season.

For hours at a stretch, the captain and *practico* had been continuously sounding the depth all along this part of the river. Here in the *Mal Paso* (evil passage) the river divided into two arms, one broad and one very narrow, split by a long island. Maybe the navigator thought that sailing through the meandering curves of the wider section would mean a long delay. Whatever the reason, they decided to steer the ship through the narrow part of the waters.

Just as she had done on every previous day, Eva sat down for lunch with her fellow passengers. She was just squeezing some lemon juice into her teacup, when all of a sudden the bow of the *Cenepa* seemed to lift itself up out of the water with the most terrible screeching noise. All the crockery slid off the table and shattered into a thousand pieces, while the passengers were flung off their seats. The *Cenepa* had run aground on a sandbank. The two freighters were torn apart immediately and floated off down the river in the strong current, while the riverboat—not designed to sail without the support of the ballast of its freighters—sat transfixed on its own.

It was a moment of supreme suspense: without the reinforcement of its freighters would the top-heavy *Cenepa* capsize? Breathlessly they waited for the inevitable catastrophe to happen—it would mean certain death, as it was extremely unlikely that the frightened civilians could save themselves by swimming to the shore. In diving off the stricken boat, they would all end up being immediately crushed as it capsized. The passengers were fearful of course, but in spite of their incipient collective panic they behaved reasonably well. Immobile on their seats, not moving for fear of disturbing the equilibrium of the boat, they remained glued to the middle of the ship. Only mothers scrambled to grab their children, huddling together in the centre. Eva had no child with her, but at that moment, face to face with death, she felt such an acute longing for her daughter that it caused her actual physical pain.

The *Cenepa* did not capsize. Carefully she began to extract herself from the sand, and inch by inch they reversed into deeper waters. They were saved. Eventually the two freighters were captured and roped together. Fortunately the river had stranded them on the nearby banks. Meanwhile, the three crewmen who had fallen overboard were finally picked up again after a long period of searching, much to the relief of all on board. God had been gracious. Nobody had been hurt and no damage had been done—with the exception of every bottle in the galley being smashed, losing every drop of alcohol on board, together with just three barrels of petrol. More than anything the fact was driven home to Eva, that had they got lost in that far-off region of the deep jungle it would have taken weeks or possibly months for Ursula to have been informed of her mother's fate. Even if Eva had been able to save her own life and had been stranded in one of the huts on the shore, it would probably have taken many long months before she could have expected any help from Lima.

And finally, on the tenth evening after their start from Pucallpa, the impenetrable green wall of trees that lined the banks suddenly came to an end. The river had become a wide lake by now, a lake with a tranquil and quite unruffled surface. Another wide lake opened up unannounced, and then without a single wave or any visible movement of the current, another even more immense lake expanded in front of the boat. The riverbanks disappeared completely, while the horizon, hitherto restricted by thick jungle to either side, dropped away to infinity. In the light of a round, copper-coloured moon an immense expanse of water lay below Eva's eyes: the Amazon! Majestically, powerfully, soundlessly, the impressively wide river extended before her, a water-world of its own, in which earth and virgin forest no longer played any part.

Twenty-four hours later they landed in Iquitos. This major settlement in the Loreto region is situated at the very heart of the Amazon jungle. It lies some 100 metres above sea level, but if Eva had wished to continue her journey eastwards, it would have taken her another 3,000 miles to reach the mouth of the river Amazon where it opened out into the Atlantic Ocean. After a fascinating few days exploring the region and enduring heat as hot as a furnace, Eva intended to travel back to Lima in a Catalina seaplane. It was an expensive but time-saving mode of travel. The journey was delayed for a whole week, but finally the day of departure dawned.

Just as the sun was rising in sheaves of flames above the *río* Itaya, the twin floats under the Catalina glided along its smooth, velvety surface towards the open waters of the Amazon. Their 'giant bird' spread out its wings and soared up into the deep blue dome. Hovering for a few seconds above the green island of Iquitos, the plane darted off like an arrow into infinite space.

Soon Eva was able to recognise her route on the river Ucayali, along which she had come on the steamer *Cenepa*. She saw its endless curves meandering through the trackless jungle. She saw the long, intertwined lines of silver, brown and ruddy streamlets that split up the interminable vista of trees into fragments, islets, parcels and tongues. Lagoons winked like dark eyes at the speeding clouds.

Looking round the cramped cabin, Eva noticed with some apprehension that their plane was equipped with bush-knives and flare pistols. This revealed to her in a flash what fate would hold in store for them, in the case of a forced landing. But they zoomed on, and the Catalina's trusty engines sang the song of man's victory over gravity. They ascended higher and higher as they flew towards the Cordillera. The altimeter showed a height of 20,000 feet and all at once the lack of oxygen was becoming oppressive. Eva was feeling quite light-headed and breathless, as the cabin would have been completely unpressurised.

Her attention was soon diverted, however, as the diamond-glittering snow-peaks of the Cordillera rushed up to meet them. Far below them, glaciers sparkled like icicles, seeming to cling to the roof of the earth. Chasms and crevasses plunged headlong into richly dark-blue depths. Then fog closed in all around the plane. When they finally emerged from the cloud-packs, the Pacific Ocean was heaving underneath the Catalina. Almost startled at this modern speed—which gave the passenger no time for mental adjustment—Eva could make out the first white squares of Lima. She felt a sudden wave of wistful regret for the world of virgin forest and river she had left behind. Sighing to herself, she sent it a last wordless farewell. But before she had time to ponder any further, the Catalina was already circling above the vivid green lawns of gleaming white mansions cloaked in purple bougainvillaea. With a swift and final loop they landed safely at Lima Airport.

In six hours Eva had travelled by air the distance for which she had needed twenty days to cross the country.

21

Broken Dreams

After three nights with wave after wave of bombing raids, the city of Dresden was engulfed in a terrifying firestorm that reached temperatures of 1,500 degrees centigrade. In scenes reminiscent of the worst horrors of Dante's *Inferno*, as the air above the wide area of utter destruction heated up, cold air rushed in from the ground beyond, and people were simply sucked into the flames like bits of chaff. It was 15 February 1945, and for three days the skies above the baroque city had been filled with the rumbling drone of the bombers. In the first wave, the 796 Avro Lancasters and nine De Havilland Mosquitos of No. 5 Group RAF Bomber Command released almost 1,500 tons of high explosive and in excess of 1,100 tons of incendiary bombs over the city. Some three hours later, a second raid was carried out by further groups of RAF Bomber Command, well into the morning of 14 February. Hampered by bad weather in Europe on the first day of the bombing campaign, the USAAF had to wait until the second day before sending their B-17s to drop bombs on Dresden's railway stations. Both the loss of life and the destruction of property were catastrophic.

A total of four raids were carried out over three days, with some 3,900 bombs dropped altogether. At the time there were reports that panic-stricken civilians, fleeing the ensuing firestorm that engulfed the city, were then strafed along the banks of the river by the US bombers. This would later be refuted by eminent historians, but was firmly believed by the survivors caught up in the horrors of that February. By that stage in the war, the practice of firebombing was already well established. High explosives were used to blow the roofs off; and then incendiary devices (fire-sticks) were dropped in order to ignite the buildings. So as to hamper the efforts of the fire-services battling against raging fires on the ground, further high-explosive bombs were dropped. This was a particularly effective technique in Dresden, which possessed many wooden-roofed buildings at the time.

Estimates varied wildly, but at least 30,000 civilians were killed in the bombing of Dresden. Numbers of citizens in the city itself had been dramatically increased by the influx of some 200,000 refugees fleeing westwards from the eastern parts of the German Reich before the relentless advance of the Soviet army. It was later calculated that at least 23 per cent of industrial and 56 per cent of non-industrial buildings were damaged: these included the world-renowned Zeiss precision optical works, dozens of beautiful baroque buildings, the Zwinger, the Opera House, the Royal Palace and the famous bridges over the Elbe. Most poignant of all, Dresden's cathedral of Our Lady, the *Frauenkirche*, lay in a gigantic tumble of smouldering and blackened limestone blocks. The American raids on the railway stations had effectively and totally paralysed all communications in the city.

A little further upriver in the villa by the village of Wachwitz, situated as it was some ten kilometres outside the city centre, it can only be imagined with what horror the Vollmanns and their staff watched the lurid pall of red filling the sky, as a thick shroud of choking black smoke covered the whole of Dresden. The house had escaped any major damage, apart from being covered in the ubiquitous and noxious-smelling black soot that drifted upriver from the inferno.

Controversy about the justification for the bombing of Dresden would rage for years. Another victim, however, was none other than Professor Emil Waldmann. Already dismayed by the destruction of dozens of masterpieces of art and culture in the bombing raids on the city of Wurzburg, he was so sickened by the tragic fate to befall Dresden that he took his own life. He was 65 years old, but his untimely death was soon followed by that of his wife Minerva, who was still only 59.

This particular news took years to reach Eva in Peru. Situated as she was some 5,000 miles away from the tragedies occurring on both such an epic and an individual scale, for her the last months of the war would bring turmoil of a much more personal nature. At the beginning of 1945 the British War Office, confident that the end of the war was only months away, had begun considering how to repopulate post-war Britain. While the advance of the Allied forces in Europe grew ever closer to their German targets (following the D-Day landings the previous June), troops that had spent most of the war fighting in the North African campaigns against Rommel found themselves being 'sent home to Blighty'. Included amongst these was Teddy Harman.

Having survived his five-year posting to Egypt, he was looking forward to coming back to England, and especially to seeing his wife again after all the painful years of separation. Married officers had been ordered home to their wives, to begin the process of compensating for the catastrophic loss of life, amongst both the young men lost in the forces and the civilian population at home. By this time, however, Ursula had completely different plans in mind. On his arrival in London Teddy was greeted by devastating news: Ursula wanted a divorce from her husband. Not only that, but she had found somebody else. Utterly bereft, Teddy turned to his own family for consolation. Ursula's hard-hearted coldness, towards a husband who had remained faithful to her for the entire duration of the war, cut Teddy to the very quick. Feeling unable to compete with an unknown Canadian officer fighting on the ground amid the Allied advance into Nazi-occupied Europe, Teddy agreed to an almost immediate separation.

This allowed Ursula to continue receiving the short but impassioned love letters sent by John, stationed 'somewhere in Germany' with his Canadian battalion. Eva meanwhile found herself in an almost impossible situation. She had been extremely fond of her English son-in-law, and it hurt her immensely to receive news of the impending divorce not from her daughter, but from Teddy's father Bertie. Whilst she did not condemn Ursula outright for allowing the war to propel her into the arms of another man, Eva did regard her daughter's behaviour as very ill-considered, in that she was broadcasting her affair so publicly. She might have been even more aghast to learn how sympathetic her brother Werner and his wife Barbara had previously been to Ursula and her lover John, inviting the couple to their home in Chalfont St Peter. The Canadian would write in one of his love letters to Ursula, 'I often think of how very kind they have been to me and realise not many others would have done the same under the circumstances.'

For Eva, the overriding quality she expected of her daughter in such circumstances was discretion. In one of her letters written in the first half of 1945, she basically berated Ursula for having 'let the cat out of the bag' so unnecessarily. 'London is a big town,' she wrote. 'You could have done whatever you wished without giving the Harmans the slightest clue.' She went on to complain, 'I must really tell you, Ursele, that women down the centuries have had affairs in every part of the world. This really is nothing new at all. But why you should not have taken every possible precaution to conceal it—this is what I do not understand.' Even worse, from Eva's point of view, was her daughter's precarious background to consider. 'You were in a particularly delicate situation,' she wrote further on. 'Being of German origin, and moreover in part of Jewish origin, you must be aware that to become part of an English family—whether middle-class or not—is an enormous asset for which thousands of other girls would have given their lives. Therefore it should have been more important than ever to show the Harmans only the good sides to your character, and keep the "other side of the coin" well hidden. You, however, on the very contrary, have carefully squashed every good trait in your character, showing them instead nothing but those primordial instincts which all of us have in the very depths of our being, but which we do our best to conceal.'

As a final point, Eva then alluded to one of the bitterest periods of her life, when she considered herself robbed of her daughter's affection by her own governess. As she wrote:

> I know you think every 'convention' a lie. But this couldn't be further from the truth. It was that cursed Franke's fault, she who had been filling your head with nothing but lies like that from the time when you were just a young girl. Sincerity is an example of a good convention; tact is another. Indeed, if you had more tact, the outcome today wouldn't be as disastrous as it is.

Ursula paid no attention to her mother, probably receiving such long-distance advice with bad grace. While millions celebrated the end of the war by dancing in the streets on VE Day, Ursula spent 8 May miserably curled up in her room while staying with her uncle and aunt in Chalfont. Her beloved John had already set sail across the Atlantic to return home to his Canadian wife. Ursula was inconsolable, but it would take another year before her divorce, which cited her lover as co-respondent, would finally be made absolute.

Before the war was brought to its ultimate conclusion with the horrific atomic bombings of Hiroshima and Nagasaki on 6 and 9 August respectively, Eva's letters were returning to a much chattier and more amusing tone of voice. By this time she had finished her book and was actively looking for a publisher. She had also been writing articles covering various facets of Inca civilisation, which she attempted to sell in the United States to such publications as *National Geographic*. She was to have little success in either regard, unfortunately, and in the end she had to be satisfied with paying privately for five copies of the book, each consisting of a quarter of a million words laboriously produced on closely typewritten and carbon-copied onion-skin paper, and hardbound with a cloth cover. With everything else going on in her life, Ursula had shown scant interest in what she regarded as her mother's long-winded escapades on the other side of the world.

Before returning to the well-worn topic of her quest for a visa to escape Peru and come 'home', Eva told Ursula about meeting a certain 'rather rum' English lady. She wrote to Ursula:

> One of these days you might receive a visitor. She is a Mrs Young, and she's coming directly from Lima, Peru to bring you greetings! Maybe she'll tell you she's my bosom-friend, which is

> certainly not the case. We did live together in the same *pension* for a few months, but then she went off to live in Chile. Just recently she popped up again, telling me that she was going straight to England. But instead of agreeing to take some little parcel with her, she merely offered to take you 'greetings from dear Ma'. It won't be very thrilling for you, but she might tell you this and that about our life here in this 'good old country', if you have the patience to listen to her ramblings. She is more or less as mad as a hatter. Of course she is convinced 100% that she is just the brightest and most wonderful person existing. In fact she's a very inept 'astrologer' besides many other things she claims to excel at—a book-writer for example. She'd be my competitor, so don't for goodness' sake mention that I am a 'fellow author'. She might also go to Chalfont—so please warn Barbara about her. But as she was so kind to offer to go and see you, I really couldn't very well tell her not to. She is apparently very wealthy, and is going home to England to try and sell her immense Tudor mansion with genuine period furniture, a place situated somewhere near Eastbourne. So now you know about everything I myself know about Mrs Everild Young.*

As if to counterbalance her obsession with returning across the Atlantic, Eva would subsequently think of her daughter's wellbeing and how she could help to mend her depleted, war-torn nerves. She suggested that Ursula might like to come over and spend some time with her in Peru—again rather a fanciful notion, given the severe austerity of the immediate post-war years. Ursula never took her mother up on her offer, as she was now directing her focus onto her own career, and how she could take her mind off her unpleasant marital situation. There had been only one truly awful occasion during the war when serious aspersions were cast on her German background. While staying with her one-time penfriend Joyce in Sussex, Ursula became the object of intense vilification by a group of Norwegian resistance fighters. They had been temporarily lodged in Joyce's substantial house after a daring escape

* Everild Young was a fellow of the Royal Geographical Society, and the author of several books on South America and the Caribbean (*The Land of Three Worlds* about her journeys in Peru was published in 1953). She has an extremely engaging style and a very good eye for detail, and it can only be assumed that Eva's 'peevish' attitude towards a 'fellow-writer' was born out of sheer envy. She married Kjeld Helweg-Larsen, also possibly an explorer (with a Scandinavian background), co-authoring several books with him and with whom she might have lived in the Bahamas. Date of death unknown.

from their Nazi-occupied homeland. With their understandable but deeply entrenched hatred of all things German, the group found it impossible to believe that Ursula was not a spy in the camp. Nevertheless, by the time she had reached her 31st birthday at the end of September 1945, the graduate of the Courtauld Institute was well on her way to achieving her first professional qualification: as an interpreter.

In Germany itself, the aftermath of war brought almost unbearable living conditions. Already utterly demoralised by their second total surrender and capitulation in less than 30 years, the majority of the German population was subsisting like rats in a hole, on starvation rations and in the bombed-out craters of cellars and underground passages. In the capital itself, beleaguered Berliners had welcomed the advancing Americans with open arms. Those in Dresden and its surroundings, however, were to be put immediately into the Soviet sphere of influence. Having survived the Nazi regime and all the horrors of war, Richard Vollmann as a former factory owner now found himself a legitimate target of the Russians. Holding to the Marxist ideology that 'property is theft', Richard was told that his factory would be confiscated and his house turned over to the State. Refusing to relinquish his ownership of the villa, to Ilse's terrified consternation her husband was summarily arrested and marched off to an uncertain fate by officers of the NKVD.* He would spend 270 days incarcerated by the Russians, while his whereabouts remained completely unknown even to his immediate family.

During the master's absence, Russian soldiers began ransacking the villa above the Elbe. Ever loyal to the last, it was the housekeeper Helene who had the presence of mind to dispose of the seven boxes that had spent the war years in the cellar. She changed the labelling to 'Steinthal', and challenged the soldiers that as the boxes obviously did not belong to the owner, they must be handed over at once to the State Art Gallery in Dresden. By some miracle the gallery was still functioning to a small extent, and the boxes were safely installed in the copious rabbit warren of underground tunnels beneath their depository at Schloss Pillnitz on the banks of the Elbe. The castle had miraculously escaped relatively unscathed from the firebombing, and many works of art would remain ensconced deep underground for decades to come.

* This was the successor of the OGPU, the original State Political Directorate that was subsequently known as the People's Commissariat for Internal Affairs. The NKVD was the forerunner of the KGB.

On 20 November 1945 the international trial of 22 high-ranking Nazi officers opened in the city of Nuremberg. This was to be a landmark trial for many reasons, not least of which was that it would last for a total of 315 days. For a start, the unconditional surrender of the Axis powers was unusual, and this 'showcase of judicial process' would lead directly to the creation of international tribunals. On the linguistic front, it was the first time in history that a trial would be conducted simultaneously in four languages. And seated on a hard bench amidst the phalanx of multi-lingual interpreters, all wearing uncomfortably large headphones, was Ursula.

The original Morgenthau plan for the 'denazification' of Germany had collapsed with the death of Roosevelt in April 1945 (who never lived to see the end of the war or the defeat of Japan). Morgenthau's vision, approved at the time by both the American and British governments, was for a similar structure to the Treaty of Versailles; in other words punitive retribution in the form of deportation, forced labour and economic repression. Roosevelt's successor however, Harry H. Truman, was strongly in favour of the notion of judicial process as preferred by the Russians. And so a plan was drawn up by the US War Department for the 'Trial of European War Criminals'.

Although Berlin had originally been suggested by the USSR as the most suitable place to hold such a showcase trial, in the end Nuremberg was chosen. Not only was the city in the American sector, but its Palace of Justice was also spacious and had remained relatively undamaged by the wartime bombing raids. Moreover, it was uncomfortably evocative as the site of the infamous Nazi Party rallies of the 1930s. It would take many months of concerted effort, however, before the four victorious powers would concur—not only on the choice of prosecutors to untangle the gigantic mass of evidence, but also on the judges to lead the extremely complex and lengthy proceedings. And Nuremberg itself was not without its own inherent dangers. The entire legal team had to be protected whenever they went out into the city, because of the still persistent danger of German snipers.

5,000 miles away in distant Peru, Eva must have felt considerable alarm for her daughter's state of mind. She had already expressed concern when she learned that, on successfully qualifying as an interpreter, Ursula had very quickly been recruited by the Allied Control Commission. Not only that, but instead of remaining in London to sort out her tangled marital affairs (Eva was still holding on to the faint but irrational hope that her daughter would somehow reconcile her differences and get back together with Teddy), Ursula was being sent back to Germany.

In the makeshift military encampment erected in the bombed-out city of Düsseldorf, headquarters of the British Sector in Germany, Ursula was to meet many linguists—some with Jewish backgrounds similar to her own; others from the USA, France, the USSR and Britain. Amongst her new acquaintances was an English girl by the name of Evelyn, as gifted for languages as Ursula. Recruited from the WRNS, she had spent the latter war years at Latimer House, a top-secret detention centre based in a manor house in Chesham in Buckinghamshire, where high-ranking German and Italian prisoners-of-war had been interrogated.* Yet like her 'colleagues' involved in the decoding of the captured Enigma machine at Bletchley Park, it was a period of her life about which she was absolutely forbidden to utter a word.

The experience of working at the Nuremberg Trials was as new for the interpreters as it was for the presiding judge, Sir Geoffrey Lawrence. It was the International Business Machines Company (later immediately recognisable as IBM) who would provide the solution to an initially insurmountable problem: how to allow every word uttered to be conducted in four languages at once. They supplied headphones for everyone: prosecutors, judges, interpreters and prisoners. It was also the first time, however, that interpreters all trained in consecutive translation would have to interpret simultaneously. Despite the deeply traumatic nature of all the evidence presented, and the close proximity to such reviled Nazi figures, Ursula found that she took to the task of interpreting without much difficulty. Whilst each prosecutor would have his chance to present his case, it was Chief Prosecutor Justice Jackson's brilliant opening remarks that would make an impressive and historic impact.

In a speech lasting for the better part of a day, he said, 'May it please your honours, the privilege of opening the first trial in history for crimes against the peace of the world imposes a grave responsibility.

'The wrongs which we seek to condemn and punish have been so calculated, so malignant, and so devastating that civilization cannot tolerate their being ignored because it cannot survive their being repeated.

'That four great nations, flushed with victory and stung with injury, stay the hand of vengeance and voluntarily submit their captive enemies to the judgment of the law is one of the most significant tributes that

* This manor house belonging to the Cavendish family had been requisitioned by the War Office in 1942 and disguised as a supply depot called 'Number One Distribution Centre'.

power has ever paid to reason.'*

Given Ursula's background, the most shocking part of the trial would come just a month into the proceedings that were to last the best part of a year. On 29 November, the prosecution dropped a bombshell with the showing of a documentary film entitled *Nazi Concentration Camps*. This film, created from motion pictures taken by Allied forces liberating concentration camps and from Nazi films discovered by the OSS, showed for the first time the utterly horrific crimes perpetrated by the Nazis. The impact on the courtroom was immediate: the presiding judge walked out without adjourning, while most of those present stood or sat transfixed in shock. For Ursula, this was perhaps the defining moment that would cause her to suppress all memories of this experience almost to the end of her life. The very notion that her own uncle Eduard, or even worse her frail and aged great-aunt Tante Anna, could have numbered as part of the Final Solution in the heaps of emaciated bodies so gruesomely depicted on the films shown in court—that was simply too much to bear.

On Tuesday 1 October 1946, the well-respected Munich paper *Süddeutsche Zeitung* published the judgments laid down by the Nuremberg Trials, together with photographs of all the prisoners. Twelve of the original 22 Nazi prisoners were condemned to death by hanging. The French had argued that none of the condemned merited a firing squad (which was considered a more dignified death). In an extraordinarily chauvinist gesture by the presiding judges, however, on the day sentences were to be decided, all the female interpreters including Ursula were told to leave the courtroom. Despite the months of unrelentingly terrible evidence they had been translating, it was considered unseemly for women to be present when the death sentences were pronounced.

The end of the Nuremberg Trials marked the last vestiges of Ursula's marriage to Ted Harman. With her heart perhaps hardened against any further such painful relationships, Ursula continued living in Germany and working as an interpreter. While she would later accompany high-ranking American and British officials on 'peace visits' to the bombed-out remains of German cities, Ursula must have felt even more detached and remote from her mother. Eva meanwhile was continuing to have all her hopes of returning to Europe constantly dashed. Her last

* The Robert H. Jackson Center in Jamestown, New York, contains the foremost collection of memorabilia relating to the Nuremberg Trials. For an eye-witness account by one of the interpreters at the Nuremberg Trials, see the report by the late Patricia Vander Elst (a member of the professional interpreters' association AIIC) at http://www.aiic.net.

surviving letters from Peru, however, were full of chatty news about her South American 'family', and included the usual mixture of advice and what she considered amusing anecdotes about her travels.

While in one letter she had implored Ursula to return to what she liked to call a 'decent' lifestyle in London, in the very next one she was telling her the story of her nearby neighbours in Miraflores and what a marvellously unpretentious yet honest life they had forged for themselves. She wrote:

> Recently I went to visit a very hard-working young couple. He is the librarian at San Marcus University and she runs a studio making dolls and toys. These young people live in the most likeable way I have seen for a long time. With their meagre savings they bought a grey and dusty plot of land, which they enclosed with a wall made of adobe mud-bricks. Inside they constructed a rectangular, single-storey house with a corrugated iron roof. It consists simply of living room in the middle, small writing room on the left, small bedroom and small bathroom on the right; then a little kitchen-house in the garden with a maid's room attached. All the rest is garden and already today, after just a month, their lettuce, spinach, carrots and radishes are all thriving. But the most enjoyable part of all is their furniture; nothing but the very, very simplest things—yet how attractively painted, and so prettily covered with woven Peruvian Indian materials. Their bookshelves are of the most primitive type—and the floor is simply made of brick. But the whole place gives the impression of 'little pioneers', who have minimal wants and tastes, who live spiritually and do not need any luxuries, and who have created their own set-up according to their liking. It just goes to show that you can also live with modest furniture in an inexpensive house—and be just as content with your life.

As a contrast to this interesting visit, Eva had also been to see 'one of the richest women of Lima', whom she regarded not only as intelligent and cultivated, but also as a person pursuing very worthwhile interests. These included patronage of the arts, such as collecting 'vast sums' for the organisation of chamber concerts. Most impressive of all, as far as Eva was concerned, was this lady's effective and meritorious work for the protection of children against abuse and slavery.

While Ursula was surviving back in Germany, Eva's dearest and oft-repeated dream of returning to England was broken yet again. Even making use of unlikely people like her former son-in-law's father in

London, it had simply proved impossible for Eva to wade through the impenetrable tangle of red tape. Her last surviving letter from Peru was still dated 1945, but it would take another four years before she was finally able to return to Europe. Once again, Eva's moods could change from one extreme to the other. Although not even in her mid fifties, she would sometimes write as if she were a doddery old grandmother. During a pre-war Christmas holiday, Ursula had presented her mother with the gift of a book by 'some Russian author', from which Eva now quoted in this particular letter, 'What other pleasures in life are there left to an old woman but just to pick her nose?'

Then in a complete volte-face, she went on to describe the latest wedding in the Ferreyros family. Her description, both of the sumptuousness of the banquet and extravagance of the presents, was perhaps somewhat tactless. Rationing was still fully in force in post-war Europe, and throughout her time in Germany Ursula would have to become inured to army food.

'The bride was extremely pretty with her long veil and orange blossoms, wearing a glistening white silk dress with a beautiful long train,' wrote Eva. After a simple Catholic ceremony, everybody joined the happy couple for lunch at the Country Club. Eva went on to describe the scene.

> The most interesting feature was the gorgeous buffet with amazingly good food. It struck me as very funny that at one long table seats had been prepared for the bridegroom and his bride as well as for their parents, together with the oldest members of their close family. Apart from this there were only three tiny tables, at which people could find somewhere to sit. Some of the guests stood about the place, balancing their plates and cutting up their meat one-handed, while others simply sat on the floor. Of course as life here is based on Spanish customs, the whole affair was rather stiff and formal. Only when the young couple were about to leave on their honeymoon (a two-month holiday in Brazil, Buenos Aires and Chile), did everybody run to the wedding car and decorate it tastelessly with flowers and empty tins, chalking amusing things all over it and drawing pictures of hearts on the bonnet. Then as Rosita and Alfred came out, they were duly pelted with handfuls of rice, which pricked my conscience as it is so scarce nowadays.

Just two days previously, Eva had been invited to examine the presents given to the young couple, of 'unimaginable quantity and value' as she wrote to Ursula. There were apparently 'at least four metres' of silver goods: large silver platters, substantial silver containers, tea- and coffee-sets and trays. The lucky pair were further given jewels and beautiful carpets, pictures and card-tables; small but very attractive articles of furniture; items in suede for their writing desk; half a dozen lamps and clocks; china and glassware for twelve place-settings—a 'flood of things', as she described it. The bride's parents gave her a beautiful bracelet with diamonds, and her father-in-law presented her with another lovely bracelet all the way from Cartier in New York.

Eva's final description of life in Peru was quite affectionate. She wrote:

> Of course I thought of you, my darling child, not because of all the presents which you certainly wouldn't have appreciated, but for the 'promise of happiness' contained in every wedding. How easy it is for people in this country to be happy! They simply don't have any of the problems we do. If they are well off, life will be a never-ending bundle of laughs, with nothing but happy prospects and no snags whatsoever. How far away they are from the war-torn struggles of Europe. People here have serene and good-natured temperaments, and 'passion' is a rare thing. Even if you are not happy, you just bear it and make the best of it, as it is a Catholic country and divorce exists only in exceptional cases. More often than not, in this blessed country you simply marry and are happy ever after.

After ten years of separation from her native land, Eva's eventual return across the Atlantic in 1949 was certainly no such 'happy ever after'. Despite being used to the worldwide shortages whose effects were felt even in Peru, nothing could have prepared Eva for the austerity of conditions in post-war Europe. Ursula, who by now was forging her own successful career as an interpreter, had absolutely no desire to meet up again with her mother. And as for the surviving siblings, Eva was to find that their erstwhile cosy and companiable friendship had almost dissolved. The terrible havoc caused by war was reflected in the turbulent and troubled relationship that would rumble on amongst her remaining family.*

* Despite having most of his vast wealth confiscated by the Nazis, Max Steinthal had been able to ensure that a lump sum was transferred to a bank in London before the eventual exile of his children. Because Erich had remained in Germany, Werner as next surviving oldest son was put in charge of safeguarding the remaining siblings' money donated by their father. Werner's refusal to communicate with his sister in Peru, however,

It was an equally difficult time for the Vollmanns in Saxony. Now living entirely in the Russian sector, the year of Eva's return to Europe would mark the creation of two German nations: the Federal Republic in the west and the Democratic Republic in the east. When Ilse had finally been allowed to greet her husband after his nine-month absence in a Russian gaol, his appearance was so altered that she had not at first been able to recognise him. Within months, however, Richard had decided to make good their escape to the west. Even though he was now branded an 'escapee of the Republic' by the East German authorities, he managed to get permission for Ilse to stay behind in Wachwitz for a few more weeks, in order to pack up the one crateful of furniture allowed. The faithful housekeeper Helene was sent back to her native town of Pirna. Once all its former occupants had left, the villa itself was immediately requisitioned by the local authority, and an inventory made of all the rooms and remaining furniture. The ground floor consisted of: the erstwhile Belgian consulate, a dining room, a hall, a sitting room, the garden room and a vestibule. On the first floor there was a hallway, a master bedroom, a lady's bedroom with its own sitting room, three further bedrooms, dressing rooms and a guest room. And on the second floor there were the servants' quarters, an ironing room, a small guest room, three maids' rooms and the cook's room, and finally the tower room that had once been used as the nursery. Below stairs there were the kitchen and cellars.

Without compunction, this one-family villa house was converted into ten separate apartments—each one destined for a family of at least four—while part of the ground floor would soon be utilised as the village kindergarten. Another inventory was made of the remains of Richard's extensive collection of Peruvian and other ethnic artefacts, which was shipped off to the local folk museum. In the end Richard Vollmann was able to fashion a new life for himself just outside the town of Trier in the Rhineland Palatinate, on the far side of West Germany close to the Luxembourg border. Approaching his 70th year but with the vigour which typified many industrious Germans (and which would later lead to the 'Economic Miracle'), he 'reinvented' the firm of Mey & Co., and soon Trier would boast its own successful factory producing artificial silk flowers.

had meant that Eva would be forced to remain reluctantly in contact with her former son-in-law's family, because they also had information about Eva's bank account in London. Meanwhile, her brother Peter, living in Sussex, had sent her a 'very nasty' letter in which he accused his sister of 'being stupid' for making no effort to return to England. These recriminations from her brothers left Eva feeling hurt and resentful.

In an odd twist of fate, it was the second marriage of their daughter that would eventually bring Eva and Richard back into contact. While taking a short break in Geneva, Ursula had met an Englishman by the name of Richard Thonger, whom she would later confide to her mother had been 'very kind' to her. Through contacts at the Belgian embassy, Eva had by now set up home in another apartment in Brussels. Her first meeting with her daughter, perhaps in Düsseldorf, must already have been a shock to her system. The sight of the bombed-out remains of once-proud German cities, many of them with their cathedrals standing forlornly with blackened spires—even now, some five years after the end of the war—must have saddened Eva terribly. What distresed her even more, however, was her daughter's relationship with a man she considered to be entirely unsuitable.

Eva's disapproval had nothing to do with her future son-in-law's background. He came from just as 'middle class' a background as Teddy, and had just managed to complete his degree in languages at Cambridge before the onset of the war. Together with his completely impulsive and untrained, yet impassioned fellow students, in 1936 he had already been caught up in the struggle against Fascism, fighting Franco in Spain. Coincidentally, this other Richard had also been trained in Signals, just as Teddy had, but he had spent his war with the Eighth Army in Italy and northern France. After the cessation of hostilities, Richard Thonger had decided to indulge his lifelong fascination with German expressionist theatre, film and art by remaining in the devastated city of Berlin, learning German from scratch by befriending members of the burgeoning Berlin Radio. All of this would have impressed Eva but for one serious flaw: Richard had never had a civilian career. Ursula seemed quite unable to grasp that in direct consequence of his fanciful and ill-conceived business ideas, this Richard would never be able to provide his intended wife with a stable income.

United in a mutual fear for their daughter's future, and 11 years after their pre-war separation, Richard Vollmann met up with Eva again at the wedding. This took place quietly in Düsseldorf in the middle of November 1950, about two months after Ursula's 36th birthday. Her new husband was three years younger than his wife, and had never been married. At the event, Eva was even able to confront her 'nemesis' Ilse without too much discomfort; it was the first time too that Ursula had met her stepmother. Less than two years later Ursula was pregnant with her first child, an event that possibly propelled the couple into making a definite decision: to return to England to live in London. This news made Eva even more determined to live in the same country as her daughter. She wrote an impassioned and forceful letter directly to the

Prime Minister, Clement Atlee, begging him to grant her domiciliary rights to live in England to be near her only daughter. The officious reply she received was curt in the extreme, ending along the lines of 'Please go away. We already have enough mouths to feed.'

Resigned to living for the rest of her life *'in der Verbannung'* (in a state of banishment), Eva set about making a real home for herself in her pleasant, first-floor apartment in Brussels. Amongst the carefully bought reproduction furniture, in pride of place stood a display cabinet showing off Eva's eclectic collection of Peruvian artefacts. Her reduced circumstances had now finally forced her to learn how to cook in order to survive. Her only domestic assistance was in the form of a rather bad-tempered, Flemish lady by the name of Louise, who would turn up twice a week at the flat in order to clean and iron.

In the year of her 60th birthday, Eva's first grandchild came into the world. She had 'rushed over' to London to be at Ursula's side for this momentous event, despite her continued dislike and suspicion of her new son-in-law. Less than two years later, Ursula presented her young daughter with a little sister. As they grew up, neither girl had the slightest idea that at the time of their birth their grandmother had been a Peruvian.

It would be well into the late 1950s before Eva could change her Peruvian passport and revert to her original German nationality. And it would take even longer for Eva, together with her remaining five siblings, to receive their just reparations from the West German government. Through years of a frequently acrimonious exchange of letters between the siblings from Brazil, Switzerland, France, England and Sweden, it was Richard Vollmann who was able to unite the Steinthal 'children' in their quest for compensation for having been exiled from their homeland.

Eva was never able to achieve her dearest wish: to live with her closest family. Yet her frequent visits to London to see her granddaughters did facilitate a rapprochement between mother and daughter. And for the rest of his life, Richard Vollmann kept up a regular and affectionate correspondence with his former wife.

Afterword

This narrative finishes with many unanswered questions. What happened to the other five of Eva's surviving siblings? Did Eva's misgivings about her new son-in-law turn out to be true? Was she ever able to live in England with her daughter and granddaughters? Would she return to Germany? And did the seven crates of pictures ever survive the war? The truth is that there remains a wealth of family archives and possessions—belonging to both the Steinthal and the Vollmann families—still to be recovered. It is my intention to continue the story in a second book.

CT

The SS *Orduña*

Eva during her first months in Peru

Eva & Packard in the Cordillera

Richard's second marriage to Ilse Schmidt (1940)

Eva's white hair (1941)

Peruvian mother and child

Indian of Puno in *chullo*

Exchanging news in Cuzco

Llamas

Burial tower at Sillustani

Huascarán (Peru's highest mountain in the Cordillera Blanca)

Machu Picchu

Patio in Ayacucho

Colonial façades of Jesuit church, Arequipa

Women at Sunday market

Virgin forest (with nests of *oropendulas,* weaver birds)

Girls in Moyobamba

Chunchu Indians

Tigrillo (ocelot)

A typical riverboat

The jungle town of Pucallpa (with stilt-huts)

The river Ucayali

Ursula as a land-girl on Brenda's farm (1940s)

Ursula in her Allied Commission uniform (Nuremberg 1946)

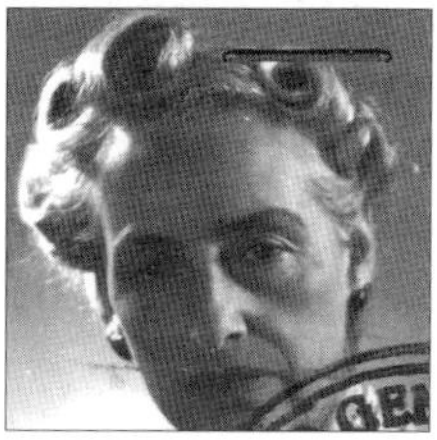

Eva's passport photo 1950 (with Peruvian nationality)

Ursula & Eva around 1950

The ruins of the villa on Uhlandstrasse 1944

A Brief Note on Research

If writing this complex family biography has taught me anything, it is that family reminiscences cannot always be relied upon. During my interview with my mother, undertaken in London when she was in her 85th year and around four years before her death, she inadvertently gave me some information that would send me off on completely the wrong track for years afterwards. Always extremely reluctant to talk about the past, especially anything to do with war, she firmly believed that her mother Eva had sailed to Peru from Southampton. It was only within the last two years that I finally unearthed a letter mentioning the Adelphi Hotel. That gave me the clue to Liverpool, but it took many further hours of painstaking research in the National Archives at Kew, before I finally found the correct passenger lists for the *Orduña*. I can distinctly remember the frisson of excitement I experienced when I saw my grandmother's name amongst those of the other passengers sailing on that fateful day in 1939. The whole process had taken me nearly five years of searching.

Much more disturbing, however, were my researches at the State Archives in Berlin. To sit there and stare at the carefully preserved copies of letters stamped with swastikas and *'Gestapo'* in bold and black Gothic script, all recording in intrusive detail the lives of my own relatives, was a truly horrifying experience. Nevertheless, it is entirely due to German efficiency and immaculate record-keeping that I was able to view, for example, all the building plans for my great-grandfather's grand designs for his family 'villa' on the Uhlandstrasse.

This project has also taught me how important it is to preserve family history. Over the course of some 20 years I have been lucky enough to retain in my possession: an interview on tape with my grandmother (recorded in 1986 in the Brussels flat by my sister); my own personal copy of my grandmother's South American journal; notes of my own interview with my mother from summer 1999; and within the last two years talks with my sister in Holland, my mother's maternal cousins in Berlin, and my mother's paternal cousins elsewhere in Germany, as well as various German friends of the family. I am particularly grateful to my mother's cousin in France, an indomitable lady in her 90th year with whom I spent five days, recording her astoundingly clear memories of the Steinthal family.

Further useful information came from a writing friend whose father was a merchant sailor before 1912; and the wartime friend of my mother's working at Latimer House, the top secret debriefing location for high-ranking German and Italian prisoners of war, during the Second World War.

Following my mother's death in 2003 I was able to gain access to a previously hidden treasure-store of family letters and other material. My first task, however, was to preserve these unbelievably fragile papers in permanent form, some documents dating back to the early 1850s. My other 'Berlin cousin' Brigitte Schmitt provided me with a wonderful Steinthal family tree, while relatives in Trier contributed further papers and effects belonging to my grandfather, grandmother and mother. Most precious of all is my collection of black-and-white and sepia-coloured family photos.

I will conclude with a word about translations. All the family letters I uncovered during my research (Eva's letters to her brother Werner during the First World War, the 'Waldmann' letters and the exchange of letters between Eva, her mother and Richard Vollman both before and during the Second World War) have been translated from the original German by me, as have other family and official documents mentioned in the text. I have also translated letters written in French and those including phrases in Italian. The letters sent by Eva to her daughter from on board the SS *Orduña* and consequently from Peru, have been slightly edited from her original English for the sake of clarity and brevity.

A Short Bibliography

Burland, C.A., *Inca Peru*, Hulton Educational Publications, London, 1957.

Bruhns, Wibke, *Meines Vaters Land*, Ullstein, Berlin, 2005.

Hague, Arnold, *The Allied Convoy System 1939–1945*, Chatham, London, 2000.

Insight Guides to Peru (1999 and 2006 edns).

Ladd, Brian, *Ghosts of Berlin*, University of Chicago Press, Chicago and London, 1997.

Lonely Planet Guide to Peru, 4th edn, 2000.

Meiche, Professor Dr Alfred, *Die Familie Vollmann*, Dresden, printed for private circulation, 1922.

Richie, Alexandra, *Faust's Metropolis: A History of Berlin*, Harper-Collins, London, 1998.

Smith, Michael, *Foley. The Spy Who Saved 10,000 Jews*, Hodder & Stoughton, London, 1999.

Steinthal, Fanny, *Max Steinthal on His 70th Birthday*, Berlin, printed for private circulation, 1920.

Stendell, Carola (pen-name of author's grandmother), *Along the Roads of Peru*, Lima, Peru, printed for private circulation, 1945.

Sulzbach, Herbert, *With the German Guns: Four Years on the Western Front*, Leo Cooper (Pen and Sword Books), Barnsley, 1973. Originally published in Germany in 1935 as *Zwei Lebende Mauern*, translated by Richard Thonger, the present author's late father.

Tatzkow, Monika, *Max Steinthal*, Proprietas-Verlag, Berlin, 2004.

Young, Everild, *Land of Three Worlds*, Andrew Melrose, London, 1953.

Zinneker, Liselotte, 'Eric Steinthal und seine Buchsammlung', Zurich, n.d. (typescript thesis).